HANNAH ARENDT AND SIMONE WEIL

Also Available from Bloomsbury

The Bloomsbury Companion to Arendt, ed. Peter Gratton
Mirror of Obedience, ed. Silvia Caprioglio Panizza and Philip Wilson
Venice Saved, ed. Silvia Caprioglio Panizza and Philip Wilson

HANNAH ARENDT AND SIMONE WEIL

Unprecedented Conversations

Edited by

Kathryn Lawson and Joshua Livingstone

BLOOMSBURY ACADEMIC
LONDON • NEW YORK • OXFORD • NEW DELHI • SYDNEY

BLOOMSBURY ACADEMIC
Bloomsbury Publishing Plc, 50 Bedford Square, London, WC1B 3DP, UK
Bloomsbury Publishing Inc, 1385 Broadway, New York, NY 10018, USA
Bloomsbury Publishing Ireland, 29 Earlsfort Terrace, Dublin 2, D02 AY28, Ireland

BLOOMSBURY, BLOOMSBURY ACADEMIC and the Diana logo are
trademarks of Bloomsbury Publishing Plc

First published in Great Britain 2024
This paperback edition published 2025

Copyright © Kathryn Lawson and Joshua Livingstone, and Contributors, 2024

Kathryn Lawson and Joshua Livingstone have asserted their right under the Copyright,
Designs and Patents Act, 1988, to be identified as Editors of this work.

Series design by Charlotte Daniels
Cover image: Ceiling of the Stanza della Segnatura (1508) Raphael Rooms
(tanze di Raffaello) Raffaello Sanzio da Urbino (1483–1520), Vatican Palace, Rome, Italy
(© Peter Horree / Alamy Stock Photo)

All rights reserved. No part of this publication may be: i) reproduced or transmitted in
any form, electronic or mechanical, including photocopying, recording or by means
of any information storage or retrieval system without prior permission in writing from
the publishers; or ii) used or reproduced in any way for the training, development or
operation of artificial intelligence (AI) technologies, including generative AI technologies.
The rights holders expressly reserve this publication from the text and data mining
exception as per Article 4(3) of the Digital Single Market Directive (EU) 2019/790.

Bloomsbury Publishing Inc does not have any control over, or responsibility for,
any third-party websites referred to or in this book. All internet addresses given
in this book were correct at the time of going to press. The author and publisher
regret any inconvenience caused if addresses have changed or sites have
ceased to exist, but can accept no responsibility for any such changes.

A catalogue record for this book is available from the British Library.

A catalog record for this book is available from the Library of Congress.

ISBN: HB: 978-1-3503-4446-4
PB: 978-1-3503-4445-7
ePDF: 978-1-3503-4447-1
eBook: 978-1-3503-4448-8

Typeset by Newgen KnowledgeWorks Pvt. Ltd., Chennai, India

For product safety related questions contact productsafety@bloomsbury.com.

To find out more about our authors and books visit www.bloomsbury.com
and sign up for our newsletters.

With thanks to each of the generous contributors to these unprecedented conversations and to the lives and minds of Hannah Arendt and Simone Weil who ask us to imagine a brave new political world.
Also, to our families.
—Josh and Kate

CONTENTS

List of Figures ... ix
Foreword ... x
List of Abbreviations ... xi

INTRODUCTION: UNPRECEDENTED CONVERSATIONS IN AN
UNPRECEDENTED TIME ... 1
    Joshua Livingstone and Kathryn Lawson

Part I
POWER, VIOLENCE, AND THE ADVERSARIES OF FREEDOM

Chapter 1
ON POWER IN SIMONE WEIL AND HANNAH ARENDT: CONTRASTS
AND CORRELATIONS ... 19
    Lissa McCullough

Chapter 2
TYRANNY WITHOUT A TYRANT: HANNAH ARENDT AND SIMONE
WEIL ON BUREAUCRACY ... 43
    Marina Lademacher

Chapter 3
LIVING IN DARK TIMES: THE SEDUCTION OF TOTALITARIAN EVIL ... 59
    Marie Cabaud Meaney

Chapter 4
POLITICAL VIOLENCE: A CONTRADICTION IN TERMS ... 77
    Rose A. Owen

Part II
SOCIETY, WORLD, AND THE NEED FOR POLITICAL ROOTS

Chapter 5
WE COME AND GO: THE WORLD IS HERE TO STAY—HANNAH
ARENDT AND THE WORLD AS COMMON ... 97
    Elvira Roncalli

Chapter 6
AN ETHICS OF GOD'S GRACE TO BALANCE A POLITICS OF WORLDLY AFFLICTION: A WEILIAN COMPANION TO RONCALLI ON ARENDT   113
  Kathryn Lawson

Chapter 7
REROOTING "WE REFUGEES": CONSIDERATIONS ON CONDITIONS OF DISPLACEMENT FROM HANNAH ARENDT AND SIMONE WEIL   127
  Scott B. Ritner

Chapter 8
ATTENTION AS A CONTESTED ETHICAL AND POLITICAL RESOURCE: SIMONE WEIL AND HANNAH ARENDT ON THE INNER ORIGINS OF FREEDOM   141
  Paolo Monti

Part III
ART, AESTHETICS, AND THE VULNERABILITIES OF POLITICAL APPEARANCES

Chapter 9
PAYING ATTENTION TO AFFLICTION: HANNAH ARENDT AND SIMONE WEIL ON TRAGIC STORYTELLING   157
  Pascale Devette

Chapter 10
EMBODYING THE IN-BETWEEN: AN ARENDTIAN REFLECTION ON SIMONE WEIL'S *VENICE SAVED*   179
  Thomas Sojer

Chapter 11
BEAUTY AS THE BEGINNING AND END OF JUSTICE: AESTHETIC POLITICS IN HANNAH ARENDT AND SIMONE WEIL   199
  Catherine Craig and Sara MacDonald

Chapter 12
ON THE POWER OF WORDS   215
  Ian Rhoad

List of Contributors   227
Index   231

FIGURES

5.1	Elsa Oliva with her partisans' companions	106
6.1	Sister Dianna Ortiz, 1996	120

FOREWORD

In this book, two of the greatest thinkers of the twentieth century intersect in a dialogue that is at the same time impossible and necessary. Divided by their life experiences, they are united by the tragedy of war and exile, which they both suffer, but also by their common interest in the world and social life. Despite an undeniable difference in inspiration, Hannah Arendt and Simone Weil share a series of topics—community, responsibility, political action, intellectual work, but also war, violence, evil—that connect them in a network of common references. The authors of the essays, collected by Kathryn Lawson and Joshua Livingstone, trace the intersections—manifest and secret—between two great philosophers, elaborating them in an acute and original way. The result of this volume is a constellation of great philosophical intensity that illuminates one of the most difficult and richest seasons in contemporary history.

Roberto Esposito

ABBREVIATIONS

Hannah Arendt

BPF	*Between Past and Future*. New York: Penguin, 2006.
CJ	*Hannah Arendt, Karl Jaspers, Correspondence: 1926–1969*. Edited by Lotte Kohler and Hans Saner. Translated by Robert and Rita Kimber. New York: Harcourt, 1992.
DT	*Men in Dark Times*. New York: Harcourt, 1995.
EJ	*Eichmann in Jerusalem: A Report on the Banality of Evil*. New York: Penguin, 2006.
EU	*Essays in Understanding: 1930–1954*. New York: Schocken, 1994.
HC	*The Human Condition*, 2nd ed. Chicago, IL: University of Chicago Press, 1998.
LMT	*The Life of the Mind*. "Thinking." New York: Harcourt Brace, 1978.
LMW	*The Life of the Mind*. "Willing." New York: Harcourt Brace, 1978.
OR	*On Revolution*. New York: Viking Press, 1963.
OT	*The Origins of Totalitarianism*. New York: Harcourt, 1951.
OV	*On Violence*. New York: Harcourt Brace, 1970.
PA	*The Portable Hannah Arendt*. New York: Penguin, 2000.
PP	*The Problems of Politics*. Edited by Jerome Kohn. New York: Schocken, 2005.
RJ	*Responsibility and Judgment*. New York: Schocken, 2003.

Simone Weil

APP	*On the Abolition of All Political Parties*. Translated by Simon Leys. New York: New York Review of Books, 2013.
FLN	*First and Last Notebooks: Supernatural Knowledge*. Translated by Richard Rees. Eugene, OR: Wipf and Stock, 1970.
FW	*Formative Writings 1929–1941*. Edited and translated by Dorothy Tuck McFarland and Wilhelmina Van Ness. Amherst: University of Massachusetts Press, 1987.
GG	*Gravity and Grace*. Edited by Gustave Thibon and Thomas R. Nevin. Translated by Arthur Wills. Lincoln: University of Nebraska Press, 1997.
HP	"Human Personality." Translated by Richard Rees. In *Simone Weil: An Anthology*. Edited by Siân Miles, 69–98. New York: Grove Press, 1986.
IC	*Intimations of Christianity among the Ancient Greeks*. London: Ark Paper Backs, 1957.
IF	"The Iliad, or the Poem of Force." Translated by Mary McCarthy. In *Simone Weil: An Anthology*, 182–215. London: Penguin Books, 2005.

LP	*Lectures on Philosophy*. Translated by Hugh Price. Cambridge: Cambridge University Press, 1978.
NB	*The Notebooks of Simone Weil*. Translated by Arthur Wills. London: Routledge, 2004.
NR	*The Need for Roots*. Translated by Arthur Wills. New York: Routledge, 1952.
OL	*Oppression and Liberty*. Translated by Arthur Wills and John Petrie. Amherst: University of Massachusetts Press, 1973.
SE	*Selected Essays, 1934–1943*. Translated by Richard Rees. Eugene, OR: Wipf & Stock, 1962.
SWA	*Simone Weil: An Anthology*. Edited by Siân Miles. New York: Grove Press, 1986.
SWR	*The Simone Weil Reader*. Edited by George A. Panichas. New York: David McKay, 1977.
VS	*Venice Saved*. Edited and translated by Silvia Panizza and Philip Wilson. London: Bloomsbury, 2019.
WG	*Waiting for God*. Translated by Emma Crauford. Introduction by Leslie A. Fiedler. New York: HarperCollins, 2009.

INTRODUCTION: UNPRECEDENTED CONVERSATIONS IN AN UNPRECEDENTED TIME

Joshua Livingstone and Kathryn Lawson

O, wonder!
How many goodly creatures are there here!
How beauteous mankind is! O brave new world,
That has such people in't!

—Miranda, *The Tempest*[1]

It is well known that Hannah Arendt and Simone Weil, despite sharing a common world, and despite being born less than three years apart, never had the chance to meet. Although they both thought deeply about many of the same political events and philosophical issues, they were not fortunate enough to think together. Theirs is a relationship of quiet divergence, narrow misses, and unfortunate timing. As a result, a near-complete silence lies between them.[2]

No doubt, one of the primary reasons for this regrettable silence was the chaotic state of the world they inhabited. The early years of the twentieth century were some of the most turbulent and unstable in human history. Global wars powered by devastating advances in technology shook the earth from one end to the other. Monstrous acts of inhumanity, against which words seem to crumble in our mouths, exposed the limits of understanding. Authoritarian regimes rose and fell, emerged, and collapsed in dramatic fashion as vicious cycles of force took countless victims and left few victors. Altogether, the various forces of Arendt and Weil's world, both human and inhuman, worked tirelessly to push people apart rather than bring them together. Between the bombs, the camps, and the trenches, there was little time for café conversations, academic conferences, and public panels.

In addition to such atrocious worldly conditions, another key reason for the silence between them is the tragic shortness of Weil's life. Leaving the world at the tender age of thirty-four, Weil remained mostly unpublished in her lifetime.

While alive, she was a relatively obscure figure largely unknown to those outside her immediate circle. Little did she know the impact her work would have on her peers and generations to follow. Those, like Albert Camus, who would eventually bring her into the spotlight of public attention would have to do so in her absence. Similarly, it wasn't until eight years after Weil's death, in 1951, that Arendt would publish her first well-known work, *The Origins of Totalitarianism*. Prior to that, hers was a life lived on the run, uprooted, unsettled, and under constant threat. Trapped in the perilous and vulnerable condition of statelessness, a fate that befell so many in the early years of the twentieth century, Arendt, too, remained a relatively obscure figure until she was well into her forties. As a result, during the period where a meeting might have taken place, Arendt and Weil were likely completely unaware of the other's existence. This innocent ignorance further limited the already slim opportunities for dialogue.

In the end, whether it was the chaos of their time, the tragedy of Weil's death, or simple mischance that prevented their meeting, one thing is clear; the silence that lies between them represents a missed opportunity on a grand scale. One can only imagine what might have transpired, what insights might have been gleaned, what disputes might have given way to new trains of thought, and what possibilities might have been unlocked had this silence been replaced with fruitful dialogue. Sadly, in the absence of such an event, we are left to speculate on how these two great thinkers might have impacted one another. Indeed, we are left to wonder how Arendt's secular humanist account of politics might have impacted Weil's thinking about freedom and oppression, or how Weil's spiritual-ethical approach to politics might have altered Arendt's thinking about judgement and moral responsibility. Without a clear answer to such questions, the possibilities seem boundless.

Martin Buber, the man Arendt once referred to as "German Judaism's incontestable guide,"[3] famously argues that the act of dialogue is a turning toward the other that opens a portal to the present.[4] Against a Platonic tradition that sees dialogue as a means of transcending the illusory realm of the everyday, Buber argued that genuine dialogue does not lead to ultimate Truths or final conclusions, nor does it provide us with the technical knowledge needed to solve the many problems and dilemmas that we face on a daily basis. Instead, what dialogue does is release us from the enclosures of historical precedent and predetermined ways of being that objectify and constrain the possibilities of the present moment. When genuine, dialogue allows us to shed the weight of the past to confront a reality that is radically new, spontaneous, and unprecedented. Borrowing (and perhaps misusing) Wittgenstein's famous metaphor, we might say that dialogue releases us from the fly bottle of reflexive monologue to face one another and the world anew.

Echoing this sentiment in a 1966 address, Arendt writes that "by talking … about the unprecedented and by making decisions as we must, even though they may one day prove wholly inadequate, I believe we will become better able to deal with the underlying crisis even if we fail to define it" (TB 331). The crisis she refers to here is not any one particular crisis, such as the crisis in education or the crisis in culture, but rather the general state of crisis that seems to define the modern world. It is the all-pervasive crisis brought on by the explosive force of totalitarianism, which, Arendt argues, collapsed the bridge of tradition and rendered its whole stock of readymade universals, concepts, rules, values, and norms utterly inadequate. For Arendtian thinking, whether it's the climate crisis, the post-truth crisis, the financial crisis, the global health crisis, the crisis of democracy, or any other such crisis, what binds all crises together is the simple fact that they involve a breakdown of judgement. In times of crisis, "not even common sense makes sense any longer" (PP 102). Crises are events in which the hitherto unknown looms before us, demanding our attention and calling on us to think without the banisters of tradition. Dialogue, Arendt suggests, is but one way of heeding that call. By simply talking with one another, sharing opinions and perspectives, we can confront a mystifying and boundless present without allowing the event of crisis to develop into catastrophe.

The result of this "talking" is not necessarily the insertion of new concepts into the collective reserve of ideas. It is primarily a means not of bolstering support for a collapsing tradition but rather of enacting a kind of self-transformation or second birth that can make us better prepared to carry on in the wake of difficult and tragic circumstance. To converse, in its originally Latin formation (as *converso*), means to "turn over." Partners in dialogue take hold of a shared present, turning it over, again and again, in order to examine it from a variety of unique perspectives. As Jürgen Habermas puts it, dialogue enacts "the reciprocal interpenetration of the perspective of those involved."[5] For Arendt, the ideal result of this process of turning over is what Kant calls an "enlargement of the mind" (LK 40–6). By combining perspectives and widening our otherwise narrow view, the thought is that we become better positioned to see reality for what it is, without the blinders of prejudice and individual motivation. We are liberated from the limitations of the self to judge on the basis of a plurality; that is, we are enabled to see from the perspective of the many unique *whos* that comprise our communities. Conversation, therefore, can be seen as a kind of conversion—a transformation of the self that leaves its mark on our very being. For Arendt, it is the width of one's perspective, not their adherence to rational principles and logical operations, that determines the validity and the strength of one's judgement.

For Weil, conversation comes from true friendship, which is rare and divine, but it can also come from the more pedestrian love of one's neighbor. Weilian friendship is a form of Pythagorean harmony not in that it harmonizes the contraries of the I and the other, but that it allows for a void to open up between them. Only when such a gap exists can God, the Good, and the mysterious emerge to fill that gap. To be truly friends is to allow a space for difference and divinity and to seek an accord that can produce justice. The friendship between humans is modeled on the originary friendship of the Divine Trinity and on one's relation to God (IC 176–7). For Weil, the harmony that we seek with other people and with God is cultivated by our intelligence, which is a "specifically and rigorously individual thing" (WG 34). Weil cites Jesus's claim, "Wheresoever two or three are gathered together in my name, there am I in the midst of them," and argues that it is in these close conversations that truth and justice can be brought about through balance: "He said precisely that he always forms the third in the intimacy of the tête-à-tête" (WG 35). Conversing makes possible a harmony among humans and a space for the divine, balance, and justice. Because a true friendship is a connection to the divine for Weil, it is not something that can be forced. For it will arrive only with God's grace. And while such friendship is rare, we must continually attempt to cultivate these just conversations with others without hope of friendship (FLN 37).

Weil notes that we can and should strive to cultivate a love for the unknown and often misunderstood neighbor, and that this love should be generated by giving that neighbor our attention. This attention requires careful cultivation but is simultaneously quite simple. As she explains, "The love of our neighbor in all its fullness simply means being able to say to him: 'What are you going through?'" (WG 64). It is on the basis of this simple ability to open a dialogue with one another that divine love and ethical action is possible. Because the neighbor need not be a friend, there is an equality in this attention. As such, our attentive, thoughtful conversation offers the highest possibility of friendship *and* the ethical foundation of political action.

From this perspective, the silence that takes the place of a dialogue between Hannah Arendt and Simone Weil also takes the place of this opportunity to mix perspectives, to form friendships, and to undergo that dialogical self-transformation that enlarges each person's view and enhances their capacity for judgement. Being unable to come together to talk and to confront the unprecedented present, Arendt and Weil lost more than the mere chance for pleasant conversation. And while the loss of this opportunity does not entail a diminishment of either thinker's creative capacity or power of judgement, one still wonders what might have been gained had a dialogue taken place.

In the spirit of such conversation, therefore, the authors of this volume seek to join those few who have already attempted to make up for this missed opportunity. Those, like Roberto Esposito, Lyndsey Stonebridge,[6] Robert Chenavier,[7] Emmanuel Gabellieri,[8] Mary Dietz,[9] Sylvie Courtine-Denamy,[10] and others, who remain dissatisfied with silence.[11] By bringing Arendt and Weil together to confront a present they themselves did not live to see, our hope is that, even in the absence of living speakers, we may still be able to instigate a dialogue by breathing our own life into it. While this might not be a wholly sufficient replacement for a genuine in-person dialogue, the hope is that the exercise alone may embolden us and help us address the endless stream of aporias and challenges that plague our own time. By bringing the insights of Arendt and Weil to bear on our own present, the aim of this collection is to enrich our ability to confront a world of crisis that has not so much improved in the intervening century since their deaths as it has simply evolved and intensified.

Of course, there are inherent difficulties in staging a conversation between two thinkers who never met. For one, we are forced to speculate on what they might have discussed, what topics they might have covered, what trajectories their conversation might have taken. Whenever two people come together in dialogue, no single outcome or definitive conclusion is guaranteed. Something inevitably remains outstanding. Still, provided there is a large enough body of work to draw upon, such speculation may not be completely arbitrary. In both cases, we are lucky to have access to a large collection of writings on a wide range of subject matter, much of which overlaps and intersects with the writings of the other. In fact, there are even a few rare moments in which a dialogue (albeit one-sided) begins to emerge between Arendt and Weil before withdrawing back into deafening silence. These moments in Arendt's work, which appear as minor footnotes and off-hand references to the thought and person of Simone Weil, offer tantalizing insight into the character, shape, and possible direction a conversation might have taken.

The first of these references occurs in *The Human Condition*, in the section on labor. There Arendt praises Weil for her lack of "prejudice and sentimentality" in dealing with the so-called labor question (HC 131). What this all-too-brief mention reveals is that there is a kind of kinship between the two thinkers with regard to the way they approach their craft. Indeed, if there is one thing that can equally be said of Arendt and of Weil, it is that their way of thinking abhors the detached analysis of the atomized subject or the mawkish romanticism of the privileged academic.[12] Neither thinker had much time for the excessively abstract pleasures of leisurely philosophizing or nostalgic reflections on times past. Questions about angels dancing on the head of pins or the *Beyng* of beings represented for them a kind of thinking divorced from political realities and worldly conditions. And though both took inspiration from the oft-romanticized ancients, the Greeks, in particular, neither sought a return to ancient conditions or traditions. Instead, Arendt and Weil, each in their own way, sought to enact what Arendt calls an "unpremeditated, attentive facing up to, and resisting of, reality—whatever it may be or might have been" (OT xiv). Similarly, Weil suggests the cultivation of an "attentive intelligence" through which we "give birth to reality" in the sense that we can perceive the world and the ethical balance we might, by our actions, bring to that reality (IC 188). This kind of thinking is grounded in the concrete realities of modern life—its painful struggles and alienating circumstances. And yet, it is also not a pessimistic thinking. Resisting the extremes of what Arendt calls "reckless optimism and reckless despair," both thinkers seek to chart a middle way—one that is not overly enthusiastic nor unfairly cynical, but which is authentic, realistic, and remains hopeful even in the face of overwhelming odds (OT vii).

Stateless and fleeing the totalitarian explosion in Nazi Germany, Arendt had barely become acquainted with adulthood when she found herself forced into the dark background of difference in which human beings are reduced to the meager existence of what Giorgio Agamben calls "bare life."[13] Stripped of her status as a unique and dignified "who," a person with equal rights and value, Arendt endured almost two decades without citizenship, belonging to no nation or state. Her political theory is in many ways a protest against the conditions that stole the dignity and the humanity of so many like her. Her aim, in spite of these conditions, is to carve out a space in which she might take back what was stolen. Acutely aware of the despair that seems to accompany the misguided optimism of her fellow "newcomers," those *parvenus* that find themselves caught in a vicious cycle of assimilationist hope and crushing rejection, Arendt chose to take the path of the conscious pariah (JW 264–74). Her emphasis on the uniqueness of the self and the power of individual action emerges as a response to the loss of the self and imposed impotence of those without rights. Her middle way lies between the extremes of optimistic assimilation and pessimistic resignation.

Like Arendt, Weil, too, was forced to confront the rise of totalitarian evil as one whose Jewish background marked her as a target. And yet, even when her own life was in danger, Weil was always quick to reject the comforts of home in order to thrust herself into the fray and to join those less fortunate in their fight against oppression. Weil states that while she would inevitably delight in being a part of a group, "I feel that it is not permissible for me. I feel that it is necessary and ordained that I should be alone, a stranger and an exile in relation to every human circle without exception" (WG 13). This commitment is evident in her biography, which reads as a series of dramatic acts of self-sacrifice, service and support, and her philosophical writings, which express similar passionate sentiments of love and devotion. And when eventually she was forced into exile, Weil's emphasis on selflessness, attention, and divine intervention never wavered. Never did she put herself before others, even when doing so might have spared her great suffering. Instead, Weil consistently and unrelentingly dedicated her life to the cause of freedom and to the project of building a more just world. Like Arendt, Weil argues that the individual ability to think and pay attention is what keeps one from falling into the social collective emotions that masquerade as an *ersatz* form of ethical truth (WG 12). Paradoxically, the ultimate selfless act, for Weil, is to maintain an attentive sense of self rather than falling into the ease of collective thought. As T. S. Elliot puts it in his foreword to *The Need for Roots*, Weil was a "woman of genius, of a kind of genius akin to that of the saints" (NR viii). Her middle way is a consent to necessity and an active fight for justice. It lies between the divine optimism of friendship, beauty and love, and the pessimism of the godless force that creates war, death, and destruction.

Contrary to the detached perspective all too common among political scientists, Arendt and Weil write from the perspective of one on the ground, so to speak, whether it's the perspective of one directly involved in political action or one adversely impacted by it. Together, they paint a picture of the political realm as a place of phenomenal richness. For Arendt it is a place of glory and heroism, where actors are free to become themselves, where new beginnings are begun, and new relationships are forged that weave together a web of relations capable of bestowing the world with meaning. For Weil, it is a place of dark necessity, important in its own right but filled, nonetheless, with tragic suffering and oppression. Weil argues that "the essential tendency of all political parties is towards totalitarianism, first on the national scale and then on the global scale" (APP 14). But this is not just the case for politics. Weil argues that in Plato's *Republic*, "Human society, and any collectivity contained within that society, is likened to the great and powerful beast" (IC 134). Thus, this extends also to collective systematic philosophizing.

For both thinkers, traditional forms of philosophical thinking about the political are not only overly abstract but also highly dangerous. The solitary nature of philosophical thinking, its character of disinterested withdrawal, its ego-centric approach to life, and its overemphasis on harmonious order and unity not only erode the philosopher's capacity to appreciate plurality and see the world as others do but also bring them into easy alignment with totalitarian systems of domination. Spending their days in the no-where, no-time of the thought landscape that Arendt calls the *nunc-stans*, the philosopher, even more so than her peers, is susceptible to the insidious influence of ideology (LM 202–13). As Arendt puts it, reflecting on her narrow escape from Germany in 1933, "among intellectuals *Gleichschaltung* was the rule, so to speak. But not among others. And I never forgot that."[14] Here, we might also be reminded of Arendt's famously controversial declaration that "there are no dangerous thoughts for the simple reason that thinking itself is a dangerous enterprise" (TB 408).

When it comes to philosophy, Weil's rejection of collectivity is a matter of her desire to keep open contradictory poles and her refusal to "resolve" history through dialectic. She states: "What is intelligible in the famous 'dialectic' is nothing more than the idea of relation, which can be seen much more clearly in Plato than in Hegel. As for the famous 'negation of the negation,' it is pure rubbish" (FLN 17). To be thoughtful and attentive is to reject any absolute dialectical resolutions or understanding of history as progress. Instead, we attend, think, and balance force with love. There is no end to this cycle.

Another of Arendt's sparse references to Weil appears in a 1968 piece, printed in the *New York Review of Books*, humorously titled "He's All Dwight" (TB 397). The article is a reflection on the publication history of the relatively short-lived New York political magazine, *Politics*, and its editor, Dwight Macdonald. Deliberately trying to avoid nostalgic sentiment, Arendt praises Macdonald for both his willingness to publish the work of "leftist refugees" and for his keen ability to recognize radical thought before fame. There Weil is cited as one such thinker—a radical who genuinely seeks "to grasp the matter by the root" (TB 397). This suggests that Arendt did see Weil as not only an unsentimental thinker, someone who does not fall prey to romantic or nostalgic inclination but also a profoundly deep thinker, a radical who strives to always get to the heart of any political matter, which, for Macdonald, means keeping the human person always in view.

Macdonald's article "The Root Is Man," which would grow into a book by the same title, makes the case that political theory suffers from a crisis of vocabulary. He suggests that with the bewildering emergence of totalitarian regimes, Nazi and Stalinist versions alike (both of which combine ideas from across the political spectrum), the distinction between left and right has been rendered inadequate, and he argues that to confront these new political realities, political theorists are in desperate need of a whole new set of terms and distinctions by which to frame their ongoing conversations.[15] By continuing to view politics through the traditional left-right lens, Macdonald thinks, theorists risk falling into a state of detached dogmatism. Instead, he proposes that theorists ought to move toward a political theory centered on a "progressive/radical" distinction. The progressivists are "those who view the present as an episode on the way to a better future," while the radicals are "those who reject the concept of Progress, who judge things by their present meaning and effect, who think the ability of science to guide us in human affairs has been overrated and who therefore redress the balance by emphasizing the ethical aspect of politics."¹⁶ For Macdonald, the radical is a thinker who places real, flesh-and-blood human beings at the root of all politics rather than abstract ideals and historicist ideologies.

By putting Weil in the camp of the radicals, Arendt acknowledges another point of commonality between them, namely, an unwillingness to view history and politics through the lens of progress. Unlike so many of her Marxists colleagues, Weil does not see history as a linear development, a series of moments moving steadily and surely toward some utopian future—a view that so often justifies the unjustifiable. As Czeslaw Milosz explains:

> There is a contradiction between our longing for the good and the cold universe absolutely indifferent to any values, subject to the iron necessity of causes and effects. That contradiction has been solved by the rationalists and progressives of various kinds who placed the good in the world, in matter, and usually in the future. The philosophy of Hegel and of his followers crowned those attempts by inventing the idea of the good in movement, walking toward fuller and fuller accomplishment in history. Simone Weil ... combatted such solutions as illegitimate. Her efforts were directed toward making the contradiction as acute as possible. Whoever tries to escape an inevitable contraction by patching it up is, she affirms, a coward. (APP 49)

Instead of striving to overcome contradictions, Weil's approach to politics is grounded in a profound appreciation for the fallenness of human beings and ever-present need for redemption. For Weil, any honest look at history will reveal that in overcoming one set of problems and challenges, we almost always find ourselves falling back into another. This is the very nature of Weilian *force* and human existence. We find balance, we lose balance, we try once again to find balance. Contra the enlightenment hope for a future of perpetual peace, what we should expect is a future of ongoing struggle and oppression. As she explains in *Oppression and Liberty*, "human history is simply the history of servitude which makes men—oppressors and oppressed alike—the plaything of the instruments of domination they themselves have manufactures, and thus reduces living humanity to being the chattel of inanimate chattels" (OL 66). For Weil, politics is a constant and unending struggle against the relentless forces of oppression and violence.

In *The Need for Roots*, Weil argues that to have even a modicum of success in this struggle requires one to set down roots in a human community. She claims that rootedness is "perhaps the most important and least recognized need of the human soul" (NR 43). For her, this does not mean belonging to a particular national, cultural, or racial group, but more simply, it means having a place to call home. It means belonging to a living community while being treated as a valued and dignified member of that community. When human beings are reduced to their place within the greater forces of history and their role in furthering the development of those forces, politics is degraded to a kind of servitude, and oppression is seen as a justifiable means to some greater end: "Instead of thinking, one merely takes sides: for or against. Such a choice replaces the activity of the mind. This is an intellectual leprosy" (APP 34).

Conversely, when divine love forms the center of an ethical community built between human beings, then, Weil thinks, the meaning and purpose of politics radically changes: "It is when we desire truth with an empty soul and without attempting to guess its content that we receive the light" (APP 22). This individual thoughtful attention allows for a recognition of our obligation "towards the human being as such," an obligation that should be the basis of our politics, according to Weil (NR 5). Any government, law, or institution created by that community will no longer be seen as a means of control or of bringing its members into alignment with some vision of historical development. Instead, they will be implemented as a means of uplifting the people and promoting freedom.

Arendt, like Weil, also sees history in nonprogressivist terms. Following her friend and fellow Jewish refugee, Walter Benjamin, Arendt sees history as "one single catastrophe which keeps piling wreckage upon wreckage."[17] Contra Hegel and Marx, Arendt's view of history is a tragic one, full of unexpected and volatile events, events that could not have been predicted from the perspective of the present. It is a view of history grounded in the human capacity for new beginning. "Limitations and boundaries," she explains, "exist within the realm of human affairs, but they never offer a framework that can reliably withstand the onslaught with which each new generation must insert itself" (HC 190). Only by taking a reflective perspective, Arendt thinks, can we look back on the past and say that one event led to another. And it is only by denying human freedom that we are able to do so. From the perspective of the present, the future appears as an open sea of possibilities, some good, some bad, but all effectively unprecedented. If nothing else, Arendt holds that the explosion of totalitarianism at the beginning of the twentieth century proved this to be the case.

One of the consequences of this nonlinear view of history, for Arendt, is that we are continuously confronted by new events and happenings that challenge our sense of understanding and being at home in the world. To root politics in the human being, as Macdonald desired and as Weil set out to achieve, is to place oneself in the position of always having to negotiate with an ambiguous present. One can never arrive at a point where perfect understanding can be achieved. Instead, for Arendt, understanding is a lifelong process of settlement and resettlement. As she explains, in her essay "Understanding and Politics (The Difficulties of Understanding)," understanding is not a state of being but rather "an unending activity by which, in constant change and variation, we come to terms with and reconcile ourselves to reality, that is, try to be at home in the world" (UP 308). Indeed, as totalitarianism has all too clearly revealed, there are times when the world around us begins to unravel, to wobble and shake from the ground up; times when our capacity to tell real from unreal, true from false is disrupted; times when the world we once knew is replaced by a previously unfathomable constellation of chaotic happenings. In these dark times, we can relatively easily, in fact, become unsettled and thrown into a kind of homelessness.

Paradoxically, it is during such times of upheaval and potential disaster that so many are driven into the consolations and reassurances of mass existence and nonthinking. Indeed, Weil notes that such a thing is initially "so comfortable! It amounts to having no thoughts at all. Nothing is more comfortable than not having to think" (APP 27). In a letter, Weil confesses her personal fear of this collective seduction, noting that the comradery and patriotic songs of a group of young Nazis would surely capture a part of her soul into their brotherhood (WG 11). This fear of the comfort of collective "thinking" (or, rather, the absence of thinking) motivates Weil to remain ever on guard and to continue to dedicate herself toward intellectual pursuits. The uprootedness that she observes in France during the Second World War is a loss of "real, active and natural participation in the life of a community" (NR 43) and can happen either quickly or over many years without our realizing it when we offload our thinking onto the collective.

In the end, what Arendt's brief but enticing references to Weil's work reveal is that both thinkers share an ability to assess honestly and without sentiment the political realities of any given moment and to respond to those realities with hope that things will get better without appealing to the forces of history or ideology. Any speculative conversation between these two thinkers, therefore, ought to do two things: (1) it ought to take the middle way between excessive optimism and excessive despair, and (2) it ought not to skim the surface of the issues it concerns itself with but to dive deep into the radical ground of politics. Whatever the subject of the conversation might be, Arendt and Weil are fellow travelers in these two crucial respects.

This, of course, is not to say that there are no conflicts or disagreements between them or that their shared lack of sentimentality and appreciation for depth means that they would inevitably come to the same conclusions. Indeed, Arendt's secular humanism, her emphasis on heroic action, and her rejection of the strictly moral approach to politics contrast starkly with Weil's religious approach, her faith in the power of divine Goodness, and her other-centric ethic of suffering and affliction. As Roberto Esposito puts it, the difference in perspective between Arendt and Weil is so great that we can conceive of them as a "contrasting overlap" in which "each thinks in the inverse of the other's thought, in the shadow of the other's light, in the silence of the other's voice, in the emptiness of the other's plenitude."[18]

Such dramatic differences, however, do not in and of themselves reject the possibility of fruitful dialogue. Quite the opposite in fact. What these differences suggest is that any conversation between Arendt and Weil promises to be immensely productive. By acknowledging the ways in which their ideas challenge one another and reveal the limitations of the other's thought, the authors of this collection hope to instigate a kind of *Auseinándersetzung* or productive struggle in which the interpenetration of perspectives leads to new political insights. Without attempting to overcome the tension between them, Esposito sought to exploit it, to crisscross the partition line and draw out of each what the other failed to see. In so doing, he discovered that Arendt and Weil share the same apparently contradictory insight, namely that the origin of the political is its apparent opposite—war. Politics, he explained, "is born at the heart of a *polemos* whose outcome is the destruction of a polis."[19] He recognized that both Arendt and Weil draw heavily on the Homeric account of the Trojan War as the beginning of a political tradition spanning the centuries right up to today. And what they discovered was a sense of the political in which politics becomes an attempt to rescue human relations from the utter destruction of all-out war. By sublimating the agonal spirit of war into the region of peace, politics became a means of securing the human community against the onslaught of nature's indifference and the meaninglessness of violent struggle.

In a similar spirit, this collection aims to follow Esposito by bringing Arendt and Weil into a dialogue of "reciprocal complication."[20] This is a dialogue that strives, through instigating antagonisms and clearing common ground, to reveal hidden insights and possibilities previously unseen and underappreciated. Building on the dialogue opened by Esposito, the authors of this collection carry the conversation forward to address the concrete challenges and ambiguities of our current moment in time. The essays gathered here bring Arendt and Weil together to discuss timeless political themes of power, freedom, violence, justice, resistance, responsibility, attention, aesthetics, and human vulnerability, as they relate to the pressing political challenges of our unprecedented era—challenges like the ongoing migration crisis, literary censorship, increasing bureaucratization, the social media revolution.

The basic framework of this collection is organized around three main sections, each of which covers a distinct theme. Part I includes four chapters on "Power, Violence, and the Adversaries of Freedom." Part II includes another four chapters on "Society, World, and the Need for Political Roots." And lastly, Part III contains a final four chapters on the theme of "Art, Aesthetics, and the Vulnerabilities of Political Appearances." Altogether, these three sections are comprised of twelve imagined conversations, each interweaving with the next to form a broader conversation about the state of politics today.

The first chapter, by Lissa McCullough, presents a dialogue on the nature of power that identifies a sharp distinction between Weil's coercive account of power and Arendt's cooperative account of power; where the former relates power to necessity, oppression, and the cyclical struggles of those seeking to dominate, the latter relates it to freedom, the overcoming of necessity, and the boundless possibility of political action. Cutting across this harsh incongruity, McCullough discovers a shared awareness of the dangers of centralized systems of power and a shared desire to protect and preserve the freedom of individuals.

Marina Lademacher then carries this theme forward by directing the conversation toward the hazards of the ever-increasing bureaucratization of politics. According to Lademacher, Arendt and Weil see bureaucracy as a means of fitting human life into a centralized system of power and molding that life around a perverse kind of utilitarian calculus. Confronting this monstrous new reality, Lademacher shows how Arendt and Weil, each in their own way, promote a decentralized, democratic approach to politics that struggles to resist and push back against the ever-rising tide and totalizing ambitions of a bureaucratic system that reduces human beings to the status of the anonymous "nobody."

Next, Marie Cabaud Meaney turns the conversation toward the question of what draws human beings into totalitarianism to enact an evil that is as radical as it is banal. Meaney argues that, for both Arendt and Weil, the extreme and nonsensical nature of totalitarianism is oddly seductive, as a source not of pleasure but of obligation. In totalitarian states, evil is normalized so that even the ordinary person, the average everyday citizen, finds themselves committing acts of unfathomable cruelty. Meaney points out that, for Arendt, it is thoughtlessness that seduces people into evil, while, for Weil, it is the fallen nature of human existence that places us eternally on the precipice. Comparing their differing solutions, Arendt's secular-humanist emphasis on judgement and "thinking without a banister" and Weil's ethical-religious emphasis on moral decision-making, Meaney concludes with a sober reminder that evil, while seductive, can never last and that by converting evil, through love, into suffering, we can resist.

Closing out the first section, Rose Owen brings Arendt and Weil together to discuss the nature of violence and its relation to politics. Owen begins by pointing out that, for Weil, violence is understood in terms of force, which turns human persons into things as a kind of cruel form of reification. For Arendt, on the other hand, violence removes human persons from the public sphere, thereby undermining our capacity to engage in politics and to manifest the power to bring about new beginnings. Together, Owen argues, Weil and Arendt view violence as antithetical to politics. And yet, she is careful to remind us that neither Arendt nor Weil were themselves pacifists. Arendt's calls for the formation of a Jewish army to fight the Nazis, and Weil's willingness to fight in the Spanish Civil War and for the Free French Resistance, show that for both thinkers there are times when violence is necessary and can serve to help bring people back to the bargaining table of politics.

Shifting the conversation away from the weighty topics of evil, power, and violence, Elvira Roncalli and Kathryn Lawson open the second section with complementary essays on the notion of "world" in Arendt and Weil. First, Roncalli considers what it means to maintain a world in the Arendtian sense, one that is both ubiquitous and frail. Moving from the fullness of the political world as common to the emptiness of wordlessness and the loss of the political, Roncalli emphasizes the crucial role of plurality in the very foundation of the world. And with reference to the example of Italian Resistance fighter Elsa Oliva, she argues that without a plurality of unique and individual persons, the world as such is liable to fall in ruins.

Mirroring Roncalli's three-scene structure, Kathryn Lawson draws out the main contrast between Arendt and Weil's worlds, namely Weil's inclusion of the divine Good as an ethical ballast for the affliction of earthly existence. Radically different from Arendt's political center, the center of the world for Weil is in-between people in the form of a divine Goodness that is not of this world. Using the example of catholic nun and activist Sister Dianna Ortiz, Lawson argues that finding such a balance allows for just political action in a shared community through a life that is profoundly marked by both intense divine love and extreme existential suffering.

From the discussion of worldliness in Arendt and Weil, Scott B. Ritner then turns our attention to the phenomenon of uprootedness. Acknowledging the fact that Arendt and Weil themselves suffered under refugee conditions and so spoke with first-hand experience, Ritner presents Arendt's figure of the refugee—as outlined in her famous essay "We Refugees"—as an intensification of the figure of the *déraciné* in Weil. This conversation is carried out with a view towards critiquing nationalist conceptions of belonging and state efforts to arbitrate identity. Ritner concludes by applying the insights derived from this conversation to the ongoing migrant crisis in the United States and around the world while also looking ahead toward future crises related to climate change and the inevitable mass migrations to follow.

Closing out the second section, Paolo Monti then carries the discussion from the physical realm into the digital sphere, bringing Arendt and Weil to bear on the "grand technology of attention," that is, social media. In particular, Monti considers the impact social media has had, both good and bad, on democracy by considering it within the framework of attention and moral responsibility, as understood by Arendt and Weil. Recalling the way totalitarian regimes enact two crucial mechanisms of domination, "uprootedness" and "unreality," through the suspension and manipulation of individual attention, he argues that attention is a both a scarce political resource and vital civic responsibility. By cultivating attention in our social media age of inattention, Monti argues that we can counter the effects of uprooting, resist the continued dissolution of our capacity to judge, and shield citizens against the antipolitical elements of social media technology.

Leaving the theme of rootedness and worldliness, Pascale Devette then opens the final section by looking at the political role of tragic storytelling. Combining an Arendtian understanding of who-centered narrative with a Weilian sense of the anonymity inherent to affliction, Devette argues that tragic storytelling offers a means of reshaping and reconfiguring our ways of sharing the world with others and of manifesting a renewed sense of love for the world and the perishable things that comprise it. By attempting to reveal the invisible, to put words to the utterly ineffable, tragic storytelling works to secure the memory of those who suffered from the anonymity and loss of self inherent in conditions of affliction. Turning to examples of testimonial holocaust literature, from figures like Primo Levi and Jean Améry, Devette puts into context the importance of tragic storytelling at a time when the last of the holocaust survivors and those who experienced the horrors of the camps will soon be gone.

Carrying the conversation from the realm of literature into the realm of theater, Thomas Sojer gives an Arendtian reading of Weil's play *Venice Saved*, discussing the political significance of play-acting and the dramaturgical nature of politics. Blending the apparently contradictory positions of Arendt and Weil, the former emphasizing the insertion of the 'who' into the public realm, the latter emphasizing the need for decreation, Sojer works to articulate a notion of theater that makes possible a unique form of action, which simultaneously decenters the I and allows for emergent whoness. Sojer's goal is to show how an understanding of theatrical performance can reveal ways of enacting decreation, forging alliances with other bodies and, in so doing, unlocking the underlying natality that lies at the core of politics.

Catherine Craig and Sara MacDonald, then, turn to Arendt and Weil for help in imagining the role of beauty in politics. Acknowledging that both thinkers have a remarkably similar sense of the individual's responsibility to the well-being of others and to the shared world more generally, Craig and MacDonald push back against attempts to de-aestheticize politics and strip it of its aesthetical qualities. Together, they argue, Arendt and Weil show us how beauty can both offer a model for justice and open the path to its attainment. Interweaving insights from Arendt and Weil's separate engagements with Homer's *Iliad*, Craig and MacDonald make the case for beauty in politics to serve as a means of encouragement, to motivate us to seek the good of others, and to recreate images of beauty in our own political communities.

And lastly, Ian Rhoad closes the final section with a reflection on the political nature of language and the need for a new kind of rhetoric. Drawing on insights from Weil's "Human Personality" and "The Power of Words," and Arendt's *Human Condition* and *The Life of the Mind*, Rhoad offers a fresh take on the nature and role of political rhetoric and what he calls "the steering function of words." He suggests that Arendt's account of liberated judgement and Weil's insistence on loving attention together can help us overcome ancient accounts of rhetoric as an art that is useful for winning debate and attaining power over others through persuasion. Instead, the fruits of a conversation between them can help us reimagine rhetoric as a kind of responsiveness through words, which is primarily a kind of listening before it is a kind of talking.

Altogether, the authors gathered here offer up an imagined conversation between Hannah Arendt and Simone Weil that shows their continued relevance and the applicability of their political philosophies to a world they themselves could only have imagined. Indeed, as we move ever deeper into the twenty-first century, the works of Arendt and Weil warn us of what can go wrong when we fail to think about what we are doing. They also stand as calls to action, to make the world a freer, more tolerant place to live. Each in their own way asks us to join them in their efforts to open new worlds and embody new forms of political thinking. Both celebrate plurality and human dignity while working toward the perhaps impossible achievement of freedom for all. And both reveal the boundless possibility inherent in the unending dialogue that is politics.

Notes

1 William Shakespeare, *The Tempest*, third series, ed. Alden T. Vaughan and Virginia Mason Vaughan (New York: Arden Shakespeare, 2011).
2 We say "near complete" silence as there are a few brief moments where reference is made, by Arendt, to Weil and to her work. These sparse references turn out to be packed with significance and suggest the possibility of a truly generative dialogue.

3 In 1935, during a time of rising tension and growing anti-Semitism, Hannah Arendt published a brief article for *Le Journal Juif*, in which she praised Buber for his leadership in the German Jewish community. There she explains how Buber "succeeded in awakening the souls of these assimilated Jews ... because he didn't bury himself or Judaism under a great past, but knew how to rediscover the living roots of this past to build an even greater future" (JW 33). His influence on Arendt's work is undeniable, and thus his insights into the nature of dialogue offer a helpful way of framing the discussion to follow.
4 Martin Buber, *I and Thou*, trans. Walter Kaufmann (New York: Simon & Schuster, 1996).
5 Jürgen Habermas, "A Philosophy of Dialogue," in *Dialogue as a Trans-disciplinary Concept*, ed. Paul Mendes-Flohr (Boston: De Gruyter, 2015), 11.
6 See Lyndsey Stonebridge, *Placeless People: Writing, Rights, and Refugees* (Oxford: Oxford University Press, 2018).
7 See Robert Chenavier, "Simone Weil et Hannah Arendt," *Cahiers Simone Weil* 12, no. 2 (1989): 149–69.
8 See Emmanuel Gabellieri, "Vie publique et vita activa: S. Weil et H. Arendt," *Cahiers Simone Weil* 22, no. 2 (1999): 135–52.
9 See Mary G Dietz, *Between the Human and the Divine: The Political Thought of Simone Weil* (Totowa, NJ: Rowman & Littlefield, 1988).
10 Sylvie Courtine-Denamy, *Three Women in Dark Times: Edith Stein, Hannah Arendt, Simone Weil*, trans. G. M. Goshgarian (Ithaca, NY: Cornell University Press, 2001).
11 See also *Les Catégories de l'Universel. Simone Weil et Hannah Arendt*, ed. Étienne Tassin and Michel Narcy (Paris: L'Harmattan, 2003); Marina Cedronio (ed.), *Modernité, Démocratie et Totalitarisme: Simone Weil et Hannah Arendt* (Paris: Klincksieck, 1996).
12 For more insight into the "unsentimental" character of Arendt and Weil's thinking, see Deborah Nelson, *Tough Enough: Arbus, Arendt, Didion, McCarthy, Sontag, Weil* (Chicago: University of Chicago Press, 2017).
13 See Giorgio Agamben, *Homo Sacer: Sovereign Power and Bare Life*, trans. Daniel Heller-Roazen (Stanford: Stanford University Press, 1998).
14 Hannah Arendt, *The Last Interview and Other Conversations* (Brooklyn: Melville House, 2013), 19.
15 Dwight Macdonald, "The Root Is Man," *Politics* 3, no. 4 (April 1946): 99–101.
16 Ibid., 100.
17 Walter Benjamin, "On the Concept of History," *Selected Writings*, vol. 4, trans. Edmund Jephcott and others, ed. Howard Eiland and Michael W. Jennings (Cambridge: Harvard University Press, 2003), 392.
18 Roberto Esposito, *The Origin of the Political*, trans. Vincenzo Binetti and Gareth Williams (New York: Fordham University Press, 2017), 1.
19 Ibid., 13.
20 Ibid., 2.

Bibliography

Agamben, Giorgio. *Homo Sacer: Sovereign Power and Bare Life*. Translated by Daniel Heller-Roazen. Stanford: Stanford University Press, 1998.

Benjamin, Walter. "On the Concept of History." In *Selected Writings, Vol. 4*. Translated by Edmund Jephcott and others. Edited by Howard Eiland and Michael W. Jennings. Cambridge: Harvard University Press, 2003, pp. 389–400.

Buber, Martin. *I and Thou*. Translated by Walter Kaufmann. New York: Simon & Schuster, 1996.

Cedronio, Marina (ed.). *Modernité, Démocratie et Totalitarisme: Simone Weil et Hannah Arendt*. Paris: Klincksieck, 1996.

Chenavier, Robert. "Simone Weil et Hannah Arendt." *Cahiers Simone Weil* 12, no. 2 (1989): 149–69.

Courtine-Denamy, Sylvie. *Three Women in Dark Times: Edith Stein, Hannah Arendt, Simone Weil*. Translated by G. M. Goshgarian. Ithaca, NY: Cornell University Press, 2001.

Dietz, Mary G. *Between the Human and the Divine: The Political Thought of Simone Weil*. Totowa, NJ: Rowman & Littlefield, 1988.

Esposito, Roberto. *The Origin of the Political*. Translated by Vincenzo Binetti and Gareth Williams. New York: Fordham University Press, 2017.

Gabellieri, Emmanuel. "Vie publique et vita activa: S. Weil et H. Arendt." *Cahiers Simone Weil* 22, no. 2 (1999): 135–52.

Habermas, Jürgen. "A Philosophy of Dialogue." In *Dialogue as a Trans-disciplinary Concept*. Edited by Paul Mendes-Flohr. Boston: De Gruyter, 2015, pp. 7–20.

Macdonald, Dwight. "The Root Is Man." *Politics* 3, no. 4 (April 1946): 97–115.

Nelson, Deborah. *Tough Enough: Arbus, Arendt, Didion, McCarthy, Sontag, Weil*. Chicago: University of Chicago Press, 2017.

Stonebridge, Lyndsey. *Placeless People: Writing, Rights, and Refugees*. Oxford: Oxford University Press, 2018.

Tassin, Étienne, and Michel Narcy (eds.). *Les Catégories de l'Universel. Simone Weil et Hannah Arendt*. Paris: L'Harmattan, 2003.

Part I

POWER, VIOLENCE, AND THE ADVERSARIES OF FREEDOM

Chapter 1

ON POWER IN SIMONE WEIL AND HANNAH ARENDT: CONTRASTS AND CORRELATIONS

Lissa McCullough

Critics have remarked of both Simone Weil and Hannah Arendt that their writings lack systematicity, sometimes even coherence, each for different reasons. Weil, who was formed with the turn to rigorous method in Descartes and Spinoza as her model, was more intent on achieving coherence and consistency than was Arendt, who embraced the freedom of peripatetic thought to roam where it will in its process of discovery. Arendt lived twice as long as Weil, which gave her ample time to write after the Second World War, and she did so on her own terms, discovering her subject matters anew with no sense of obligation to keep consistent with what she had previously written. Weil, by contrast, captured thoughts while almost continually on the move from place to place, task to task, and died in 1943 at age thirty-four, never to see a postwar calm in which to write. Weil sought fundamental principles because for her, a constraining necessity governs all life as such; there is no escaping its grip, one can only work within it: "Forces in this world are supremely determined by necessity" (NR 287). Her thinking never loses sight of the reign of necessary limits, constraints imposed by the conditions of existence, the interplay of physical forces, the presence of mechanistic pressures, and the irresolvable paradox that "human life is impossible" (NB 311). In her later religious thought, God voluntarily subjects himself to necessity in the act of creation, a crowning instantiation of her consistency in this respect.

This means that for Weil, political action, like all human activity, begins as an engagement with necessity in one form or another, and only a reshaping of action under the constraints of necessity defines a space for a relative, conditional freedom. Arendt, on the other hand, subscribes to an Aristotelian model of political life in which, once basic necessities are taken care of by labor within the realm of nature, a space of appearance can emerge between human peers for advancing novelty in the realm of free action. Thus Arendt separates off the political as a zone of freedom from the constraints of necessity by definition—a move that would not be possible in Weil's world of thought given that necessity is universally inescapable; never do we draw a breath without being subject to it. Arendt asserts, to the contrary, that "power, like action, is boundless," it has no physical limitation in human nature or bodily existence. Because this interhuman power is conditioned by the sheer givenness of ontological plurality, she posits that power can be divided without decreasing it and "the interplay of powers with their checks and balances is even liable to generate more power, so long, at least, as the interplay is alive."[1] The only limit to power's potential omnipotence is that it cannot be stored, it can only be created in actual intercourse and requires continual renewal as a living actualized phenomenon.

Such claims—that power can be divided without decreasing it, and that the interplay of powers is liable to generate more power—are prima facie absurd within Weil's world of thought, unless the latter claim is taken to mean that more and more power is relentlessly marshaled in a quest to vanquish all competing powers. This immediate absurdity signals how incongruous are the core notions of "power" under consideration by the two thinkers. The semantic content invoked by each when treating power translates notions from discrepant cultural-intellectual traditions. In *The Human Condition*, Arendt references *dynamis* with the ancient Athenian model of the polis primarily in mind, as well as the Latin *potentia* and the German *Macht*, noting that both words bear the root connotation of potentiality (HC 200). Weil's invocation of *pouvoir* articulates a range of valences, positive and negative, starting from the individual body's power to act as a means to order experience of the world, to work, and to effect action, ranging to the power to coerce, to oppress, aligned with violent force, the power of domination and conquest as discussed in her treatments of the might of the Roman Empire, the tyranny of absolute monarchy, modern revolutionary terror, and the totalitarianisms of National Socialist and Soviet regimes.

Arendt's political thinking foregrounds a notion of power as cooperative "nonviolent power," the positive empowerment of political actors aligned with freedom—though to be sure she also often employs the word *power* in a more Weilian register to describe coercive and destructive forces that brutally negate freedom.[2] No reader of *The Origins of Totalitarianism* can claim that Arendt ignores the crucial question of how modern capitalist economic power and exploitation drive imperial conquest and war. But Arendt's core constructive interest is to set forth a depiction of the positively creative power of politics, having observed all too clearly in her lifetime where the brute power of coercive agency leads. Indeed, according to A. Dirk Moses, Arendt judged that it was precisely the weakness of the republican political tradition in Germany that rendered that nation particularly vulnerable to Nazism, being the Western nation least imbued with classic virtues of civic and civil behavior.[3] This was for her the high-stakes crux of the matter to be thought: the constructive, creative promise of politics when it is not quashed by brutality.

Arendt asserts that under the conditions of human life, the only alternative to power in this constructive sense is violent force. While force can destroy power, it can never succeed in becoming a substitute for it. This is her crucial point. Impotent forces spend themselves in utter futility, incapable of creating anything, impotent to leave a positive monument or testament or trace. Tyranny, a classic example of this, condemns both rulers and ruled to impotence and futility; by instilling a vacuous space of isolation between each and all and spreading pervasive suspicion and fear, tyranny prevents the development of power. Following the lead of Montesquieu, she affirms that tyranny is not a form of government at all but rather contradicts the essential condition of plurality, the acting and speaking together, that is the precondition of all forms of political organization (HC 202). In *On Violence*, likewise, she contrasts power grounded in freedom, an engagement in voluntary political action, with power grounded in force, an involuntary subjection to violence or the threat of violence.

Weil's thinking, in striking contrast, foregrounds oppressive-coercive power, synonymous with force (Fr., *oppression, force*), driven to increase itself by an inflexible quasi-mechanistic necessitation. Yet, she nonetheless explicitly also advocates for the free power to act of the thinking individual as the primary hope for fostering an authentic civilization, one that actually *civilizes* through the formation and cultivation of roots, therein generating a culture that responds to the needs of the soul and abates and reduces reliance on force.[4]

It is the diametric differend between the two thinkers with respect to freedom and necessity that issues in a differend with respect to defining the nature of power when each invokes the word. This effectively reveals the discrepant axial starting points of their political analyses. To specify the difference more sharply: Weil begins with unfreedom in the form of necessity to understand under what conditions it may be possible to exercise a relative, conditional, unstable freedom. Arendt understands political freedom's emergence from the default givenness of cyclical "nature" by positing the in-between of the public realm, then analyzing the conditions in which free political cocreation either actively blooms or turns to unfreedom through an inability to sustain itself "alive." Yet the dynamic of freedom vis-à-vis necessity, and the analysis of power in the context of this dynamic, is a keen focal interest for both, and the case can be made that they end up remarkably close in their overall analyses and concerns—far closer to one another, indeed, than one might expect upon first glance at their patent differences. This essay seeks to explore how key differences in their thinking on power compensate each other's blind spots, producing a certain complementarity and a mutual affirmation.

Weil's thinking lacks Arendt's central focus on the creative freedom of the political actor, though she does profoundly advocate for its importance—as we shall see—in a vein that positions her surprisingly close to her contemporary. Arendt's republican model of power, meanwhile, lacks Weil's strong systematic analysis of coercive power: the relentlessly mechanistic, self-aggrandizing aspect of social-political-technical organizations (parties, governments, military forces, corporations, cartels, and other collective agencies) that subvert and supplant free political association, binding actors into an unfree system through coordination of coercive and persuasive ("stick and carrot") methods, marshaling ideological, technical, financial, legal, and other methods in tandem. Whereas Arendt's constructive focus falls on discerning the phenomenological space of free action, the better to shine light on where and why it is lacking, Weil begins with unfreedom, the mechanisms of force and coercion, the better to shine light on conditions in which a relative freedom from force might stand a chance to arise. The question to be pursued is, can the discrepant approaches of Arendt and Weil be correlated in a way that is productive for modeling political freedom and unfreedom in relation to the primary forms of coercive power in the modern world: powers of State, big capital, and their collusion in credit-debt systems, militarism, imperialism, control by surveillance, intelligence, and legal regulation?

Arendt: Power as Freedom to Engage in Political Action

Arendt's notion of power reserves an essential role for political culture, a context of collaboration and contest shared between peers who experience cenobitic joy in being together in the world, existing in concert as plural and multiform, "the joy of inhabiting together with others a world whose reality is guaranteed for each by the presence of all" (HC 244). Observing a sharp deficit of any such political joy in modern liberal democracies—not to speak of fascist and totalitarian regimes—she seeks to articulate what free political action looks like, what conditioning factors need to be in place, what institutional and interpersonal arrangements enable political power to be cultivated. Freedom is posited in and through political action, the cooperative enactment of power: "Power is what keeps the public realm, the potential space of appearance between acting and speaking men, in existence" (HC 200). This appreciation of cooperative power as a way of life, the ideal form of political action, has allowed scholars to interpret Arendt's thinking vis-à-vis anarchism and even Confucianism.[5]

Arendt and Weil share an enthusiasm for the legacy of Florentine civic humanism extending from Machiavelli through Rousseau to Hume, which Weil terms "syndicalist democracy" (NR 294). For both thinkers, this republican tradition provides the regulative ideal for political action among and between free citizens. But such freedom only exists when and where it is actually manifested in world-creating deeds of political actors. Arendt fully appreciates Rousseau's point that a people that is represented is not free because the will cannot be represented, and she disparages the emergence in modern history of "party-driven democracy," which claims to represent the people even though "the people themselves have never believed it."[6] Weil, equally possessed with this concern, wrote her essay "On the Abolition of All Political Parties."

Arendt disdains the way John Locke, for example, construed social contract theory as a *surrender* of rights and powers to either government or community. In her reading, this transaction is conceived by Locke "not at all as a 'mutual' contract but as an agreement in which an individual person resigns his power to some higher authority and consents to be ruled in exchange for a reasonable protection of his life and property."[7] In Arendtian terms, this is to sell out the locus of the political wholesale: it is to trade the power of political action, a way of being, for enjoyment of wealth, a way of having and acquiring. Locke's political theory is fundamentally a device for disempowering political action and substituting in its place an authoritarian structure to defend with force the possessions of elite individuals.

With this ideation of political freedom in place, several of Arendt's works are concerned with analyzing the reasons for the devolution and loss of the fragile, unstable, unfixable potency of freedom. *On Revolution* in particular studies the ways in which the republican aspirations of the French and American Revolutions went awry, made fatal errors, fell into unfreedom—and the rest was *history* rather than *action*. History draws its storyline from the past, whereas action effects a new creation, a live and living unscripted eventfulness unfolding in present actuality among and between its enactors.

Arendt's analyses of modern revolutions highlight what she calls "the problem of the absolute" (OR 149). While medieval theory recognized legitimate rebellion, its aim was to replace one authority with another—say, a usurper or tyrant with a lawful ruler—not to challenge the authority of rulers or the established order as such (OR 30). Emancipation of secular power from the Roman Catholic church issued in an epochal crisis of authority, a deficit of legitimation that ever after produced instability in sundry forms, as the very task of foundation repeatedly suffered shipwreck. Secularization thus generated the conditions for the possibility of both absolute totalitarian sovereignty or dictatorship and absolute rebellion or revolution and, in addition, the frequent reversals from one to the other. The nondivine, all-too-human absolute monarch had cut himself loose from any higher power, from divine and natural law to which previous rulers had been subjected. And yet, following the footsteps of the divinely sanctioned king, European absolutism identified the sovereign will as the source of both power and law. Revolutions only exposed this dubious nature of government in the modern age, a merely human construct illegitimately laying claim to divinely sanctioned powers. This divided the realm of political opinion between two uncomprehending formations: "conservatives" who pined anachronistically for a divine order already wholly moribund, and "radicals" who failed to understand the ultimacy of the political problem and its stakes. The problem of the absolute would call for rivers of blood yet still remain unresolved (OR 150-4).

In France, the revolutionaries committed a "fatal blunder" in believing that power and law come from the same source, entirely patterned on the model of the absolutism it was proclaiming itself to replace. For Arendt, this elision explains the rapid slide into revolutionary dictatorship (OR 154-6). Here she details the transformation of Robespierre, who reversed his position completely between 1791 and 1793 from freedom to tyranny. Initially, Robespierre defended the rights of the societies against the Assembly, seeing in them the first manifestation of freedom and public spirit, and he denounced the "conspiracy of the deputies of the people against the people," but then reversed himself once he came into power and turned against the societies (OR 232-4). The Revolution had turned into a conflict between the people and a "mercilessly centralized power apparatus which, under the pretense of representing the sovereignty of the nation, actually deprived the people of power" and persecuted the feeble power organs created by the Revolution (OR 236). It was no longer the citizen as political actor but the individual's elective alliances of interest that set in place the solid structure of a class society (OR 155). Thus, the finest hour of the *citoyen* rapidly gave way to the era of the regnant bourgeoisie, and the principle use of power was now to appropriate wealth (OT 79, 137).

Compared with the French Revolution, which ended in disaster, the American Revolution was for Arendt a relative success, if not a lasting one. Unfortunately, in the romantic mythology or typology of revolution imprinted in modern popular imagination, the French disaster won preeminence over the American success (OR 45–6). The French Revolution became the dominant model that "set the world on fire" because the American Revolution was far away across the ocean and conditioned by factors unrepeatable in the Old World with its immense population of poor. As for the Russian Revolution, Arendt opines that it was doomed precisely by the "magic spell of historical necessity" cast by Marx's determinism, as the revolutionaries modeled their strategies on the fiasco of the French revolutionary playbook instead of laying claim to their actual freedom in history, making revolution in free acts of novel instauration, without model or precedent: "It was the course of events, not the men of the Revolution, which they imitated … . They knew that a revolution must devour its own children" (OR 47–8). Because Marx, the greatest theorist of revolution, was far more interested in history than in politics, he did not concern himself with how the foundation of freedom is won but abdicated freedom from the get-go in favor of the dictates of historical necessity (OR 51). In her eyes, he conceded political freedom before it stood a chance to see daylight.

Revolutionaries, free political actors, are only as free as their manifest actions stake a claim to free thought and free deeds—to power—in interaction and cooperation with their fellows, which is why Arendt is intent to articulate what freedom looks like, how one can know it when one sees it, and also how to recognize when it has been lost, persisting in name but not in substance. Arendt's standard for what constitutes a *revolution*, properly speaking, is narrowly political, as historian Neil Davidson notes critically, not concerned with the broader scope of society. He disparages her "relentless fixation on the political at the expense of the socioeconomic," applying a strict political criterion that winnows out all preceding revolutions as not up to snuff, and she finds only in the American context the gold standard she is looking for.[8] But this is not fair, not respecting the specific focal task she has assigned herself to think. There exists a surfeit of social histories of 1776. She is not doing history; she is tracing *power* in her specific sense.

Arendt admits that the American political success was gained for a singular complex of reasons that are inapplicable in other social-cultural and historical contexts, and moreover its glory was soon lost. The new American republic was a "good poor Man's country" in the words of William Penn, and this was to a considerable degree due to "black labor and black misery" (OR 61) and the abundance of land and natural resources expropriated through genocidal dispensation of the indigenous population. The novelty that excites Arendt about the American case, however, is that it presents "an entirely new concept of power and authority, an entirely novel idea of what was of prime importance in the political realm" (OR 166). The seat of power lay in the people—and this was understood not as a Roman-style founding fiction lodged back in the mythic past but was rather a "working reality": the organized multitudes of the colonies met, constituted themselves as townships, then duly elected delegates to speak and act on their behalf. She invokes Tocqueville's observation that "the doctrine of the sovereignty of the people came out of the townships and took possession of the state" (OR 157). The process of constitution began from the bottom up in the multitude of primary-level political bodies. This new American concept of power had long functioned pragmatically before its principles began to emerge as a consequence of the revolution, which demanded explicit articulation of operations that had been laid down in colonial practice, in the use of covenants such as the Mayflower Compact that was drawn up and signed even before landing. The American Constitution simply repeated on a national scale the constitutional processes practiced among the citizenry who founded the colonies themselves.

The most important distinguishing factor in the American experience for Arendt was the "radical separation of law and power" (OR 137). Legitimacy and stability are most susceptible to being maintained when law is above power, and power is only a means of law's enforcement (OT 256). Authority to legislate was stipulated by the US Constitution and invested in representative bodies, while the legitimating power ratifying the constitution was directly fed to it "live" by the constituent will of the people. Yet this authorizing flow of live, operational political activity and consent from the townships feeding into the counties and districts as authorizing agents, which Arendt prizes as the invaluable New World innovation, all too quickly perished. Already under the impact of the revolution, she notes, the revolutionary spirit in America began to wither.[9]

Only Thomas Jefferson among the principal leaders of the American Revolution thought to pose the essential political question as to how to preserve the revolutionary spirit of the citizenry once the revolution as an event had come to an end. Others took this spirit for granted, lulled by complacency, thus remained unaware of the fateful failure of the US Constitution to incorporate and constitute—to found and establish in writing and in principle—the "original sources of their power and public happiness," that is, the townships and the town hall meetings of the original colonies. Arendt observes that this failure amounted to a death sentence for them (OR 230–1). Jefferson repeatedly promoted in vain what Arendt describes as his most cherished political idea: a plan to divide the counties of the new nation into wards in order to create "elementary republics," and he feared the absence of such a systematic subdivision constituted a vital threat to the very existence of the republic (OR 241). This was a vision of systematically networking the citizenry within a "live" political structure that would remain active and communicative from roots to branches and back, a currency enlivening the body politic as one people actively delegating power "live" in situ.

Given her keen objection to political representation as a game-over compromise, we may surmise that Arendt would agree with the assessment of Henry James Sr., father of Henry and William James, who articulated the view in 1852 that the apparent American success was wholly negative, leaving the United States with an undefined political system. "Democracy," James wrote, "is not so much a new form of political life as a dissolution and disorganization of the old forms. It is simply a resolution of government into the hands of the people, a taking down of that which has before existed, and a recommitment of it to its original sources, but it is by no means the substitution of anything else in its place."[10] The resort to representation shut down the beehive of constituent action, the currency of legitimation, the political way of life of the citizenry, the very wellsprings that gave birth to the new nation, and the rest is history. Jefferson alone among the founders, Arendt notes, feared that the abstract political system of democracy lacked concrete organs constituted by the people as political actors (OR 227).

Weil: Power as Coercive Mechanism

Arendt's ideal of political action is closely shared by the early Weil as a young syndicalist, trade union activist, and volunteer in a republican militia in Spain. Later, in her last book *The Need for Roots*, Weil expresses solidarity with the French revolutionary tradition, noting that even the spirit of revolution must nourish itself out of the past because "like all human activities, the revolution draws all its vigor from a tradition" (NR 51, see also 54, 110), though she, like Arendt, is severely critical of the revolution's turn to absolutism once in power. But she detects that a watershed change has occurred in the twentieth century: since the beginning of the Great War in 1914, Weil observes, there has been a complete destruction of the integral fabric of social life: "There is no longer a collective life, there are only dead collectivities …. Greatness, in our day … can only be solitary, obscure, and without echo" (FLN 46–7).

The early Weil, attempting to define the ideal of true liberty, asserted that the notion of liberty must not be a childish fantasy; it must have a realistic and realizable concrete meaning. By this she means to insist that liberty is not the absence of necessity, not an "unconditional surrender to caprice," but is rather a relationship between thought and action, the product of an encounter with necessity (OL 87). We might ask, does this already discount Arendt's notion of political action freed from necessity as a childish fantasy? Yes, probably so—at least as a fantasy, if not a childish one. The inescapability of necessity is an axiom for Weil. She then proceeds to define an instrumental notion of freedom using a nautical metaphor:

> The intelligence is powerless to get its bearings amid the innumerable eddies formed by wind and water on the high seas; but if we place in the midst of these swirling waters a boat whose sails and rudder are fixed in such and such a manner it is possible to draw up a list of the actions which they can cause it to undergo. All tools are thus, in a more or less perfect way, in the manner of instruments for defining chance events. (OL 89)

Note that Weil's example does not concern itself with whether the ship serves the peaceful aspirations of a high civilization or the uprooting designs of conquest and war. The power attained through the deployment of instruments as a means may be directed toward radically discrepant or ambiguous ends, and those ends may suddenly shift.

Only months before Hitler's decisive seizure of power in the first half of 1933, Weil journeyed to Berlin and Hamburg to spend several weeks absorbing the atmosphere and meeting various contacts to better grasp "upon what the strengths of Nazism rested," according to her friend and biographer Simone Pétrement. Looking for action but finding "complete calm," Weil reported to her parents that "politically, everything is still quiet," and Berlin "is at the moment the calmest city in the world."[11] Yet her writings on Germany during this period analyze the aggressive use of rhetoric and the manipulation of public fears by the Hitlerite movement.[12] This bid to understand its mechanism occurred a couple of years before she worked out her seminal analysis of coercive power, "Reflections Concerning the Causes of Liberty and Social Oppression" (1934), containing the key subsection titled "Analysis of Oppression."[13]

Weil's analysis of oppression can be said to extend the "sails and rudder" example just quoted on a broad societal scale to grasp the coercive manipulation of *social* forces, either instead of or in conjunction with natural ones. Here we need to retrace a few key elements of her argument concerning coercive power: power attained through manipulation of social forces produces a virtually automated, self-propelling mechanism, giving an impression of "relentless" force. Yet power harbors an inherent instability that derives from two intersecting features: the incapacity of power to be stored and the impossibility of power as a pure means to establish an end: "There is never power, but only the race for power" (OL 67). This unstable dynamic of power—as always relative in being tested against other powers and necessarily bound to grow because it is essentially unsecurable—leads to excessive growth, overextension, decline, and fall, its nemesis. The pressure is structural: systemic power must seek to either grow relentlessly in its competition with all other powers or commence to decline and perish. It cannot relent, downsize, or fail to marshal every possible resource available to be turned into a means to more power (OL 73). Thus, the race for power enslaves everybody, strong and weak alike, in response to the "brutal spur" of necessity (OL 68, 63). Weil frequently quoted with admiration the Athenians' position reported by Thucydides: "It is a necessity of nature ... that each one, whether god or man, exercise all the power at his disposal" (NB 182, 198; *The Peloponnesian War* 5.105.2).

Weil's Marx-inspired analysis of power's conditioning factors ultimately hinges on the inexorable eventuality of death. Death as full stop, as the always impending absolute ontological deprivation, constitutes an absolute threat to existence that provokes reactive refusal—an unfreedom in the face of the ultimatum—that fuels the demand to possess and shore up power. Arendt offers a similar insight, writing that "death is the real reason why property and acquisition can never become a true political principle," then launches into a probing analysis of Hobbes, identifying him as the primary forerunner of the Lockean ideology alluded to earlier. Hobbes, whose philosophy advanced the political needs of the rising bourgeoisie, set forth the fundamental insight that a never-ending accumulation of property must be based on a never-ending accumulation of power—even if, as Arendt wisely interjects, personal death renders the whole thing a delusion (OT 144–5).

Per Weil, who offers a less political, more probing philosophical reading, the quest for power is a reaction formation against powerlessness, the constitutive impotence of the finite creature. Power's inherent instability and quest for death-forfending conditionality goads the automatic mechanistic bid for more and more. Fear of decline and loss of power drives the craven involuntary *voluntas* of power-seeking. Weil's analysis stresses the relentless pressure exerted by power's inherent instability, which ultimately necessitates that all elements within a power structure obey its logic.

The core of Weil's argument is that "power-seeking, owing to its essential incapacity to seize hold of its object, rules out all consideration of an end, and finally comes, through an inevitable reversal, to take the place of all ends" (OL 69). Successes and gains are as tightly governed by necessity as is avoidance of failure. This is exemplified in how the very successes of Hitler's movement amplified and goaded the need for power, as sociologist Norbert Elias has observed: "The Fuhrer, seemingly the spring and fountainhead of all oppression, was anything but a free arbiter of his decisions … . Hitler was as little able to escape the demands his followers made on him as they were able to escape from his. The greater his pressure on them, the greater their pressure on him."[14] The whole system, with the Fuhrer at the top and the Nazi *Weltanschauung* as a binding and driving force, "developed a dynamic of self-perpetuation and self-reinforcement."[15] This perfectly instantiates Weil's analysis of systemic power.

In her 1939 essay "Some Reflections on the Origins of Hitlerism," Weil aims to identify the most compelling historical precedents for the unlimited character of the Hitler movement's power-lust. In the ancient world, she points to the Roman Empire first and foremost (SE 90, 144; NR 161), noting that although ancient Germania was fierce in defense of its liberty, it was not at all prone to seek expansion and conquest or to enslave others (SE 96–101). Looking for the closest modern precedent to Hitlerism, she finds no German forerunners but rather points to seventeenth-century France, especially the adulation of the French State by Cardinal Richelieu—Hitler's closest historical forerunner, she opines (SE 94)—and the "already totalitarian" reign of Louis XIV (NR 117). Richelieu invented not only the modern State, a historically unprecedented concentration of despotic power, but simultaneously also the attitude of its idolization (SE 91–6; NR 110, 114–15). Under Richelieu, the divine right of the Crown was surreptitiously supplanted by the power of the State, which led soon enough to a competition between them—and eventual regicide. Weil perceives that the entire structure of the so-called Third Republic in France (1870–1940) was derived from the expansionist empire; it constituted a "republic" in name only, without a shred of republican political substance. A couple of years after its fall, in 1943, she remarked: "The English have a kingdom with a republican content; we had a republic with an imperial content," adding that the French people's love for abstract logic makes them easily deceived by labels (NR 119).

Her essay on Hitlerism critiques the group-think that animated French public discourse in its hostility to German aggression, bandying about the mottos "eternal France" and "unchanging Germany"—with the implication that France is eternally divinely chosen because of her innate goodness, whereas Germany is "unchanging" in its perfidy (SE 91–6).[16] This us-versus-them dichotomization gives license to the idea that "they" are inherently evil, whereas "we" in our goodness can do no wrong. Weil argues, on the contrary, that history only confirms that violent conquest and oppression are the natural modes of functioning of any self-aggrandizing centralized power structure—whether Roman, French, German, or American—and the pattern of relentlessly converting all ends to means is repeated. A "basely civilized state" such as ancient Rome or Hitler's Germany manages to "infect all those it threatens and all those it conquers with moral corruption, and thus not only to destroy in advance all hope of resistance but also to disrupt, brutally and finally, the continuity of spiritual life" (SE 144)—that is to say, it destroys the living cultural roots that nourish life, replacing them with uprooting power-lust and money-value. Power, in order to be stable, must appear as something absolute and sacrosanct; thus, the powerful, even in secular States, always believe that they command by divine right, and every oppressive society is cemented by this religion of power (OL 73). This is what makes prestige, an illusion, the very essence of power (SE 168).

Like Arendt, Weil points to the increasing centralization of power as the primary menace rising in the twentieth century globally, judging that all progress in the growth of centralized power implies irreparable losses of everything that is most precious in civilized and indigenous societies (SE 80). Centralization has bred and spread rootlessness, corruption, and loss of the past, which, once lost, will never be restored (NR 8, 52, 119). Weil identifies a nihilistic drive inherent in the dynamics of the limitless pursuit of power. Whether gradually or rapidly, the inevitable dynamic becomes manifest when the quest to augment power resorts to assimilating or crushing any and all qualitative ends that stand in the way. Life itself is the end in itself that will be crushed by the will to aggregate unlimited power. One is compelled to give orders pitilessly—commanding first of all oneself, then others—when draconian necessity bears down once the technical ability to vie for power takes organic form in a refusal of vulnerability and mortality, a futile bid to stave off helplessness, suffering, and death.

In comparison with Arendt, Weil's thinking on means and ends is more systematic and thought through, giving it more substance and weight. Even if Arendt affirms that "the end is in danger of being overwhelmed by the means, which it both justifies and needs" (OV 4), Weil can counter that power as a pure means is actually unable to establish any end other than itself, its own maintenance and cancerous growth. It is compelled to secure its unsecurable object, pure potency, eclipsing all real questions of good. Only a quest for good rather than force is able to establish and honor ends.

When Arendt also invokes the instability of power due to its merely potential character, her emphasis is once again on free political action, not on necessity or compulsion. Power is always, she writes, a power *potential* and not an unchangeable, measurable, and reliable entity like force or strength. Power springs up between people when they act together and vanishes the moment they disperse. It can only be actualized, never fully materialized (HC 200).

> If power were more than this potentiality in being together, if it could be possessed like strength or applied like force instead of being dependent upon the unreliable and only temporary agreement of many wills and intentions, omnipotence would be a concrete human possibility. For power, like action, is boundless; it has no physical limitation in human nature, in the bodily existence of man, like strength. Its only limitation is the existence of other people, but this limitation is not accidental, because human power corresponds to the condition of plurality to begin with. (HC 201)

One may apply Weil's analysis in critique of Arendt's claims that "power is to an astonishing degree independent of material factors, either of numbers or means" and that a comparatively small but well-organized group of men can rule almost indefinitely over large and populous empires (HC 200). Concerning the first point, to assert that power can be independent of material means is for Weil nonsensical given that power per se is pure means; thus, all convertible means directly correlate with its increase. Concerning the second, for Weil, numbers and means cannot be lumped together in this way. A key point of Weil's analysis is that numbers are always a disadvantage, *ceteris paribus*, because mass numbers are difficult or actually impossible to organize. Numbers are only as strong as their actual organization into organs of methodical action, and "that unanimity which is produced in the heat of a quickening and general emotion is incompatible with any form of methodical action" (OL 144). The few, precisely because they are few, form an organized whole with methodical power over numbers (OL 143). It is functional organs, not numbers, that are indispensable to power, and mass numbers cannot be transformed into functioning organs, even if their passivity or support can be arranged through fear, cooptation, or neutralization (OL 58–9). She invokes Richelieu's point that, in terms of numbers, rebels are always only half as strong as the defenders of official power for this reason (NR 124).

In this view, Weil adopts and adapts Étienne de La Boétie's understanding of power as a concerted organ of collusion of the few against the many (OL 141).[17] A free people would be one capable of recognizing this collusive structure, disabling it, and militating for a legal-political system that effectively disallows and forefends it. There is need for the free society to institutionalize a ban on the formation of organized coercive power. Accordingly, she remarks that Rousseau was right to see Machiavelli's *The Prince* as a handbook advising the citizen, not the prince (SE 73). Being a "revolutionary," as the early Weil defined it for her own self-understanding, is not a struggle to realize a once-for-all utopia but rather a "calling forth by one's wishes and helping by one's acts everything which can, directly or indirectly, alleviate or lift the weight that presses upon the mass of men, break the chains that degrade labor, reject the lies by means of which it is sought to disguise or excuse the systematic humiliation of the majority" (OL 153). The later Weil asserted that "social progress depends upon a pressure from below sufficient to change effectively the relations of power and thus to compel the actual establishment of new social relationships" (SE 163). This revolutionary stance is perennial: it is aspired to and willed at all times as a duty and a vocation; it is not a teleological interpretation of history or a bid to defeat the social mechanism; thus, it is never susceptible to becoming relieved of its task. Once again, this shows Weil very close to Arendt: politics is a live activity of actors, enacting deeds in situ, not a passive immersion in historical events or movements.

Just as a strictly mechanical system of forces is subject to a blind and rigorous necessity, Weil observes, the same applies to "that non-tangible matter" that is the substance of our thoughts. "Thoughts are subject to [*soumises à*] a mechanism which is proper to themselves," she writes, "but it is a mechanism." This mechanism in the realm of thought is deeply elusive, she affirms, as it is especially difficult to conceive the laws of this necessity to which human thought is submitted, or to grasp a notion of force that is nontangible (OL 178).

> Imagination is always the fabric of social life and the dynamic of history. The influence of real needs and compulsions, of real interests and materials, is indirect because the crowd is never conscious of it. To become conscious of even the simplest realities one needs to pay attention. Nor, from this point of view, do culture, education, or social position make much difference ... . Anyone who invented a method of assembly that could avoid the extinction of thought in each of the participants would make a revolution in human history comparable to the discovery of fire, or of the wheel, or of the use of implements. (SE 150–1)

Arendt's political thought arguably seeks to articulate—in the positive register—precisely such a "method of assembly" that avoids the extinction of thought. Here again, the two thinkers are closely aligned, notwithstanding their patent and important differences.

Moreover, Arendt's analysis of the ideologies of the pan-movements of the twentieth century can illustrate Weil's point about mechanistic laws operating in the realm of thought. For Arendt the ideological absoluteness of the pan-movements distinguished them from the differentiating partialities and class interests that characterize party structures. In pan-Germanism and pan-Slavism, the "particular reality of the individual person" shrank into a negligible quantity and was submerged in the dynamic movement of the spurious universal; the difference between ends and means evaporated together with the personality, and every idea and value vanished into the concretization of the historical force of the movement itself (OT 249). The consequential impact of such spurious universals in modern history exemplifies how a mere idea—an abstract "unreal" notion—can become a manipulative vehicle to move mass numbers via the widespread extinction of thought.

Weil and Arendt on Modern Power

Reflecting on the sociology of the new financial order of capitalism as "an abstract way of measuring power," Lewis Mumford observed how this system liberated the European bourgeoisie from all previous traditional social and economic limitations: "No glutton can eat a hundred pheasants; no drunkard can drink a hundred bottles of wine at a sitting; [but] once he could exchange the potential pheasants and Burgundy for marks or thalers, he could direct the labor of his neighbors, and achieve the place of an aristocrat without being to the manner born."[18] The modern bourgeois liberal order gains this ascendency by dissolving the Pauline-inspired social body tradition of medieval Christendom.[19] Breaking down all social bonds, it positions the individual counterfactually *outside* society, then preconditions all participation within a new notion of society that is rendered impervious to political transformation in advance by defining, prophylactically, the proprietary conditions of "entering into" the social contract—that is, into the social body—at all. The actual fact of participation in society is simply erased by this new regnant political myth of original nonparticipation. The myth thus forfends the very permissibility of an all-inclusive, sustaining holistic social order, erecting a legal-political-economic prophylactic against it. The entire purpose of Hobbesian-Lockean liberal thought, for Arendt, is to enshrine a specific propertied elite in power by blocking social-political transformation from either above or below. This prophylactic against the political in favor of the propriety is what makes the Glorious Revolution so glorious. Political power, understood in Arendt's specific sense, is frozen out by the pseudo-primordial mythic ideology of a powerful economic elite that would rise up to command the organs of State and private finance in tandem.

For both Weil and Arendt, the mechanisms of State capitalist power are imperial and colonial at their roots. Arendt cites Rosa Luxemburg's observation that imperialism is the political expression of the accumulation of capital in its competition for the possession of the remainders of the noncapitalistic world. This dependence of capitalism on the noncapitalistic world is palpable in the need for new markets, supplies of raw materials, and the need to export capital to equalize the national profit rate. Arendt, quoting Rudolf Hilferding, notes that late modern imperialism suddenly uses again the methods of the original accumulation of capitalistic wealth, that is, the "original sin of simple robbery" (OT 148). Thus, primitive accumulation, Marx's term, is continued in what might better be denoted as *privative* accumulation: the use of coercive means to achieve present-day dispossession of land, rights, property, and human time and energy (labor).[20]

But such coercive privative methods, once exploited to exhaustion abroad, inevitably come home to be deployed against neighboring and domestic populations. The situation in Europe, threatened by Hitler's power, is not that of a civilized people fighting a barbarian, Weil avers, but rather the "much more difficult and dangerous one of independent countries threatened with colonization" (SE 144). The colonial subjection so widely practiced by European nations abroad had come home to roost internally on the continent in the naked will to power of Hitler's movement. Weil perceived this "disorder in bureaucratic form" as only the first fruits of a civilizational destruction on its way: "When chaos and destruction have reached the limit beyond which the very functioning of the economic and social organization becomes materially impossible, our civilization will perish" (OL 116).

The State, as a bureaucratic organization par excellence, itself "incapable of constructing," concentrates in itself the most powerful means of coercion and destruction. It tends more and more to become the center of economic and social life, and the struggle for economic power consists far less in building up than in conquering, with an increasing subordination of economic to military interests, creating an "inextricable mixture of the military and the economic" (FW 241). Thus, the State capitalist system, while appearing outwardly more or less the same as fifty years earlier, "is wholly turned towards destruction" as this "diffused economic war" issues in literal war (OL 115). Given that power is always essentially vulnerable, it is bound to defend itself with all its might, and "it is nearly always believed by all parties, with or without reason, that the only defense is attack" (SE 169). War, self-defensive attack, is the principal aspect of the will to power, and the so-called national interest of every State consists in its capacity to make war for the purpose of safeguarding or increasing its capacity to make war (SE 158). War, she notes, the one sport that really inflames human lust, is the sport whose objective is the domination of others, and "having once taken up this sport it is not easy to drop it … since it calls for unlimited resources, in armaments and other things."[21] In passing, she refers to armaments as "the real heroes of modern wars" (FW 241).

The species of power pursued within and between modern nation-states and aggregated transnational blocs has virtually nothing to do with political statecraft, which is inessential and subordinate, and everything to do with resource strategizing: developing armaments, obtaining military intelligence, controlling energy, land, transportation routes, waterways, precious minerals and metals, patents and inventions, and fungible human resources understood in the broadest sense. Only a "highly organized State" is able to paralyze adversaries by overpowering their imagination with its pitiless mechanism, "a mechanism for seizing every advantage undeterred by human weakness or human virtue, and equally able to pursue this aim by lies or the truth, by simulated respect for convention or open contempt for it" (SE 144). Weil discerns in State fascism and State communism, "almost identical political and social conceptions" in which the State seizes control of almost every domain of individual and social life. Meanwhile, the real and valuable distinction between dictatorship and democracy, understood as two diametrically opposed structures of society, is lost when these are reified as things in themselves rather than applied as heuristic points of reference, ideal types by which to judge the health of a society that is always in fact a compound of the two (SE 160–1).

The relentless pressure to increase power—its mechanical demand for unlimited growth—mandates a coercive endgame of possession, control, fixation, predictability, which is to say it requires a constraining unfreedom to secure the conditions of increase. Mechanisms of power qua "instruments for defining chance events" (in Weil's phrase cited earlier) seek to eliminate freedom and erect a command structure so that the functioning can achieve as high a degree of automation as possible, for example, in the military, in corporations, in factories and factory farms, in prisons, and even in schools for their conditioning benefit. Contingent factors that hinge on human decision and preference must be annulled for the social command mechanism to predominate as a power structure.

Arendt argues in a wholly positive vein that humans make promises and contract with each other to gain predictability, harnessing "the force of mutual promise in contract." Promises and contracts are needed to arrange predictability because "the basic unreliability of men" means they can never guarantee who they will be tomorrow; the human inability to rely on oneself is the price human beings pay for freedom, for plurality, and for reality—"for the joy of inhabiting together with others a world whose reality is guaranteed for each by the presence of all" (HC 244–5). When promises and contracts are agreed to in freedom among equals, it realizes her ideal of political life, but when they are agreed to in the context of coercive constraints, these contracts slip into the domain of Weil's pessimistic realism about power.

Describing the mechanism of State capitalist oppression, Weil wrote: "Marx showed clearly that the true reason for the exploitation of the workers is not any desire on the part of the capitalists to enjoy and consume, but the need to expand the undertaking as rapidly as possible so as to make it more powerful than its rivals" (OL 40). Since no human organization has absolute power, *relative* power is the functional index of power competitions in the world. The whole array of promise, contract, coercion, social consensus, and so on is mobilized to ensure aggrandizement of relative power. As the expansive gray area between voluntary and involuntary is exploited, power becomes grounded in constraining agreements enforced with coercive consequences. One "voluntarily" agrees to contract one's labor thanks to manifold surrounding pressures and constraints—such as the desire for oneself and one's loved ones to live, or to live well, rather than die or live poorly—that necessitate one to sign on or sign up.

For State capitalism to achieve the predictability of a command structure, securing coercive power, it is necessary to set up conditions of no choice (unfreedom) through "voluntary" contract, constraining all subtending human factors to function as a mechanism. Thus the political economist Ernesto Screpanti has argued that the most fundamental institution of capitalism is the employment contract, which can take different specific forms without changing its essential characteristic, that is, "its ability to generate the workers' obligation to obedience and the employers' prerogative to command."[22] Institutions exercise corporate-bureaucratic coercion through asymmetrical legal agreements, property claims, and employment contracts that effect control in ways that are seemingly nonviolent, ostensibly relying on free choice and persuasion rather than coercion.

Arguing along Nietzschean-Arendtian lines, indeed, sociologist Maurizio Lazzarato posits that the primary object of capitalist expropriation and appropriation is the experiential freedom of human time, freezing the openness of the future according to fixed contractual relations: "The future and its possibilities, quashed by the huge sums of money mobilized by finance and devoted to reproducing capitalist power relations, seem to be frozen. Debt simply neutralizes time, time as the creation of new possibilities, the raw material of all political, social, or aesthetic change."[23] He proceeds to analyze the debt-based economy as a process of *subjectivation*—a coercive regime that forces acceptance of this freezing the future in the name of capital gains. Systemic subjectivation produces the "entrepreneur self," whom capitalism demands and compels in every area to take on the costs and risks externalized by the State and corporations.

Conclusion

Reading Arendt and Weil in tandem as political thinkers alerts us to the increasingly massive power of centralized systems, public–private collusions, that clothe unfreedom in ringing Orwellian descriptors and neutralizing dissimulations. Both thinkers warn against becoming passive dupes of the appealing language of freedom, while the reality actually presented is a charade, a diametric falsification. For both, freedom is an activity actualized by and between individuals, not a reifiable attribute, not a legal claim, not a birthright or civil right, not a consumer good, not a glorious historical achievement once for all time. Human interrelations are only as free as the actors who make them so in their interactions, once again, in this or that identifiable manifestation; freedom cannot be stored any more than power can. When actors step forth to actualize it politically, it suddenly shows its place and its power. The sempiternal problem is therefore how to construct and defend a place for the practice of politics to operate outside the killing and deadening forces of domination, coercion, cooptation, intimidation, surveillance, and secrecy by more and more massive power blocs, governmental–private collusions, national and international monopolies and cartels.

Since the decades in which Weil and Arendt wrote, such massive interests are increasingly technologically enhanced, organized into coordinated automated systems, threatening to eclipse entirely the human wellsprings of authentic politics. Both thinkers grasped that for generations the fiercest battles that constitute this long-running war have been fought by colonized peoples around the world, that this struggle has been their daily bread of existence, and furthermore that the coercive forces of imperialism always necessarily requisition at home the means to wage war and administer oppression abroad, then retire back home to pillage friends and neighbors.[24] In the draconian logic of power as pure means, an increasing power of external subjection necessitates an increasing subjection internally within national borders and corporate walls. It is the first interest of coercive power to strangle or smash the free desires of creative life, bonds of love in family, friendship, loyalty to anything other than rootless abstractions, as George Orwell depicted so unforgettably in his fiction and nonfiction.

Writing for the Free France movement in London during the German occupation in 1943, Weil urged that the "veritable genius" of France must be discovered once more in the depths of its misfortune. Its spiritual conscience must be awakened while the country is in defeat, building a patriotic resolve that is rooted in love and loyalty toward the collective past, because when victory comes, it will unleash individual appetites seeking power and competitive advantage and will spur renewed competition among varied economic and political interests in the face of which the spiritual solidarity created under foreign occupation will rapidly dissolve and vanish. She hoped that the Free France movement could generate this degree of inspiration and courageous resolution, carrying "a living, warm environment, full of friendly intercourse, companionship, and kindness that is the sort of humus in which the unfortunate French, uprooted by the disaster, can live and find their salvation both in war and in peace" (NR 212–13). This is striking language: in view of the deep-seated religious faith Weil developed in the preceding few years, she is surely not using the phrase *find their salvation* lightly. She expressly believes that there is such a thing as political salvation: a wholeness, health, and joy achieved specifically through political process and belonging, through a just and creative communion uniting the wide diversity of lives in society that mirrors, on the earthly plane, the spiritual salvation of the soul.

The modes of political engagement outlined by Weil in *The Need for Roots* require discipline and discernment, a high degree of concentration of the same quality required for creative work in art or science. She inquires, "Why should politics, which decides the fate of peoples and whose object is justice, demand any less concentration than art or science, whose respective objects are beauty and truth?" Weil posits that politics is a creative *art* that can only aspire to justice when inspired by "desire for perfection," aiming for the Good in a fully spiritual-religious sense. She argues that politics has a very close affinity to arts such as poetry, music, and architecture in which simultaneous composition occurs on several planes at once, which is the law—and the special difficulty—of these forms of creative activity: "Politics cannot but be as much in need of efforts of creative invention as are art and science" (NR 215). A sort of prayer for good should inspire the people as a whole, their leaders and administrators: it should inspire a desire that the good incarnate itself in their midst. Weil's affirmative vision of politics as a living communal art in *The Need for Roots* is no less lofty than the one laid out by Arendt, but she acknowledges that politics is almost never looked upon "as an art of so high a category" because we have for centuries been accustomed to regard it principally, if not solely, as "a technique for acquiring and holding onto power" (NR 216).

On this point, Arendt is fully in accord, noting a widespread prejudice against politics because it is conceived as "a fabric of lies and deceptions woven by shady interests" or as "the exercise of raw power" (PP 98). Her own understanding of political power as emerging endemically between individual actors implies the mandate to achieve widespread decentralization of power as the one centrifugal dynamic able to check the formation of coercive centralized power mechanisms, including the abstracting force of spurious ideologies. Weil, in her turn, affirms that "the enlightened goodwill of men acting in an individual capacity is the only possible principle of social progress" (OL 60). But on the powerfully pessimistic side, we must note that individual actors regularly submit and convert, folding themselves into authoritarian power structures under pressure of circumstance, as Arendt repeatedly observes in *On Revolution* and *The Origins of Totalitarianism*. The modern form of totalitarianism is in a profound sense truly apolitical, she asserts, as in it "alleged higher, impersonal 'historical forces' and processes are unleashed, and human beings are enslaved to their service" (PP 98), eliminating wholesale the domain of free political action.

Both thinkers remind us that freedom is as freedom does; by the vitality of its deeds you will know it, not by glorious proclamations. Free political creation is an *activity* that real actors continually enact anew; it does not exist "out there." Anywhere individual actors are self-empowered to engage with peers; there lies freedom's health and hope. The deep congruence of their understandings of positive political power is telling and instructive—but it points to an ideal distant from us, rendered almost inapplicable in a world stunned by technological enhancements allowing the total anonymization and opaque secrecy of power complexes. Political power understood as human self-empowerment to think, speak, and act as cocreators of the world is extremely frail and fragile in the face of such technically arrayed power, in part because thinking itself is highly vulnerable to persuasive-coercive forces, as well as the passivity of complacency, apathy, and dejection. Thomas Jefferson identified lethargy as "the forerunner of death to the public liberty."[25] Despite modern democracies' uneven and inadequate efforts to safeguard the ideal of political freedom, "freedom" and "democracy" are as susceptible as other political ideations to devolve into ersatz imitations mouthed in perfectly mindless invocations. Actual free acts and deeds are all too easily substituted for by ringing vacuous phrases. As Weil put it, "The whole intellectual climate of our age favors the growth and multiplication of vacuous entities" that prevent us from even seeing that there is a problem to be solved instead of a fatality to be endured (SE 170).

In her thinking about thinking, Arendt commented that no other human capacity is so vulnerable that "it is in fact far easier to act under conditions of tyranny than it is to think" (HC 324). If she could assert that "the meaning of politics is freedom," she could also immediately ask in a more aggressive, pessimistic tone: "Does politics still have any meaning at all?" (PP 108). Weil, a keen reader of Hobbes and Machiavelli, remarked that a dose of cynicism is essential for perspicacity, and that "everything can be found in the ranks of social democracy except a really free mind" (SE 153). Thinking is able to transcend oppressive power in principle, if not immediately in the world, which makes thinking on the basis of essential values subversive, Weil affirms. Because social-political force is bound to be accompanied by lies, by false disguise, "all that is highest in human life, every effort of thought, every effort of love, has a corrosive action on the established order" insofar as it is ceaselessly creating a scale of values that insists on establishing its place *in*—but not *of*—this world (OL 145).

Notes

1. Hannah Arendt, *The Human Condition*, 2nd edn., introduction by Margaret Canovan, with a new foreword by Danielle Allen (Chicago: University of Chicago Press, 2018), 201. Hereafter this work is cited in the text as HC followed by the page number.
2. Arendt employs the term "nonviolent power" in *On Revolution*, introduction by Jonathan Schell (New York: Penguin, 2006), 240. Hereafter this work is cited in the text as OR followed by the page number. Key criticisms of Arendt's political thought are summarized by Maurizio Passerin d'Entreves:

   > Arendt is, in fact, unable to acknowledge that a modern capitalist economy constitutes a structure of power with a highly asymmetric distribution of costs and rewards. ... She maintains that all questions pertaining to the economy are pre-political, and thus ignores the crucial question of economic power and exploitation ... By insisting on a strict separation between the private and the public, and between the social and the political, she is unable to account for the essential connection between these spheres and the struggles to redraw their boundaries. ("Hannah Arendt," section 3: Arendt's Conception of Modernity, *Stanford Encyclopedia of Philosophy*, 2006. https://plato.stanford.edu/entries/arendt)

   While these criticisms hold true of Arendt's theoretical political thinking in *The Human Condition*, it must be noted in objection that she offers abundant astute analyses of imperial and capitalist power structures in *The Origins of Totalitarianism*. The discrepant specific purposes of the two works, and how they relate to each other, must be taken into account, thus avoiding excessive blanket statements.
3. A. Dirk Moses, "Das römische Gespräch in a New Key: Hannah Arendt, Genocide, and the Defense of Republican Civilization," *Journal of Modern History* 85, no. 4 (December 2013): 867–913, quote on 874. Moses's claim concerning Arendt's "inability to manage genocidal settler violence and the consequently limited scope of her much-vaunted critique of imperialism" (879) falls short of the nuanced correlation that is needed to reconcile her constructive political thought with her historical treatments. At the very least, her scathing treatment of Boer settler-colonials in South Africa in *The Origins of Totalitarianism* (Part 2.7: Race and Bureaucracy) argues against any such sweeping dismissal.
4. For the early Weil's vision of such a civilizing society, see "Theoretical Picture of a Free Society," in *OL*, 83–108. The later Weil's vision of such a society is laid out in *The Need for Roots*.
5. Brian Smith, "Anarcho-Republicanism? Arendt and the Federated Council System," *Science & Society* 83, no. 1 (January 2019): 87–116; Joel Olson, "The Revolutionary Spirit: Hannah Arendt and the Anarchists of the Spanish Civil War," *Polity* 29, no. 4 (Summer 1997): 461–88; Sam Crane, "Arendt and Confucius," https://uselesstree.typepad.com/useless_tree/2009/01/arendt-and-confucius.html.
6. Hannah Arendt, *The Promise of Politics*, ed. and with an introduction by Jerome Kon (New York: Schocken, 2005), 98. Hereafter this work is cited in the text as PP followed by the page number.
7. Hannah Arendt, *On Revolution*, introduction by Jonathan Schell (New York: Penguin, 2006), 160. Hereafter this work is cited in the text as OR followed by the page number.

8   Neil Davidson, *How Revolutionary Were the Bourgeois Revolutions?* (Chicago: Haymarket, 2012), 352–3.
9   Annelien de Dijn, in *Freedom: An Unruly History* (Cambridge: Harvard University Press, 2020), looks at how the modern negative conception of freedom as an absence of state interference emerged as an antidemocratic reaction by elites who wanted to curtail state power. Later this counterrevolutionary conception of freedom invented in the 1790s was reimagined as the very essence of Western civilization, and even Arendt accepted this overextended retrospective narrative in her sharp critique of it (339–40).
10 Henry James Sr. is cited by Lewis Mumford, *The Golden Day* (New York: Boni & Liveright, 1926; reprint, Boston: Beacon Press, 1957), 10–11.
11 Simone Pétrement, *Simone Weil: A Life*, trans. Raymond Rosenthal (New York: Pantheon, 1976), 129, 131, 133.
12 Simone Weil, "The Situation in Germany," in *FW*, 91–147.
13 Simone Weil, "Réflections sur les causes de la liberté et de l'oppression sociale" and "Méditation sur l'obéissance et la liberté," in *Œuvres completes, Vol. 2: La Condition ouvrière (1934–7)*, ed. André A. Devaux and Florence de Lussy (Paris: Gallimard, 1988), 27–110, 128–33; English translation: "Reflections Concerning the Causes of Liberty and Social Oppression" and "Meditations on Obedience and Liberty," in *OL* 37–124, 140–6.
14 Norbert Elias, *The Germans: Power Struggles and the Development of Habitus in the Nineteenth and Twentieth Centuries*, ed. Michael Schröter, trans. Eric Dunning and Stephen Mennell (New York: Columbia University Press, 1996), 385.
15 Ibid. These paragraphs reiterate points made in Lissa McCullough, "Simone Weil's Analysis of Oppression: From La Boétie to the Neoliberal Present," in *Simone Weil and Continental Philosophy*, ed. A. Rebecca Rozelle-Stone (Lanham, MD: Rowman & Littlefield, 2017), chapter 9, 167–85.
16 Weil's analyses of us-versus-them thinking are found in "The War of Religions," in SE 211–18, and *On the Abolition of All Political Parties*, passim.
17 See Étienne de la Boétie, *The Politics of Obedience: The Discourse of Voluntary Servitude*, trans. Harry Kurz, introduction by Murray N. Rothbard (Auburn, AL: Ludwig von Mises Institute, 2008).
18 Mumford, *The Golden Day*, 9.
19 For some general background to this claim, see Richard Henry Tawney, *Religion and the Rise of Capitalism* (New York: Harcourt, Brace, 1926; reprint, New York: Pelican, 1980);; Ernst H. Kantorowicz, *The King's Two Bodies: A Study in Medieval Political Theology* (Princeton, NJ: Princeton University Press, 1957); and John A. T. Robinson, *The Body: A Study in Pauline Theology* (Philadelphia: Westminster, 1952).
20 The intentionally obfuscated connection between classical political economy and primitive accumulation (i.e., the "brutal acts associated with the process of stripping the majority of the people of the means of producing for themselves") is traced by Michael Perelman in *The Invention of Capitalism: Classical Political Economy and the Secret History of Primitive Accumulation* (Durham, NC: Duke University Press, 2000), quote on 2. See also, for example, Saskia Sassen, *Expulsions: Brutality and Complexity in the Global Economy* (Cambridge, MA: Belknap, 2014); Vincenzo Ruggiero, *The Crimes of the Economy: A Criminological Analysis of Economic Thought* (London: Routledge, 2013); and Merete Borch, "Rethinking the Origins of Terra Nullius," *Australian Historical Studies* 32, no. 117 (2001): 222–39.
21 See "Scientism—A Review," in SWR 298; see also FW 240–54.

22 Ernesto Screpanti, *The Fundamental Institutions of Capitalism* (London: Routledge, 2001), 258.
23 Maurizio Lazzarato, *The Making of Indebted Man*, trans. Joshua David Gordon (Los Angeles: Semiotext(e), 2011), 48–51.
24 For a collection of Weil's writings on colonialism, see *Simone Weil on Colonialism: An Ethic of the Other*, ed. and trans. J. P. Little (Lanham, MD: Rowman & Littlefield, 2003); for Arendt, see especially "Imperialism," part 2 of *The Origins of Totalitarianism*.
25 Thomas Jefferson, "Letter to William Stephens Smith" (Paris, November 13, 1787).

Bibliography

Boétie, Étienne de la. *The Politics of Obedience: The Discourse of Voluntary Servitude*. Translated by Harry Kurz. Auburn, AL: Ludwig von Mises Institute, 2008.

Borch, Merete. "Rethinking the Origins of Terra Nullius." *Australian Historical Studies* 32, no. 117 (2001): 222–39.

Crane, Sam. "Arendt and Confucius." *The Useless Tree*, January 9, 2009. https://uselesstree.typepad.com/useless_tree/2009/01/arendt-and-confucius.html.

Davidson, Neil. *How Revolutionary Were the Bourgeois Revolutions?* Chicago: Haymarket, 2012.

Dijn, Annelien de. *Freedom: An Unruly History*. Cambridge: Harvard University Press, 2020.

Elias, Norbert. *The Germans: Power Struggles and the Development of Habitus in the Nineteenth and Twentieth Centuries*. Edited by Michael Schröter. Translated by Eric Dunning and Stephen Mennell. New York: Columbia University Press, 1996.

Jefferson, Thomas. "Letter to William Stephens Smith." Paris, November 13, 1787.

Kantorowicz, Ernst H. *The King's Two Bodies: A Study in Medieval Political Theology*. Princeton, NJ: Princeton University Press, 1957.

Lazzarato, Maurizio. *The Making of Indebted Man*. Translated by Joshua David Gordon. Los Angeles: Semiotext(e), 2011.

Little, J. P. (ed. and trans). *Simone Weil on Colonialism: An Ethic of the Other*. Lanham, MD: Rowman & Littlefield, 2003.

McCullough, Lissa. "Simone Weil's Analysis of Oppression: From La Boétie to the Neoliberal Present." In *Simone Weil and Continental Philosophy*. Edited by A. Rebecca Rozelle-Stone. Lanham, MD: Rowman & Littlefield, 2017, pp. 167–85.

Moses, A. Dirk. "Das römische Gespräch in a New Key: Hannah Arendt, Genocide, and the Defense of Republican Civilization." *Journal of Modern History* 85, no. 4 (December 2013): 867–913.

Mumford, Lewis. *The Golden Day*. New York: Boni & Liveright, 1926; reprint, Boston, MA: Beacon Press, 1957.

Olson, Joel. "The Revolutionary Spirit: Hannah Arendt and the Anarchists of the Spanish Civil War," *Polity* 29, no. 4 (Summer 1997): 461–88.

Passerin d'Entreves, Maurizio. "Hannah Arendt." *Stanford Encyclopedia of Philosophy*, 2006. https://plato.stanford.edu/entries/arendt.

Perelman, Michael. *The Invention of Capitalism: Classical Political Economy and the Secret History of Primitive Accumulation*. Durham, NC: Duke University Press, 2000.

Pétrement, Simone. *Simone Weil: A Life*. Translated by Raymond Rosenthal. New York: Pantheon, 1976.
Robinson, John A. T. *The Body: A Study in Pauline Theology*. Philadelphia: Westminster, 1952.
Ruggiero, Vincenzo. *The Crimes of the Economy: A Criminological Analysis of Economic Thought*. London: Routledge, 2013.
Sassen, Saskia. *Expulsions: Brutality and Complexity in the Global Economy*. Cambridge, MA: Belknap, 2014.
Screpanti, Ernesto. *The Fundamental Institutions of Capitalism*. London: Routledge, 2001.
Smith, Brian. "Anarcho-Republicanism? Arendt and the Federated Council System." *Science & Society* 83, no. 1 (January 2019): 87–116.
Tawney, Richard Henry. *Religion and the Rise of Capitalism*. New York: Harcourt, Brace, 1926; reprint, New York: Pelican, 1980.

Chapter 2

TYRANNY WITHOUT A TYRANT: HANNAH ARENDT AND SIMONE WEIL ON BUREAUCRACY

Marina Lademacher

"The speed with which bureaucracy has invaded almost every branch of human activity," Simone Weil writes in *Oppression and Liberty*, "is something astounding once one thinks about it" (OL 13). By contrast, in her essay "Kafka: A Revaluation," Hannah Arendt argues that Kafka illuminated the central predicament of the modern age, the disappearance of freedom and loss of a capacity to think and act politically, and that the Kafkaesque world was not a mere forecast but depicted what actually became our own world (EU 76–7). Arguing his "so-called prophecies were but a sober analysis of underlying structures which today have come out into the open," the nightmarish quality to Kafka's stories expresses "the true nature of the thing called bureaucracy—the replacing of government by administration and of law by arbitrary decrees" (EU 74). While those interested in questions about bureaucracy may turn to sociologist Max Weber to guide their thinking, lesser known but as richly developed are the accounts of bureaucracy articulated by Arendt and Weil. With this in mind, this chapter seeks to clarify Arendt and Weil's shared contribution to understanding, and critiquing, the modern phenomenon of bureaucratization. In so doing, I unpack the ways in which their accounts of bureaucracy come together, reinforce one another, and yet still move apart. Considered altogether, this discussion highlights how a concern with the dehumanizing, disempowering, and therefore violent consequences of bureaucracy ebbs and flows throughout Weil and Arendt's political thought.

The phenomenon of bureaucratization is connected, for Arendt and Weil, to the more general phenomenon of technologization and its movement toward unlimited progress and process efficiency. Bureaucratic organizations, tethered to a web of technologically deterministic trends that "forced us into an infinitely faster rhythm of repletion than the cycle of natural processes prescribed," funnel human beings into predetermined roles where their sense of self is derived from how they fit into the overall process (HC 296). In contrast to a positive, *rooted* rationality embedded in human intelligence and community, bureaucratic rationality, ahistorical and instrumental, separates reason from reality. The indispensability of bureaucracy to both the modern state and capitalist economy indicates the rise of the techno-scientific worldview, the worldview of *homo faber*, in which mechanical processes, not human creativity, guide work and action (HC 300). The more society becomes bureaucratized, the nearer is the entirety of public life affected by the overly strict, routine operations of bureaucracy such as obsessive record-keeping practices.

To help readers understand the numerous approaches both thinkers take to navigate the modern bureaucratic maze, this chapter proceeds as follows. First, I discuss how the modern phenomenon of bureaucratization is linked to the development of the modern capitalist state, then move to examine Arendt and Weil's conceptualizations of bureaucracy through the lens of the concept of collectivity and the category of the social, respectively. After establishing the conceptual framework, the focus shifts to a discussion of bureaucracy in politics and the economy, including Arendt and Weil's shared concern with party politics and Weil's critique of bureaucratized work.[1] In the final section, I explain how Arendt views the case of Adolf Eichmann as an important example of the ways in which bureaucracies encourage conditions of nonthinking within which evildoing can flourish.

Bureaucracy, Capitalism, and the Nation-State

Within *The Origins of Totalitarianism*, Arendt anchors the emergence of modern, imperial bureaucracies in the context of racial imperialism. In this way, bureaucratic systems of governance developed as a vehicle for European imperial powers to racially administer, manage, and dominate colonial populations at a distance and without limit. Along with the influence of colonial rule on the expansion of bureaucratic systems of governance, Arendt looks at its evolution through the lens of increasingly complex societal conditions requiring government interventions in the economy and elsewhere across society.[2] Maintaining marketized democracies' inequities in privilege and power means that economic interests become the nation's general interests: political administration reproduces capitalist relations of exchange and production, mitigates against the contingencies of capitalism, protects the interests of the propertied classes, and puts itself at the service of commercial necessity.[3] Yet the bureaucratic ethos, as both thinkers observe, is not confined to the political sphere, diffusing across other areas of society, from education and housing to the sciences and everyday modes of interaction.[4] Alert to the veracity with which mechanical concepts can shape our forms of life, Weil writes that "the speed with which bureaucracy has invaded almost every branch of human activity is something astounding once one thinks about it" (OL 13).

Although to Arendt and Weil the gradual bureaucratization of society is connected to a confluence of interrelated practices—economic, political, philosophical, and technical—its development is interwoven with the historical evolution of capitalist market societies and the centralization of social functions at the hands of the modern capitalist state. On the one hand, bureaucracy provided the superior institutional mechanism for upholding the system of private property and for protecting the interests of large-scale enterprise. On the other, the external pressures on government machinery to respond to the increasingly complex socioeconomic needs of the national population reinforce the state's need for an organizational form capable of monitoring and managing the masses at a distance (BPF 154). This means that the motives of government and capitalism, rather than being in antagonism, jointly benefit from the creation of a more bureaucratized society that reproduces conditions favorable to capital.[5] Undergirding the bureaucratic form of organization through which the state coldly governs, therefore, is a techno-scientific principle of rationality where what matters most is the efficiency and utility maximization of process, not the ends to which means are directed.[6] With knowledge compartmentalized and action severed from understanding, the result is a world almost entirely devoid of mystery.

So far, this picture obscures the common prevalence of bureaucratic oppression irrespective of the ideological differences.[7] Whether the society in question is capitalist, fascist, or communist, the inherent tendency of bureaucracies to expand and exert an increasing influence over individuals leads Arendt and Weil to perceive bureaucratic power as a distinct form of oppression.[8] Modern state-centric systems, which appear to be an interconnected matrix of centralized power, comprise an intricate bureaucratic machinery that includes not only government and the relationships between various branches but also the entire state apparatus, including the military and police forces. The constant preparation for war as a permanent condition, for example, in the context of war being the "recognized form of the struggle for power when the competitors are states," results in a gigantic, bureaucratic war machine whose functions are opaque and inscrutable, but which justifies social life being centered on the authority of the central power (OL 109). In bureaucratized environments, Weil observes, the functions of coordination and management are entrusted to a "curious machine, whose parts are men, whose gears consist of regulations, reports and statistics, and which is called bureaucratic organization" (OL 109). Arendt, by contrast, argues that when describing such state-centric systems necessarily, it is

> inevitable that we speak of all persons used by the system in terms of cogs and wheels that keep the administration running. Each cog, that is, each person, must be expendable without changing the system, an assumption underlying all bureaucracies, all civil services, and all functions properly speaking. (RJ 29)

Weil too draws a link between bureaucracy and anonymity, pointing out that the social functions "most connected with the individual," those consisting in coordinating, managing, and deciding, exceed any individual's capacity and in so doing become to a certain extent "collective and, as it were, anonymous" (OL 104).

Weil's Collectivity

Bureaucratic organizations and the collective mindset they generate exemplify (1) the domination of individuals under collective structures and (2) the machine-like qualities of its oppression that affect the mechanization of thought itself. When addressing bureaucratic oppression, Weil employs the concept of collectivity to conceptualize and unpack the tense relationship that exists between the social and the individual.[9] Dietz suggests we understand Weil's idea of collectivity—abstract, social, and general—in opposition to persons—concrete, individual, and particular.[10] The collectivity thus forms the conceptual backdrop to the concrete, bureaucratic form in which individuals are dominated and molded by collective structures, with the concept used to analyze three institutions in particular: centralized bureaucracy, giant industry, and the state itself.[11] Drawing on Plato's notion of the great beast, Weil sees collectivities as things that form a social mentality dominated by "ersatz reality" or illusions.[12] Simultaneously, an oppressive collectivity sets itself up as an absolute value in this world, that is, as an end and "object of all idolatry."[13] For Weil, the most powerful representation of the abstract and false sense of the sacred offered up by modern collectivities is, ultimately, the state itself, which "naturally reaped the desire for unity—'unity of death'—which had developed around the belief in national sovereignty" (NR 115). Although, by "the nature of things, the person is subdued to the collectivity" (HP 81), Weil calls attention to the particular force of bureaucratic oppression in this specific historical moment: "Never has the individual been so completely delivered up to a blind collectivity, and never have men been less capable, not only of subordinating their actions to their thoughts, but even of thinking" (OL 102).

The dehumanization that occurs when people are reduced to machine-like things denied the chance to develop their capacities of thought, and attention in complete freedom is crucial to Weil's analysis of oppressive collectivities.[14] As Weil argues, bureaucratic machines have "almost reached the point of taking the place of leaders," while "in all spheres, thought, the prerogative of the individual, is subordinated to vast mechanisms which crystallize collective life ... to such an extent we have almost lost the notion of what real thought is" (OL 104). Part of bureaucracies' destructive impact on individuals and social life, critically, stems from their collective inability to *think*. Not only are all "organs of expression" individual, but "a collectivity is not someone, except by a fiction; it has an abstract existence and can only be spoken to fictitiously" (HP 78). Moreover, only the individual, not the collectivity, has a *mind* capable of producing thoughts. By definition, collectivities cannot engage in the thinking process that allows the individual to understand situations and adapt to circumstances, possessing only the capacity to say a vague, dangerous but debilitating *we* (HP 76). The need to constantly think for oneself and engage attention independently is clouded from the perspective of the human person whose fate and freedom is determined by the arbitrary allocation of power within the collective hierarchy. As a result, when caught in the grip of blind collectivities with a proclivity to fabricate lies, action becomes thoughtless. According to Weil, a decoupling of thought and action is built into the fabric of collective structures; McCullough notes that its force lies in the proclivity for the collective "we" to be asserted over the individual capacity to discern, deliberate, and judge.[15] It is in this sense that Dietz understands the collective mentality as Weil sees it in terms of an "imprisoned mind, unable to achieve a vantage point from whence it can begin to gain a perspective on and act in the world."[16]

Arendt's Social

In *The Origins of Totalitarianism*, Arendt examines the historical connections between racism and bureaucracy, focusing on the racialized bureaucratic practices that emerged within the European colonial and slave regimes of the modern world (OT 241).[17] In conceptual terms, the supervision and control of colonial populations at a distance by faceless imperial bureaucracies exemplifies the instrumentalist mentality of the social, which views human beings as objects or isolated things rather than unique and plural agents (OT 185–7). As the form of government in which the social and critically the "rule by nobody" unfolds, the division of administration into minute tasks disperses bureaucratic duties across impenetrable hierarchical structures that make it impossible to assign responsibility to any one person or group of people (OV 81). Consequently, the rule by nobody is the most "tyrannical" state affairs because it is unanswerable and, crucially, absolves decision-making of democratic accountability. An interpretation of bureaucracy as "rule by nobody" is something touched on by Weil too, who notes that hardly anyone understands that power "resides nowhere, so that the dominant feeling everywhere is that dizzy fear which is always brought about by loss of contact with reality" (OL 111). With both thinkers concerned with the position of the individual in relation to an excessively complex, vertigo-inducing bureaucratic machinery remote from human will, Arendt would no doubt agree with Weil's claim that "man is not meant to be the playthings of blind collectivities" (OL 93).

Arendt connects the expansion of bureaucratic forms of governance in mass capitalist societies with the substitution of conformity and behavior for conversation and action as the reality of politics when she describes bureaucracy as the "most social form of government" (HC 40). For Arendt, the conquering of the political by the social involves the dissolution of what traditionally was termed government and state into "pure administration"; politics becomes "nothing but a function of society" (HC 33), while society itself "excludes the possibility of action … [expecting] from each of its members a certain kind of behavior, imposing innumerable and various rules, all of which tend to 'normalize' its members, to make them behave, to exclude spontaneous action or outstanding achievement" (HC 40). By means of statistical abstraction, human beings are bureaucratically classified according to artificial social categories within which they can be compared, measured, and targeted by the state as the objects of management, while categorical outsiders are subjected to forms of extreme violence. Even if they are grouped together under the hazy umbrella of political parties, citizens are, in Arendt's view, world-alienated creatures deprived of and denied access to the spaces of contact where meaning is created and new relationships are formed.[18] By reducing the individual person to an anonymous cog in an intricate, depersonalized machine, politics-as-administration reflects the reduction of politics *itself* into a means for something else.[19] Though Arendt sees work, the activity of *homo faber*, as vital to the built world's durability, stability, and objectivity,[20] the modern world of work, by contrast, has become entwined with the world of politics, resulting in a functionalist and utilitarian atmosphere pervading political life.[21] In this context, Arendt's *power-with* metamorphoses into Hobbesian *power-over*. While Arendt attributes Enlightenment rationalism's elevation of universals over particulars, as well as the conflation of politics with rulership and sovereignty, to impoverished understandings in modern political philosophy, she blames two philosophers in particular: Descartes and his "radical subjectivism" for conceiving of humanity as a bunch of atomized and powerless individuals, and Hobbes for transforming the public world of action and meaning-making into the world of economic interests and machine-like behavior (LM 47, 193). For Arendt, Hobbes misunderstands power as something that can be gripped and possessed, a misunderstanding that underlies a false conflation of strength with power.

Arendt's argument against the managerialization of politics, and concomitantly the decoupling of freedom from politics, should be understood in relation to her broader critique of the organization of our political systems around socioeconomic needs and, by extension, the reduction of citizens into consumers and jobholders free of the toils of political experience. When politics is reduced to administration and management, "all action is by definition under the sway of necessity," meaning a bureaucratic commitment to standardization and impersonal impartiality supersedes what is particular and contextually specific (BPF 154). In practical terms, this means rigid rules and procedures are established that formally define the boundaries within which action and communication can take place, resulting in a situation where plurality and novelty have no room to appear. Unlike work or labor, however, action, in Arendt's opinion, is the only activity that allows us to share our experiences with others and listen to their stories,[22] offering the fragile possibility for actors to reimagine and reinvent shared obligations to one another.

Arendt and Weil on the Party System

Arendt and Weil share an interest in the suffocating effects of bureaucracy on individuals and the world, which leads them to criticize party politics for its opinion manipulation and antidemocratic influence on public life. Party politics, by relying on nonexistent, nebulous abstractions such as "the people" to advance partisan interests, closes off genuine communication between government and citizens. At the same time, the maneuverings of political parties, as hierarchically layered organizations of authority that are undoubtedly bureaucratic in structure and practice, stymie the appearance of plurality within the public sphere while also impeding the creation of new public spaces in which political freedom, "a state of being manifest in action,"[23] can be experienced in the here and now (BPF 161). This is important for Arendt in particular because it is within the public spaces of the world that spontaneous, temporary experiences of political freedom are channeled into new forms of constituted power that ultimately lead to a revitalized public sphere (BPF 164). Understanding genuine democracy to mean participation rather than representation, an ongoing process rather than a product, their disdain for party politics is linked to their common concern with excessive rationalization at the state and institutional levels. For both, representative political systems do not and cannot provide citizens with the means to express their opinions on any given topic, or the opportunity to engage in constructive debate and democratic deliberation in which genuine conflicts can be navigated. While Arendt believes that it is impossible for someone to act politically on another's behalf or truly represent another's actions and opinions, Weil contends that political parties are ill-equipped to offer more than a mere caricature of the general will and are incapable of representing the complexity of choices that people would make on sets of problems pertaining to the public interest under more democratic conditions. Furthermore, Weil regards all political parties, whether they are single or multiparty systems, as toxic, coercive machines with a mendacious, totalitarian spirit at their core. As concrete embodiments of abstract collectivities (Weil) and the socialization of politics (Arendt), political parties retain the formal, customary rituals of democracy stripped of all substantive significance.

Written in 1943, Weil's essay *On the Abolition of All Political Parties* emerges in the context of her frustration with the reignition of destructive party politics and factionalism by French politicians in exile. "Political parties," Weil argues, are "organizations that are publicly and officially designed for the purpose of killing in all souls the sense of truth and justice" (APP 16). For Weil, it is not enough to pursue "democracy" as an end in itself: genuinely democratic enclaves ought to serve as a means to higher ends such as truth, justice, and goodness. Political parties, representing the dangers of oppressive collectivities, set themselves up as ends in themselves, constituting particular instances "of the phenomenon which always occurs whenever thinking individuals are dominated by a collective structure—a reversal of the relation between ends and means" (APP 12).

Weil identifies three essential characteristics of political parties: the party is a "machine to generate collective passions," an "organization designed to exert a collective pressure on the minds of all its individual members," (APP 11) while the main objective and ultimate goal of any political party "is its own growth, without limit" (APP 11). From these characteristics, Weil concludes that "every party is totalitarian—potentially, and by aspiration" (APP 11). According to Weil, though participating in public life frequently necessitates joining a political party, doing so forces one to set aside questions of morality and truth. The compulsion to conform and remain loyal to the leader, underwritten by the promise of future escalation up party ranks and enforced by penalties to punish subordination, makes it impossible for any individual party member to listen to their conscience or think independently. However, the collective mentality itself undermines the critical faculty, which allows us to distinguish between truth and lies and resist the allure of propaganda. Parties define themselves, like other artificial collectivities, through a process of inclusion and exclusion, and their divisive "thinking" takes the form of for or against, with us or against us, in ways that are likely to incite mutual animosity. Individuals intoxicated with collective passions, as a result, serve as hollow vessels through which the collective, but factional, "unified" point of view can be represented and reproduced.

Arendt's critical perspective on the party system, which draws on historical examples from the 1956 Hungarian Revolution, Russian Revolution, and French Revolution, dovetails with Weil's focus on the toxic machinations of political parties. Throughout *On Revolution*, Arendt explores how modern revolutions that do not guarantee both political freedom and/or the maintenance of participatory organs of action generate a mushrooming of bureaucratic political structures (OR 260–6). Arguing against the party system and in favor of the council system (described by Arendt as "organs of action"), political parties are understood to disempower local communities, strengthen governmental bureaucracy, and constitute "very efficient instruments through which the power of the people is curtailed and controlled" (OR 274).

Unlike the model of sovereign power embodied in the party system, councils represented the "federal principle" of the plural organization of political space, utilizing different modes of organization that attempt to make room for contingency, free association, and spontaneous creativity.[24] As they begin to resemble the state's administrative apparatuses, however, councils lose their ability to function as organs of action, turning instead into procedural organs of consumption and conformity. However, as Arendt describes, a shift toward the functional or practical emerges from demands placed on the machinery of government to carry out administrative and social management tasks (OR 277). Once burdened with administrative matters, councils face the seemingly unavoidable challenge of gradual bureaucratization and the emergence of an increasingly disconnected executive. Nonetheless, the party system as an institution assumes either that citizens' participation in politics is guaranteed by other means or is not required given representation, or that all political questions are ultimately administrative problems (OR 276). In such circumstances, politics contributes to the flattening of everyday interpersonal experiences and becomes even less capable of meeting basic human needs.

Weil on Specialization and Bureaucratic Work

The prevalence of bureaucratic oppression in both planned and capitalist societies gestures at a direct relationship between statism and the modern phenomenon of bureaucratization. To account for and explain this commonality, Weil focuses on the dehumanizing power that bureaucracies inflict on individuals, both in the context of the USSR and in the context of capitalist enterprise.[25] The Soviet Union, according to Weil, was an example of a coupling logic between a centralized administrative structure and concentrated authority, resulting in an orbit of dependency connecting the many spheres of life—political, social, economic, and intellectual—around a bureaucratic core. Consequently, a new ruling social group and oppressive bureaucratic machine that survived the capitalist economy were created as a result of the concentration of power within the party–state bureaucracy and the people's lack of control over the centralized functions of governance, coordination, management, and administration. When asserting that bureaucracy is a "new factor in the social struggle," Weil frames the problem of oppressive bureaucracy in terms of its autonomy independent of the operation of capitalism, possessing its own kind of power in need of illumination (OL 26). Furthermore, Weil is concerned about the possibility that what replaces capitalism will be a new type of oppression, namely "oppression exercised in the name of management," because the power of bureaucracy to oppress was *reinforced* after the abolition of private property (OL 9). As a result, though individuals are dominated to a greater extent by collective structures in modern, complex societies, the problem, according to Weil, arises in the division between those who command and those who execute, and in the materialization of the unstable struggle for power (OL 67).

Weil's critique of the bureaucratic power ingrained in the central coordination of economic and political life is informed by her personal experience of the brutality of factory work as well as her focus on the effects of scientific specialization on the worker's situation.[26] The power disparity between managerial and executive functions—the separation of those who do the work and those who manage the workers—continually reproduces modes of oppression in the workplace, cementing workers' degrading obedience to managers. Importantly, systems of social organization that rely on bureaucratic barriers, rooted in the control of knowledge and hyper-specialization, underpin the ability of the so-called technicians of management to maintain a position of privilege in relation to employees (OL 11). By tying an analysis of bureaucratic oppression to workplace specialization, Weil incorporates the problem of bureaucratic oppression into a critique of the misuse of attention in economic life and the conditions that maintain a separation between mental and physical labor, between thought and action.

Weil's discussion of the relationship between specialization and oppression can be understood within the context of a critique of Taylorist labor organization or "scientific management" common to both capitalist and centrally planned modes of production. According to Weil, the rise of the bureaucratic element in industry is "only the most characteristic aspect of an altogether general phenomenon: specialization" (OL 12). Specialization, which Jacques Ellul later described as the "fruit" of bureaucratic technique,[27] entails the division of projects into numerous tasks, which hinders comprehension of an individual task's purpose in relation to the whole and knowledge of any given project in its entirety.[28] Excessive administrative demands impede mutual understanding and the development of meaningful work contexts along relations of solidarity by overcomplicating and multiplying unnecessary tasks. For Ritner, this is a two-sided problem: workers are enslaved to owners and managers, as well as to the "tools and machines which had been dislodged from their proper mediating role."[29] As Ritner explains, Weil understands the real quality of bureaucratic barriers to knowledge enforced by the existence of managers in terms of the *isolation* of workers both *materially and intellectually*.[30] These interlocking forms of isolation are compounded by the fact that workers need to know and understand only the techniques involved, not the tasks and motivations of others.

The bureaucratic methods and mandates that erect barriers to knowledge in between levels of workplace organization consistently reproduce the exclusion of workers from a share in the intellectual and physical efforts of the production process.[31] By observing how the mechanism of bureaucratic oppression upholds a knowledge/power nexus, Weil connects an innate tendency of machines to expand and multiply their functions with their appearing more uncontrollable and mysterious in relation to workers under the yoke of artificial necessity.[32] Because the power to coordinate, command, and manage is connected to the control of knowledge, hierarchies of knowledge concretized within organizational structures restrict the freedom of movement for the individual worker, cementing conditions of powerlessness, passivity, and alienation. As a result, rather than making machinery more conscious and methodical, thereby increasing their soul-crushing external force in relation to workers, Weil sees actual economic liberation as entailing the creation of objective conditions that lead to the reduction of unconscious labor and the unfolding of more conscious, thoughtful, and spiritual forms of work.[33]

Bureaucracy and the Banality of Evil: The Case of Eichmann

Published in 1963, Arendt's *Eichmann in Jerusalem: A Report on the Banality of Evil* continues to provoke debate over aspects of its portrayal of Nazi official Adolf Eichmann, one of the core organizers of the expulsion of Jews from Austria and Germany and, after that, their transfer to concentration camps. As well as analyzing Eichmann, the book sees Arendt examine how bureaucracies produce a culture of nonthinking or "thoughtlessness" that devalues individual ethical judgment. Although Arendt's notion of the "banality of evil" was criticized for underplaying the severity of Eichmann's crimes, this use of the term "banality" should be viewed in the context of the contradiction she noted between the extraordinary evil nature of the Holocaust and the seemingly ordinary, cliched manner of a "desk murderer" like Eichmann.[34] What struck Arendt as particularly disturbing about Eichmann was his apparent ordinariness, describing him as "terribly and terrifyingly normal" and "neither monstrous nor demonic" (EJ 276, 159). During the trial, Eichmann's defense said he was a mere "tiny cog" in the larger machine, obeying orders as any other person would in the same circumstances.[35] Arendt rebukes Eichmann's claim that his only choice for defying orders was suicide, however, given the ease with which members of extermination squads could flee without serious repercussions (EJ 91). Indeed, many alleged that "cogs" like Eichmann were in actual fact outspoken Nazis. Despite the pleading of the agents of deadly bureaucracies to draw a line between consent and obedience, Arendt argues that "if an adult is said to obey, he actually *supports* the organization, authority, or law that claims 'obedience.'"[36]

Arendt views the Eichmann case as an extreme manifestation of the phenomenon of bureaucratization, where an intrinsic capacity for violence within bureaucracy became apparent by their being controlled by evil political forces. Further, it implies the indispensability of the Nazi bureaucratic apparatus to carrying out Hitler's Final Solution, which could only have been executed via the technical coordination of violence by anonymous bureaucratic operations. When all organizations are tightly coordinated, as in totalitarian regimes, the cold, impersonal, bureaucratic mindset can infuse all spheres of society that are already long-charged with an ideology of hatred, transforming thinking individuals into nonthinking automatons (RJ 33). At the same time, Arendt's analysis of Eichmann also underlines the difficulties that a legal system encounters when attempting to determine responsibility and legal guilt within opaque, faceless bureaucracies. In his testimony, Eichmann claimed, "he had never been told more than he needed to know in order to do a specific, limited job," and that he'd never made a decision on his own and "was extremely careful always to be 'covered' by orders" (EJ 84, 94). Indeed, in its judgment, the court "naturally conceded that such a crime could only be committed by a giant bureaucracy using the resources of government," and the task of understanding the position of the accused required deep knowledge of the "intricate bureaucratic setup of the Nazi machinery of destruction" (EJ 289, 211). For Arendt, the "rule by nobody," which is described as the political form of bureaucracy, presents multiple problems with accountability: "In every bureaucratic system the shifting of responsibilities is a matter of daily routine" (RJ 30). The obsessive technical division of administrative labor into smaller and smaller pieces, coupled with the fact that bureaucrats only need to know their specific function and not its wider outcome, means that Arendt considers the rule by nobody as "perhaps the least human and most cruel form of leadership" (RJ 31).

Extending her analysis of Eichmann to bureaucratic systems of governance in general, Arendt argues that the "essence of totalitarian government, and perhaps the nature of every bureaucracy is to make functionaries out of mere cogs in the administrative machinery out of men, and thus to dehumanize them" (EJ 289). While noting how bureaucracies can promote "de-moralized forms of conduct" that press individual technocrats into nobodies capable of committing atrocities,[37] it remains so that a cog-like job-holder "is still a human being, and it is in this capacity that he [Eichmann] stands trial" (RJ 30). Someone who plays a role in the machinery of administering genocide, irrespective of how small or seemingly insignificant their functions may appear, ought nonetheless be held morally accountable.[38] This means that no singular cog is absolved of moral responsibility, irrespective of the demoralized bureaucratic culture in which they operate. Central to the notion of the banality of evil, therefore, is Eichmann's nonthinking or thoughtless behavior that produced a moral distancing from his victims and a moral indifference in relation to his crimes. What Eichmann demonstrated, for Arendt, was a "curious, quite authentic inability to think," a *refusal* to think from another person's point of view and thus to engage in the prerequisite for moral action and judgment, the capacity of the mind to think plurally in solitude (RJ 159). This, for Arendt, can wreak "more havoc than all the evil instincts taken together" (EJ 288). Under conditions in which every legal act was criminal and every moral act illegal, what was required on the part of evildoers was a "'feeling of lawfulness' deep within themselves to contradict the law of the land and their knowledge of it" (RJ 40-1). However, totalitarian regimes are not alone in instilling a culture of nonthinking within bureaucratic structures that can normalize violence. Any institution or, to take a cue from Weil, oppressive collectivity that discourages thoughtful and adaptive examination and which encourages individuals to "hold fast to whatever the prescribed rules may be" is potentially conducive to nonthinking and nonremembrance, which means, crucially, a silencing of the voice of ethical self-consciousness (RJ 178). By contrast, Arendt considers the origins of ethical conscience to lie in the solitary dialogue with oneself, out of which past behavior is questioned and moral forms of judgment can arise, because thinking beings ultimately have to "account for themselves, to *themselves*, after they have acted."[39] In sum, like Weil's analysis of the disconnection between mind and body with overspecialization, Arendt's analysis of Eichmann's thoughtlessness considers how an inflexible adherence to rules can take root amidst the everyday mundanity of administration.

Arendt's reflections on the distancing of cog-like technocrats from the overall effects of their tasks lead her to describe Eichmann as a "new type of criminal" who "commits his crimes under circumstances that make it well-nigh impossible to know or to feel that he is doing wrong" (EJ 276). Notwithstanding the enmeshment of Eichmann and other Nazi cogs in a "labyrinth administrative structure" that produced indifference to the suffering of others, an absence of personal judgment is actually germane to bureaucratic practices. Put differently, within bureaucracies, reflections on ends, let alone ethical questions of right and wrong, are irrelevant for executing functions and obeying collective rules. In Arendt's view, what makes Eichmann's moral indifference extra compelling is its implications for her belief that human beings actually do have a basic sense of empathy for their fellow human beings. For Arendt, Eichmann's denial of thinking and, in the courtroom, his rigid appeals to authority to shield him from the reality, "that is, against the claim on our thinking attention which all events and facts arouse by virtue of their existence," center the moral significance of *thinking* (LM 5). This prompts Arendt to question whether the activity of thinking, "the habit of examining whatever comes to pass" that can dissolve norms of conduct, may actually condition people against evildoing (LM 5). At moments when the moral significance of thinking comes out, the manifestation of the wind of thought, the ability to tell right from wrong, "becomes a kind of action" (RJ 188).

Conclusion

In this chapter, I have attempted to clarify Arendt and Weil's accounts of bureaucracy and provide a richer sense of the multilayered quality of their reflections. Undoubtedly, both Arendt and Weil take a critical stance toward bureaucracies and their fateful consequences on individuals. While bureaucratic organizations dominate the institutional landscape of modern capitalist society, subsuming cog-like individuals within unresponsive structures perceived as necessary and legitimate, they are, ultimately, artificial constructions whose authority can be subverted by countervailing forms of political power. To end on Weil, there is "no means of stopping the blind trend of the social machine towards an increasing centralization," and no top-down panacea to halt the crushing force of bureaucratic oppression (OL 114). Instead, what is needed, Weil writes, is to introduce a "little play into the cogs of the machine that is grinding us down; seize every opportunity of awakening a little thought wherever they are able; encourage whatever is capable, in the sphere of politics, economics or technique, of leaving the individual here and there a certain freedom of movement amid the trammels cast around him by the social organization" (OL 114).

Notes

1 It is worth remembering that while Arendt critiques the bureaucratic party system and its assimilative effect on participatory, spontaneous political expressions of political agency from a radical democratic position, Weil's position is informed by her synthesis of anarchist and Marxist critiques of the state.
2 See Arendt's chapter, "The Public and the Private Realm," in HC 22–79. However, it should also be noted here, as Murray Bookchin observed in 2004, that "much of the social 'complexity' of our time originates in the paperwork, administration, manipulation and constant wastefulness of capitalist enterprise." Bookchin, *Post-scarcity Anarchism* (London: AK Press, 2004), 81.
3 "And the proper realm to take care of life's necessities," Arendt writes, "is the gigantic and still increasing sphere of social and economic life whose administration has overshadowed the political realm since the beginning of the modern age." "What Is Freedom," in BPF 154.
4 Weil goes on to argue that "no doubt present-day science can serve very suitably as a theology for our more and more bureaucracy-ridden society" (OL 33).
5 Indeed, as Weil argues, "it is quite natural that the increasingly bureaucratic of economic activity should favor the development of the power of the State, which is the bureaucratic organization *par excellence*" (OL 109).
6 Interestingly, Dietz argues that to Weil, bureaucracy is a "creature of modernity and a microcosm of modern society as a whole"; see Mary Dietz, *Between the Human and the Divine: The Political Thought of Simone Weil* (Totowa, NJ: Rowman and Littlefield, 1988), 51.
7 For instance, Weil observes that in the USSR, the three bureaucracies—State, capital industries, and workers' organizations—"have long since constituted one and the same apparatus" (OL 17).
8 To his credit, Karl Marx, as Weil writes, did perceive the "force of oppression constituted by bureaucracy." Problematically, however, Weil argues that "he did not ask himself whether this was not a case of an order of problems independent of the problems presented by the capitalist economy properly so called ... he did not ask himself whether the administrative function, insofar as it is permanent, might not, independently of all monopoly over property, give rise to a new class of oppressors" (OL 13).
9 Although to Weil the dispossession of individuals by oppressive collectivities is not absolute and cannot become so, she argues that it is "hard to imagine how it could go much farther than at present" (OL, 105).

10 As Dietz explains, Weil's collectivity seems "both concrete and abstract, natural and artificial, visible and invisible, 'in the world,' and a conceptual device used to talk about the world." Moreover, "Weil's collectivity *signifies* abstraction in terms of the absence of a concrete relationship between mind and world, between thought and action"; see Dietz, *Between the Human and the Divine*, 50–2.
11 Dietz, *Between the Human and the Divine*, 50.
12 Lissa McCullough, *The Religious Philosophy of Simone Weil: An Introduction* (London: I.B. Tauris, 2014), 104.
13 "The Great Beast," in SWA 141.
14 Though collectivities cannot, by themselves, meet eternal needs, they can, in their nonoppressive instantiations, serve a crucial function in service of spiritual values, as an intermediary that prepares and shapes people for participating in the eternal. If a given collectivity or social structure creates a context for individuals to develop, deliberate, and make decisions while providing access to a larger whole, it opens up opportunities for genuine, active, and natural participation that positively sustains the life of rooted communities; see Eric O. Springsted, *Simone Weil for the 21st Century* (Notre Dame, IN: University of Notre Dame Press, 2021), 160.
15 Mccullough, *The Religious Philosophy of Simone Weil*, 39.
16 Dietz, *Between the Human and the Divine*, 53.
17 See, for example, Andrew Schaap, "Inequality, Loneliness, and Political Appearance: Picturing Radical Democracy with Hannah Arendt and Jacques Rancière," *Political Theory* 49, no. 1 (2021), 28–53.
18 Arendt writes that politics in the modern age is "nothing but a function of society" and that "society, on all its levels, excludes the possibility of action … [expecting] from each of its members a certain kind of behavior, imposing innumerable and various rules, all of which tend to 'normalize' its members, to make them behave, to exclude spontaneous action or outstanding achievement" (HC 33–40).
19 This reflects a twofold reality: freedom has "shifted places; it resides no longer in the public realm but in the private life of citizens," while "freedom and power have parted company"; see OR 134.
20 To Arendt, the work of homo faber—that "who makes and literally 'works upon'" the material of the human artifice—consists in true reification. See "The Durability of the World," in HC 136.
21 David Runciman, *Confronting Leviathan: A History of Ideas* (London: Profile, 2021), 190.
22 For an excellent, in-depth account of the concept of narrative agency as a precondition for exercising political agency, see Sarah Drews Lucas, "The Primacy of Narrative Agency: A Feminist Theory of the Self" (PhD Diss., Faculty of Arts and Social Sciences, Department of Philosophy, University of Sydney, 2016).
23 Relatedly, Arendt also remarks that only where the "I-will and I-can coincide does freedom come to pass" (BPF 159).
24 See James Muldoon, *Council Democracy: Towards a Democratic Socialist Politics* (London: Routledge, 2020).
25 See Simone Weil, "Reflections Concerning Technocracy, National-Socialism, the U.S.S.R. and Certain Other Matters" as well as "Reflections Concerning the Causes of Liberty and Social Oppression" in OL 24–118.
26 Weil's concern with scientific specialization runs through her 1934 "Reflections" essay and also within her 1943 *The Need for Roots* in which Weil criticizes a culture of specialization in education and work that contributes to uprootedness.

27 Jacques Ellul, *The Technological Society* (New York: Vintage, 1964).
28 Scott B. Ritner, "The Training of the Soul: Simone Weil's Dialectical Disciplinary Paradigm—A Reading alongside Michel Foucault," in *Simone Weil and Continental Philosophy*, ed. A. Rebecca Rozelle-Stone (Lanham, MD: Rowman and Littlefield, 2017), 315.
29 Scott B. Ritner, "Simone Weil's Heterodox Marxism: Revolutionary Pessimism and the Politics of Resistance," in *Simone Weil, Beyond Ideology?* ed. Sophie Bourgault and Julie Daigle (New York: Palgrave Macmillan, 2020), 198.
30 Ritner, "The Training of the Soul," 316.
31 Additionally, in observing how "the condition of all privilege, and consequently of all oppression, is the existence of a corpus of knowledge essentially closed to the working masses," Weil foreshadows Michel Foucault's emphasis that forms of knowledge are also forms of social power (OL 33).
32 Although to Arendt and Weil natural necessity is an inescapable feature of earthly existence, bureaucratic or administrative methods built into organizations constitute an unnatural and artificial form of necessity.
33 In 1934, Weil argues that true liberty is "not defined by a relationship between desire and its satisfaction, but by a relationship between thought and action"; see OL 81.
34 Though Arendt does use the term "desk-murderer" within *Eichmann in Jerusalem*, she refers to the term specifically in her introduction to Bernd Naumann's *Auschwitz*, writing that "the desk murderers, whose chief instruments were typewriters, telephones and teletypes—were guiltier than those who actually operated the extermination machinery, threw gas pellets into the chambers, manned the machine guns for the massacre of civilians, or were busy with the cremation of mountains of corpses." See Bernd Naumann, *Auschwitz* (New York: Frederic A. Praeger, 1966), xx.
35 As authors such as Hiruta have explained, however, Eichmann was not merely playing a replaceable role but was consistently an active and imaginative leader of the "Final Solution," energetically working as "multiple cogs" in order to operate the Nazi killing machine on many fronts; see Kai Hiruta, *Hannah Arendt and Isaiah Berlin: Freedom, Politics and Humanity* (Princeton: Princeton University Press, 2021), 127.
36 "Personal Responsibility under Dictatorship," in RJ 46.
37 Finn Bowring, "Comparing Bauman and Arendt: Three Important Differences," *Sociology* 45, no.1 (2011), 58.
38 To be clear, Arendt neither considers radical evil per se to be banal nor all perpetrators of evil to be banal, but rather that Eichmann's particular banality signaled at his basic thoughtlessness. Put differently, Arendt's banality thesis can be understood through her discussion on the nature of evil itself. For an excellent account of why radical evil and banal evil in Arendt's formulation are distinct but complementary concepts, see Paul Formosa, "Is Radical Evil Banal? Is Banal Evil Radical?" *Philosophy & Social Criticism* 33, no. 6 (2007), 717–35.
39 Bowring, "Comparing Bauman and Arendt," 65.

Bibliography

Benhabib, Seyla. *The Reluctant Modernism of Hannah Arendt*. New York: Rowman & Littlefield, 2003.
Bookchin, Murray. *Post-scarcity Anarchism*. London: AK Press, 2004.

Bowring, Finn. "Comparing Bauman and Arendt: Three Important Differences." *Sociology* 45, no.1 (2011): 54–69.

Dietz, Mary. *Between the Human and the Divine: The Political Thought of Simone Weil.* Totowa, NJ: Rowman and Littlefield, 1988.

Ellul, Jacques. *The Technological* Society. New York: Vintage, 1964.

Formosa, Paul. "Is Radical Evil Banal? Is Banal Evil Radical?" *Philosophy & Social Criticism* 33, no. 6 (2007): 717–35.

Hiruta, Kei. *Hannah Arendt and Isaiah Berlin: Freedom, Politics and Humanity.* Princeton: Princeton University Press, 2021.

Lucas, Sarah Drews. "The Primacy of Narrative Agency: A Feminist Theory of the Self." PhD Dissertation, Faculty of Arts and Social Sciences, Department of Philosophy, University of Sydney, 2016.

McCullough, Lissa. *The Religious Philosophy of Simone Weil: An Introduction.* London: I.B. Tauris, 2014.

Muldoon, James. *Council Democracy: Towards a Democratic Socialist Politics.* London: Routledge Press, 2020.

Naumann, Bernd. *Auschwitz.* New York: Frederic A. Praeger, 1966.

Pitkin, Hanna. "Conformism, Housekeeping and the Attack of the Blob: The Origins of Hannah Arendt's Concept of the Social." In *Feminist Interpretations of Hannah Arendt.* Edited by Bonnie Honig. University Park: Pennsylvania State University Press, 1995, pp. 51–82.

Ritner, Scott B. "The Training of the Soul: Simone Weil's Dialectical Disciplinary Paradigm—A Reading alongside Michel Foucault." In *Simone Weil and Continental Philosophy*, Edited by A. Rebecca Rozelle-Stone. Lanham, MD: Rowman and Littlefield, 2017, pp. 187–204.

Ritner, Scott B. "Simone Weil's Heterodox Marxism: Revolutionary Pessimism and the Politics of Resistance." In *Simone Weil, Beyond Ideology?* Edited by Sophie Bourgault and Julie Daigle. New York: Palgrave Macmillan, 2020, pp. 185–206.

Runciman, David. *Confronting Leviathan: A History of Ideas.* London: Profile, 2021.

Schaap, Andrew. "Inequality, Loneliness, and Political Appearance: Picturing Radical Democracy with Hannah Arendt and Jacques Rancière." *Political Theory* 49, no.1 (2021): 28–53.

Springsted, Eric O. *Simone Weil for the 21st Century.* Notre Dame, IN: University of Notre Dame Press, 2021.

Chapter 3

LIVING IN DARK TIMES: THE SEDUCTION OF TOTALITARIAN EVIL

Marie Cabaud Meaney

In his *Divine Comedy*, Dante describes the atrocious sufferings of the damned in Hell, where despair, pain, egotism, and ugliness reign.[1] For the inferno is the city of discord, an antipolis—everything positive in a human city has been replaced by evil. And yet this inferno still pales in some respects with the radical evil epitomized in the concentration camps of the twentieth century. The pain inflicted in Hell is—according to the Christian worldview—a just response to evil committed, while the suffering of those persecuted by totalitarian regimes has no rhyme or reason. Hannah Arendt called it "radical evil." Not only are those punished innocent, selected because of their race, faith, class, or randomly chosen, but their torturers benefit in no way from their internment. Greed, a cheap workforce, even sadism cannot explain the oppressors' behavior. Yet, somehow, they are "seduced" into committing this radical evil. How we are to make sense of this is a question that has been haunting generations since Auschwitz.

There have been dark times in history—wars, torture, even genocides. But what Arendt really means by "dark times" are moments where evil causes no outrage and is not openly discussed. Though the crimes perpetrated are neither secret nor mysterious, they are not easy to perceive (DT viii). For this evil is "covered up ... by the highly efficient talk and double-talk," as Arendt explains in her preface to *Men in Dark Times*, by "speech that does not disclose what is but sweeps it under the carpet, by exhortations, moral and otherwise" that "degrade all truth to meaningless triviality" (ibid.). Totalitarianism, one could argue, epitomizes this kind of mendacity in a new form. Reality is veiled by ideological euphemisms. Nowhere else are lies held in place as strongly as in a regime built on terror and ideology. But where the seduction comes from is the daunting question.

Simone Weil's *prise-de-conscience* came during the Spanish Civil War in which she briefly participated on the anarchists' side—without ever firing a shot—in the summer of 1936. Seemingly decent human beings committed atrocities and then laughed about them. This was barbarism, as old as humanity itself. When some people are put in a separate category, as she wrote in a letter to Georges Bernanos in 1938, their lives no longer count. What defines barbarism in Weilian terms is "not the fact that one *commits* extreme evil, but that one perpetrates it *without recognizing* it as being evil," as Gabellieri aptly puts it.[2] The ideological lies have gone so far that the crimes committed are ignored or, worse, bragged about. This again would find its acme within totalitarianism.

For Arendt, totalitarianism is a modern phenomenon, a new form of government using terror to further the perceived laws of Nature or History; it therefore cannot be compared to tyranny. According to Weil, however, it has been around for a while, even if its full expression is only found in the twentieth century.[3]

Though the thought of these two women differs in many ways, it still meets at certain points. At the heart of totalitarianism lies an ideology, they believe, acted out by mindless followers and bureaucrats fulfilling their seemingly banal duty. Evil in the twentieth century, as Weil and Arendt came to see, no longer presents itself as a seduction, a promise of pleasure—at least not in an obvious way—but as an obligation. As I will try to show, it is both radical and banal—something Arendt said about it successively, sometimes dropping the one for the other. While Arendt's verdict on Eichmann—though often misunderstood and maligned—is well known, Weil's similar insights about the monotony of evil in a different context twenty years earlier are not. Though neither was attempting to establish a philosophy of evil, their thoughts on the topic are substantial enough to be assembled and compared. I will therefore focus on totalitarian evil as the epitome of dark times from an Arendtian and Weilian perspective and analyze what lies at its source in order to understand its seductive attraction and point to some responses.

The Banality of Evil: Lacking Beauty, Depth, and Transcendence

Calling evil banal, even if only in the subtitle and on the last page of *Eichmann in Jerusalem*, caused scandal. While it is misleading, Arendt nonetheless had a profound insight about an aspect of evil, the different legitimate meanings of which I will now discuss. One needs to keep in mind that hers was a journalistic and not a philosophical approach when writing *Eichmann in Jerusalem*, though she was obviously drawing on philosophical insights.

Weil's statement in her article "Morality and Literature" that "nothing is so dreary, monotonous, and boring as evil" comes close to calling it banal.[4] Written in 1941 and published posthumously in the *Cahiers du Sud* in 1944, her piece lacked the explosiveness of Arendt's *Eichmann in Jerusalem*. However, considering that Weil was writing this in a world unhinged by evil, it was still a bold thing to say. Though penned in the context of literature, her statement was about the features of evil in real life vis-à-vis those in second-rate fiction and thus carried metaphysical weight. In masterpieces and in the world, however, "nothing is so beautiful, marvelous, … continually fresh and surprising, so full of sweet and continuous ecstasy as the good" (OC IV, 1 90). Only fake goodness, like self-righteousness, is boring.

During Romanticism, evil became the new sexy, serious evildoers supposedly possessing Promethean greatness.[5] As the ideology's inheritors, we tend to think that charisma, talent, and genius come with a dose of evil, while goodness does not leave any room for creativity. In contrast, Arendt was combating (similarly to Weil) the error from the 1920s and 1930s that evil has depth, as she shared in her interview with Joachim Fest in 1964. Evil made people interesting—it was thought—while goodness was one-dimensional. Furthermore, evil supposedly moved history forward.[6] To think of evil as being somehow great and exciting is therefore an insidious lie with potentially terrible consequences. In reality, the shoe is on the other foot, Weil claims; the good is exciting while evil is nauseatingly boring.

In her *Cahiers* in 1942, Weil states furthermore that evil, unlike the good, does not possess any depth or transcendence.[7] Similarly, Arendt wrote in a letter to Gershom Scholem on July 24, 1963, that evil was never "radical," but "only extreme," possessing "neither depth nor any demonic dimension." Furthermore, it is "thought-defying," since "thought tries to reach some depth" while evil has none. She concludes: "That is its 'banality.' Only the good has depth and can be radical" (PA 396). Superficially, evil may seem appealing, falsely promising infinite pleasures. But in reality, it creates a void due to its rejection of the good, Weil would say, that leaves one dissatisfied. The good, in contrast, being infinite, discloses ever-new aspects of itself, superabundantly fulfilling the heart.

Evil, however, is finite (OC VI, 3 350). Since it has nothing to offer except by pretense, it soon becomes sickeningly tedious once the allure of novelty has disappeared, as Weil states in her *Cahiers*. What it lacks in quality, it makes up in quantity. Don Juan wants ever more conquests; the miser desires perpetually more money[8]—not because evil itself is infinite but it is addictive, eventually becoming distastefully monotonous. Furthermore, it is formless and lacks structure, as Weil writes: "Evil is unlimited in the sense of the undetermined, matter, space, time ... Only the infinite limits the unlimited" (OC VI, 3 119 and 139). Only the real infinite, only God or the absolute good, can limit formless, sprawling evil.

For Weil, this false infinity explains the blandness of evil that does not contradict its horror: "*Monotony of evil: nothing new, everything is* EQUIVALENT. *Nothing real, everything is imaginary* ... Because of this monotony, *quantity* plays so big of a role ... Condemned to false infinity. That is Hell itself" (OC VI, 2 253). Facing forever one's greed, pettiness, spirit of revenge and that of others—as one would in Hell—is truly horrible. Nothing else is left, which is horrifying.

This sickening monotony of the eternal return, according to Weil, is due to *license* or licentiousness, for example, thinking that anything goes. When yielding to the downward pull of *license*, human beings have nothing to fall back upon but themselves (OC VI, 2 256). To state this differently: the freedom to do whatever one wants, independently of any Moral Law, is ultimately enslaving. For it means being tossed about by conflicting desires and led by the *Zeitgeist* that eventually becomes tedious. Limited in scope, desires are soon satiated, no longer giving people a kick, while ideology ultimately leaves people dissatisfied by its failed promises.

Hannah Arendt, on the other hand, rejects the Natural Moral Law,[9] finding it useless, since it lost its societal significance and cannot force people to obey it—which doesn't mean she is a nihilist or a moral relativist, as Stephan Kampowski argues.[10] Her own proposed solution, by the way, cannot be enforced either, since it depends on individuals taking themselves in hand. Her approach is that of "thinking without banisters," since the pointers of morality, religion, and tradition have been dismantled. Thinking things through and realizing that one does not want to live with oneself as a genocidal murderer is her alternative to the Natural Moral Law.[11]

Eichmann and Evil

What the banality of evil was mainly referring to for Arendt was Eichmann's mediocrity. Given that he helped organize the Final Solution, was in charge of the Jews' transportation to the concentration camps, and was present at the Wannsee Conference, one would have expected a monster, Satan incarnate. Yet, as Arendt writes: "Everybody could see that this man was not a 'monster,' but it was difficult indeed not to suspect that he was a clown" (EJ 54). He spoke in clichés, was a *Spiesser*, a stuffy philistine, and a petty bureaucrat who merely followed orders without taking responsibility. Arendt believed that Eichmann had neither thought about nor judged his acts; the banality of evil in this sense would mean not having judged one's own acts.[12] Or, as Barry Sharpe puts it: "What ... [Arendt] meant by banal was that Eichmann the criminal did not seem to match the crime."[13] However, she never believed what he had done was anything but monstrous.

What she did not realize, however, was that Eichmann in captivity played the part of a mediocre bureaucrat. For Arendt did not have access to the Argentine documents (the Sassen interviews) proving that Eichmann wanted Jews killed and was proud of his part in the Holocaust. He was a rabid ideologue and had participated in horrendous policies, not just by following orders but also by initiating crimes, as Bettina Stangneth has shown conclusively.[14]

The trend at the time was to demonize war criminals. But Arendt was afraid this would make them less real, less responsible, giving too facile an explanation of how ordinary people could be led to such deeds, as she explains in her letter to Jaspers on December 17, 1946 (CJ 69). It is ironic that she was accused of doing precisely what she was trying to avoid, namely minimizing evil.[15]

Another way in which evil appears banal is when society perceives it as something "normal." In the West, many endorsed slavery into the nineteenth century. In the twentieth century, the silent deportation of people during the night due to their race, religion, or political beliefs was accepted by society. Hence, the horrible becomes habitual and loses its sting to those not personally affected by it. It is a scary thought that a majority can participate in or permit evil while thinking of themselves as civilized and good.

Ideology is key in justifying this, by setting up its own kind of morality. As Raphael Gross writes, Eichmann was "simply" following Nazi morality with its emphasis on shame, guilt, honor, and faithfulness.[16] Surprisingly, ideologues tend to see themselves as highly moral. As Claudia Koonz writes, Hitler, for example, presented himself as a "prophet of virtue."[17] Or, as Harald Welzer states, "without morality mass murder would not have been possible," giving the criminals a false sense of moral integrity.[18] Furthermore, this process of *Gleichschaltung* or "enforced conformity" is accelerated if it claims to be legal, even if a mere semblance of legality is kept up, and even more if it pretends to be scientific, like the "racial science" of the Nazis and the "dialectical materialism" of communism,[19] for it assuages people's conscience.

The Moral Law and Doxa

But all of this is only possible, according to Weil, because the Moral Law has been abandoned. By rejecting the compass of morality, human beings lose their sense of direction and become literally mad.[20] Though Eichmann was not diagnosed as medically insane by the court, he had lost contact with reality. The judges accused him of "empty talk." But while they thought he did this by design, Arendt believed he was incapable of speaking other than in his officialese (EJ 48–9, 53); how much was playacting and how much was genuine incapacity is difficult to determine. But either way real communication had become impossible, since he saw everything through the prism of ideology and had given up a central part of reality, something without which the universe becomes unhinged, namely the Moral Law.

He rejected the fundamental moral principle of respecting the inviolable dignity of every human being. The mendacity prevalent in the Nazi party, the euphemisms like "the final solution" standing for the extermination of the Jews, or of a "medical procedure" to refer to killing by gas became second nature to the point that he and his partners in crime could not see beyond them anymore. He had become trapped by his own lies.

In her piece "Auschwitz on Trial" from 1966, Arendt explains how these perpetrators of crimes against humanity acted in a completely arbitrary manner. Since, quoting the reporter Naumann, "everyone could decide for himself to be either good or evil in Auschwitz," they were subject to their own moodiness, trampling people, then sending flowers to a woman who had given birth who would be gassed the next day (RJ 252). There was no rhyme or reason to these people's actions anymore. They became like "jelly," as Arendt writes, and their "ever-changing moods" had "eaten up all substance—the firm surface of personal identity, of being either good or bad, tender or brutal, an 'idealistic' idiot or a cynical sex pervert" (RJ 254). This is similar to C. S. Lewis's description in *The Abolition of Man* of "men without chests" who end up losing their moral sensibilities after abandoning the Moral Law.

For Weil, however, losing one's reference point of right and wrong is an exception only in terms of proportions in somebody like Eichmann. For all human beings are by definition condemned to the realm of shadows following Plato's allegory of the cave. Only through grace, the help of a mentor, and the heroic courage to look beyond one's familiar world, by facing the pain that the love of truth entails, can one escape these figments of the imagination. For we live—as Weil writes in "Morality and Literature"—in a "waking dream peopled by our chatter" in which "we are amusing ourselves with lies" (OC IV, 1 92). Human beings aggrandize their importance while closing their eyes to their vices and shallowness, follow conventions while feeling original. Appearance and prestige seem more real than reality (OC IV, 2 96, 212–13).

Thus, the judges, Eichmann's attorney, the prosecution, and Eichmann himself were speaking at cross-purposes. They could not imagine, as Arendt writes, that "an average, 'normal' person, neither feeble-minded nor indoctrinated nor cynical, could be perfectly incapable of telling right from wrong," and instead concluded that he was a liar (EJ 26). They were right in that he was trying to downplay what he had done but failed to realize that he could no longer tell right from wrong other than through the lens of Nazism. As Arendt writes pertinently, "under the conditions of the Third Reich only 'exceptions' could be expected to react 'normally,'" for it takes heroic courage and great clarity to retain one's sense of right and wrong when going against the culture at large. Using Platonic terminology, Weil would say that the mass of people was swayed by *doxa* or opinion rather than being guided by truth and was therefore unable to discern the destructive reversal of values. Only heroic adherence to truth makes such perceptivity possible.

Though in agreement about the confusion of people under the Third Reich, Arendt has a different take on Plato's distinction between *doxa* and truth. Socrates, she writes, wanted "to find the truth in … [his interlocutors'] *doxa*." For Arendt, *doxa* is the truth of the world as it appears to individuals, their experience of it, and is in-between the subjective and the objective (PP 15, 19). For Weil, however, *doxa* retains its traditional negative connotation, which is that of a mob being swayed by the *Zeitgeist*.[21] If individuals do not persistently seek the truth, they will easily fall victim to propaganda and mass dynamics. For what is there to protect them? A variety of false opinions, especially when they deny the dignity of the human person, do not lead to the truth, but to confusion—to the deadly detriment of some. Anyway, Eichmann's problem for Arendt was not *doxa*, but thoughtlessness. The lesson she learned from him was "that such remoteness from reality and such thoughtlessness can wreak more havoc than all the evil instincts taken together" (EJ 288). In some respects, sadism would have been a more satisfying answer, but it doesn't hold for Eichmann nor most perpetrators, be they desktop murderers or concentration camp guards. Another explanation is needed.

At first sight, thoughtlessness seems a weak reason, but there is more to it. It is not forgetfulness, stupidity, nor insanity, but an incapacity to stop and think through what one is doing, a failure to realize that one will have to live with oneself as a genocidal murderer. Thoughtlessness also means a serious lack of empathy (EJ 49). But what about those murderers who don't mind living with themselves, those who *don't* want to think? The most enlightened principles can be ignored just like moral norms. Furthermore, isn't an absolute moral *ought* more compelling than the thought of having to live with oneself? A transgression haunts one precisely because of having overstepped an immutable norm. Besides, if one must depend on individuals' decisions, doesn't morality have a more solid foundation than fearing what one might become? Anyway, the capacity to perceive the horror of being a mass murderer presupposes a moral sense that it tries to replace.

The right choice is made more difficult, since totalitarian evil presents itself as a duty rather than a temptation, according to Arendt and Weil (which is another guise in which it appears banal). "Evil, when one is in it, is not experienced as evil, but like a necessity, or even like a duty," as Weil writes in her *Cahiers* (OC VI, 2 65, 103, 110). Evil is generally thought to come in the guise of temptation; not committing it means giving up a pleasure. Not so under totalitarianism, as Arendt writes: "Evil in the Third Reich had lost the quality by which most people recognize it—the quality of temptation. Many Germans and many Nazis ... must have been tempted *not* to murder, *not* to rob, *not* to let their neighbors go off to their doom .... But, God knows, they had learned how to resist temptation" (EJ 150).

To the Nazi war criminals, their tasks were at first sickening. Christopher R. Browning shows how those mainly middle-aged family men of working and lower middle class from Hamburg, who were ordered to shoot Jews on the Eastern Front, were traumatized at first and needed alcohol to get through it. But they were hardened fairly quickly. Social pressure, not wanting to let their comrades down or appear cowardly, little time to think, and ideology all played their part in this.[22] And a false sense of duty was an important factor as well, giving people back their bearings that they had lost upon abandoning the Moral Law. For ideology with its false absolutes fills that moral void, according to Weil (OC V, 1 252). It makes heroic demands that confirm the idea of a higher obligation, thereby hiding its ultimately self-serving nature. Although this kind of evil first seems less tempting than the usual kind, it has its own allure.

Ideology

Ideologies are highly dangerous creeds when instantiated in totalitarian systems. Stangneth's investigations into the Eichmann case led her to conclude that "systematic mass murder is not just the sum of isolated instances of sadism but the result of a political thinking that is perverted from the ground up."[23] Cruel acts are the logical result of this belief system.

Arendt distinguishes ideology from opinion in that "it claims to possess ... the key to history," the solution to the "riddles of the universe," and knowledge of the "hidden universal laws" supposedly ruling nature and man (OT 159). It can deduce everything from a single premise, as Arendt explains in the later added chapter, "Ideology and Terror," revealing history's finality. There is a certain motion contained in the idea that plays itself out, for example, that an "inferior" race or a class must be oppressed, exiled, and finally eliminated. No experience, no new idea can change its direction, since everything is contained in its own premises (OT 469–71). It is immune to reality.

Its persuasive power, as Arendt states, stems from its appeal to experience and its promise to satisfy deep-seated desires. Its scientific guise, however, gives people the false impression that it is based on facts. In reality, it appeals, I believe, to the desire for power. By pretending to give people the key to the universe's mysteries, ideologies instill a sense of control. As Arendt therefore rightly states, ideology is primarily a political weapon and not a theoretical doctrine (OT 159).[24]

Arendt comes to think that the attraction of ideologues like Hitler and Stalin resides in their capacity to bring the main idea of an ideology to its logical conclusion, overpowering their audience with its persuasive force (OT 472). Paradoxically, this logic ultimately demands going against the original idea, namely the greatness of the German nation/race or the power of the proletariat: Germany was bled to death, and the proletariat lost what little privilege it had received under the Czar. The consequences of ideologies are catastrophic. Revolutions not only eat their own children, but, as Arendt formulates it, "the real content of ideology … is devoured by the logic with which the 'idea' is carried out" (OT 472).[25]

Ideologies blind people so that they either don't notice these contradictions or are not bothered by them. The future beckons, even when complete destruction is imminent, for ideology promises paradise, thus pulling the rug from under the feet of any criticism. Insane crises like the "total war" in the final stages of the Third Reich, the artificially created famines in Mao's China, or Stalin's purges of millions of people can be brushed aside by pointing to a future utopia. Current sacrifices are necessary for the final good of humanity is the tenet. This belief, as often pointed out, requires quasi-religious attitudes. However, contrary to valid forms of religion, these substitutes demand an adherence that is contrary to reason, reality, justice, and the Moral Law in general.[26]

Weil's experience in the Spanish Civil War taught her that there is nothing more universal than barbarism. For Weil, ideology—as she would come to understand later—numbs people's moral sense, permitting them to commit atrocities without any sense of guilt. Her otherwise fraternal and decent comrade-anarchists killed people randomly, laughing about it later.[27] Making ideology even more insidious is the way it appeals to people's belief in their own goodness and enlightened virtues. As Weil states in her essay-fragment from 1939 "Réflexions sur la barbarie," the greater that belief, the faster one will abandon one's moral principles—one's supposed past goodness giving a false sense of security. Nobody, no country, no culture, no people are immune to barbarism "which develops more or less depending on whether circumstances allow for more or less leeway." The conclusion is therefore that "one is always barbaric to the weaker … except at the price of a generosity as rare as genius," or if held back by constitutions, governments, and enforced laws.[28]

Hence there are no people set apart, alone capable of becoming monsters. In her essay from 1943, "Cette Guerre est une guerre de religions," Weil writes about the Germans: "What looks to us so hideous is our own traits, but magnified" (OC V, 1 253). Similarly, Arendt states in "Nightmare and Flight": "The reality is that 'the Nazis are men like ourselves'; the nightmare is that they have … proven beyond doubt what man is capable of" (EU 134). Neither is saying that there is no difference between those who have committed such acts and those that haven't. But both emphasize that every human being is capable of horrific deeds if they so choose.

Totalitarianism

But where Weil and Arendt part ways is in their views on the ultimate source of ideology in its totalitarian instantiation. For Weil came to see that ideology is, at heart, a religious problem, a form of idolatry, turning something like a nation, race, or class, and so on, into an absolute, demanding radical sacrifices and engendering fanaticism among its followers while promising ultimate happiness. But one might well raise the question if this doesn't turn a political and moral problem unnecessarily into a religious one. Ideologues can be religious or not; one does not seem to have much to do with the other. This was part of Arendt's response to Eric Voegelin's review of her *Origins* in the *Review of Politics*. Hitler, as Arendt argues, was not a believer. To accuse him of idolatry when he didn't have much of a religious belief seems far-fetched. The place of God simply remains empty within a totalitarian system, Arendt holds. She admits that there is a connection between atheism and totalitarianism, but only by the former being a condition for the latter. Ideology or totalitarian regimes are not religions gone secular, but simply have greater success in a secular or atheistic context (PA 162).

Furthermore, the fact that two things have the same function, as Arendt rightly points out in "What Is Authority?," does not mean they are the same. Communism and religion might have the same function, attempting to fulfill people emotionally, socially, and psychologically, but their essence is quite different (BPF 101–3). Weil's account of ideology, however, gives an implicit answer to Arendt's points of criticism. Her approach is anthropological, something she holds to be self-evident following Pascal (and, through him, St. Augustine), namely that human beings need an absolute to fulfill their infinite yearning. Finite objects or ideas, when turned into absolutes, may pretend to give endless satisfaction, but ultimately cannot do so. Historical analyses are not meant to prove this, but only underpin her argument. Whether ideologues like Hitler adhere to a religion or not is therefore neither here nor there; ideology has taken the place of God in their lives. And what makes ideologies similar to religion is not primarily that they fulfill the same function, but that they take the same place in the human heart—with very different results. For only something truly infinite can fulfill human beings without undermining their freedom.

Weil appeals to a basic human experience to make her anthropological claim: "It is enough to observe what is evident to everybody, namely that all past, present or future, real or imaginary goods here below are finite and limited, radically incapable to satisfy the desire for an infinite and perfect good burning perpetually in us" (OC IV, 1 277). The initial hope that idols would be fulfilling is proven false. Sometimes, the futility of such pursuit dawns upon one, but is quickly shaken off to engage in the next fruitless chase. To wake up to the dreary truth requires death to self, accepting that nothing in this world can satisfy this infinite desire.[29]

Turning finite goods into idols doesn't just mean living a lie that is bad enough, but also becoming addicted to those lies. If individuals do not prioritize the real infinite, namely God, who alone can fulfill the unlimited longing of the human heart, then they will seek idols. As Weil writes in her American notebooks: "One can only choose between God and idolatry. There is no other possibility. For the faculty of adoration is in us and is directed toward something in this world or in the next."[30] While one tends to think of idols in terms of graven images, much more dangerous entities are prone to become idols these days. As Weil writes in her essay from 1937, "Ne recommencons pas la Guerre de Troie," words such as "nation" or "state" become treacherous once they are turned into capital-letter words thereby becoming absolutes. Interestingly, she did not yet see the problem as a religious one at that point. Intellectuals deconstructing these terms might be able to prevent wars from arising, therefore she hoped (OC II, 3 63–6).

While one might expect the idolater to care selflessly about his idol, his ego is actually at the center of his worship—even if he is willing to sacrifice much for its sake, even up to his life. In *I See Satan Fall Like Lightning*, René Girard explains in a different context how one tends to idolize one's neighbors, wrongly believing them to be absolutely fulfilled: "We congratulate ourselves on having within us a[n] [infinite] desire," Girard explains, "but we do not see what this [infinity] … conceals: the idolization of the neighbor." Then follows a key insight: "This idolatry is necessarily associated with the idolization of ourselves."[31] Hidden behind the worship of an idol is the greatest egotism, the worship of self. And this self-worship, Weil believes, is linked to the desire for *force*, a Weilian concept akin to power, while the adoration of *force* lies at the heart of totalitarianism, as she shows in *L'Enracinement* (V, 2 222).[32]

Everybody in this world is at the mercy of *force* either as oppressor or oppressed, often successively, as Weil explains in her article on the Homeric epic "L'Iliade ou le poème de la force," yet few recognize its reign. It turns people into *choses/* things, easily changes sides, and is limited, contrary to the impression it creates (OC II, 3 246–7). Prestige, however, makes force seem invincible. Prestige is created through both propaganda and the reactions of others. The actor Gustav Gründgens underlines the importance of the bystanders' reaction when stating that "the king is always played by others." The way his subjects react to him sets him off. Hence, as Stangneth so aptly puts it, "power is a phenomenon created by group dynamics, never solely by the 'powerful man.' It calls *him* into being."[33] Therefore, as Weil writes in "Réflexions sur la barbarie," *force* is key and one cannot "form clear thoughts on human relationships as long as one has not put at the center the notion of force" (OC II, 3 223). Yet, the adoration of force is so insidious since we are unaware of it in ourselves. She explains in *L'Enracinement* that: "The worst errors which distort all thought, which make one lose one's soul, which put one outside of the truth and good, are not discernible. The reason for this is that some things escape one's attention … This is why … truth is a supernatural good."[34] This lack of awareness makes erroneous worldviews and ideologies particularly dangerous. It takes a radical commitment to truth to wake up from this ideological slumber.

Another aspect of totalitarianism is the appearance of radical evil that Arendt mentions in the preface of the first edition from 1950 to *The Origins of Totalitarianism* and then again in the twelfth chapter (OT IX, 443). She speaks of radical evil as something utterly destructive of humanity. What puts concentration camps into this new category of radical evil is that there is no typical motivation present, like self-interest or profit. The juridical, moral, and physical dimensions of the inmates are destroyed successively with no benefit to their oppressors (OT 441, 443). Radical evil furthermore draws out the ultimate consequences of an ideology, peremptorily fulfilling the supposed laws of Nature or History (OT 459). Being unprecedented, it initiates a new period in history and cannot be understood in terms of traditional philosophical concepts.

Did Arendt change her mind in 1961 at Eichmann's trial, thinking evil was merely banal? Her thought shifted, though it is unclear if she abandoned the concept of radical evil for good. In her famous letter to Gershom Scholem from July 1963, she writes that she no longer believes in radical, but only in extreme evil that has no depth (PA 396). In her last work, *The Life of the Mind*, however, Arendt speaks again of evil in terms she had attributed to radical evil, that is, lacking its habitual motives (LM I 4–5). In reality, radical and banal evil are not mutually exclusive, I believe. Arendt herself uses the terms "horror" and banality in the same sentence at the end of "Some Questions of Moral Philosophy" (1964–5) to show that they can well appear together (RJ 146). This happens when people remain morally and politically indifferent, refusing to think and judge, while committing or witnessing the perpetration of evil (RJ 146). Once they buy into the lies, horrific evil can permeate society without raising any eyebrows, making it banal, common, and socially acceptable.

The banality and radicality of evil point to different dimensions of evil, I think: the first to its appearance and the other to its nature. To Eichmann and other ideologues, their acts perhaps seemed banal, yet they were radically evil. Eichmann himself appeared shallow and banal, but his acts were not. Those who were mere cogs in the system contributed to radical, horrific evil. So, when radical evil comes across as banal, that's when it is at its most terrifying and extreme, yet is ignored by those not in its immediate shooting line. It glibly pretends to be legal, scientific, even compassionate while in reality ruthlessly killing its victims. When evil appears banal, it can strike all the more easily. Hence, dark times are periods when radical evil seems banal and is ignored by a self-righteous majority believing in their own goodness.

For lack of space, I will only briefly summarize what totalitarianism means for both thinkers. For Arendt, totalitarianism is a new form of government that appeared first in the twentieth century and is essentially different from tyranny; its essence is terror, finding its ultimate expression in concentration camps. It is run by bureaucrats who obey orders without giving them any real thought. Political action has become impossible, for people cannot act freely or in concert. At its core lies an ideology that keeps the regime moving, trying to push forward the supposed Laws of History or Nature.

Simone Weil does not give a lengthy analysis of totalitarianism as such though it is implicit in parts of her *oeuvre*, especially in *L'Enracinement*. At the heart of this form of government lies an ideology, which is the idolatry of some capital-letter concept at the center of which lies the adoration of *force*. It is not a new phenomenon (already the ancient Romans employed some of Hitler's cruel techniques), but a deep-seated anthropological temptation for which the technological means were only fully available in the twentieth century. Since people live in the realm of *doxa*, ideology is connatural to them, and if made more persuasive through propaganda, it is swallowed hook, line, and sinker. But how to counter or, better, prevent this tremendous evil remains an urgent question.

Conclusions

Given their different analyses of ideology and totalitarianism, the responses of Arendt and Weil to totalitarian evil diverge substantially despite some overlaps. In her introduction to the first part of *The Life of the Mind*, Arendt speaks of Eichmann as being the "immediate impulse" for her interest in "thinking"; her sense was that his failure to think was at the root of his evildoing (LM I 3–4). Hence, it is vital to understand what constitutes thinking and realize that all people, whatever their intelligence, can think and are culpable if they refuse to engage in it. Thinking for Arendt means dialoguing with oneself and realizing one would rather not live in the company of a murderer.[35]

Judgment follows upon thinking and should be led by common sense that helps us fit into the human community and enables us to communicate through imagination and representation. This neither makes one's judgment dependent on others, nor does it turn it into something subjective, for it is valid for all who judge well rather than simply follow customs or the current *Zeitgeist* (RJ 139–42). But how reliable is common sense truly? Even if experience and consensus weathered by time (which Arendt calls tradition) shape common sense, what is there to prevent the wrong kind of tradition from being handed down? And what if a society has lost its common sense?

In any case, the right kind of thinking and judgment is meant to lead to political action, which happens for Arendt between human beings without the intermediary of things; its condition is human plurality (HC 7): "In acting and speaking, men show who they are, reveal actively their unique personal identities and thus make their appearance in the human world" (HC 179). Action sets a new beginning with unpredictable consequences, since other people chime in and might turn it in another direction (HC 178, 184).[36] Political action, which includes debate, happens within the public space. But in dark times "the public realm … los[es] the power of illumination which was originally part of its very nature" (DT 4). Though political action is made impossible in totalitarian regimes, this doesn't mean nothing can be done. People who think can shine some light into the darkness (DT IX–X, 76). Artists, poets, and writers use their imagination to create "small hidden islands of freedom," Arendt explains; hence thinking "is a creative activity which requires remembrance, story-telling, and imagination," as Richard J. Bernstein explains (BPF 6).[37]

Arendt's answer to evil, as expected, remains a secular, immanent one, founded on her anthropology and general worldview. In order to respond to evil, people must retain their individuality, yet act in concert. *Amor mundi*, love of the world, which was the original title to *The Human Condition* and which stresses the need for attachment and roots, is the answer to alienation, hence also the motivation for political action and the way to prevent totalitarianism. This is not far off from Weil's emphasis on the need for roots, whose ultimate foundation is the supernatural, however. But the question remains if a political answer to totalitarian evil suffices. Both Arendt and Weil believe in the relevance of political action to prevent and fight injustice. Weil's involvement in the Free French government at the end of her life shows that despite her religious interests, she never dismissed concrete action. However, she didn't think that the political realm yielded in and of itself the ultimate answer to evil.

For Weil, the response to totalitarian evil should start with the moral decisions and religious choices of individuals, leading to specific acts. I would have liked to discuss Weil's analysis of immoral choices as well as how to counter evil (as I have done in other publications) through attention, obedience, patience, hope, or by avoiding day-dreaming, to mention just a few.[38] But the only two items I can briefly concentrate on here are faith and self-giving love as expressed through the Cross.

"Faith is more realistic than Realpolitik," Weil writes in *L'Enracinement* (OC V, 2 282). If faith were widespread in France, then people would take action more readily against the German occupiers, sabotaging communication and rail-lines as she states in "Une Guerre de religions" (OC V, 1 257–8, 2 274–5). While Hitler recognized the power of ideas in warfare, his thinking was shortsighted when offering evil as a motive for his followers. Although evil, as Weil writes, becomes "much more easily an active motive than the good," the good alone is "the source of an inexhaustible and invariable impulsion" (OC V, 2 281). The strength of the motive depends on its source; since pure good is infinite, it never reaches its end.[39] Though faith starts small like a mustard seed, as Weil states quoting the Gospels in *Intuitions pré-chrétiennes*, this smallest and almost invisible seed becomes a big tree in which the birds of the sky can sit (OC IV, 2 153). Hence Hitler is right to take it seriously though he only uses an *Ersatz*, namely the fanaticizing power of idolatrous ideology.

Weil's project—submitted to the Free French—of frontline nurses who would put their lives at risk (she foremost) to help wounded soldiers was therefore an adequate response, spiritually speaking, against the fanaticism of Hitler's troops. As willing as the SS to die, the motivations of these frontline nurses were diametrically opposed; to transform horror through sacrifice was the goal. Similarly, the Allies needed to be motivated by radical justice, which is nothing else than a "folly of love," for being on the "right side" was not enough, as she stated in "Luttons-nous pour la justice?" (OC V, 1 248–9). This folly of love finds its most radical expression in embracing the Cross. And the Cross, as it turns out, is also the most powerful response to evil, defeating it absolutely.

One tends to react to evil by doing evil, to being hurt by passing on the hurt, for this is a way of avoiding suffering. Weil explains in her *Cahiers*: "The man who receives and transmits malediction does not let it penetrate to his core. He does not feel it. But it penetrates to the core of the man upon whom it settles, the man who stops it. He becomes a curse. One needs to be pure to become a curse" (OC VI, 3 382). Only the *être pur*, the pure being, transforms evil into suffering. However, no human being can do so consistently on his own. No finite being possesses the purity to become the perfect scapegoat, for "only that which is absolutely pure can receive our evil without being sullied by it, and therefore without ever sending it back to us" (OC VI, 3 200). Thus, "the perfectly just can only be God incarnate" (OC VI, 3 356). The defeat of evil is perfectly expressed on the Cross where Christ transmutes it out of love into suffering. Finite human beings, on the other hand, are bound to reach the end of their rope at some point (except if transformed in Christ) and hence continue the *perpetuum mobile* of sin.

Ideological utopia is an illegitimate attempt to escape suffering and avoid the vulnerability required for the descent of God who alone can fulfill the heart's infinite desires. Buttressed by a totalitarian regime, it becomes a deadly mix, generating much more suffering and oppression than what it was supposed to resolve (OC VI, 3 266).

The Cross, in contrast, reveals the ongoing dynamic of evil, that is, of transforming hurt into evil, but also shows how to bring it to a halt. It is the only adequate response to evil, when the latter cannot be prevented. Though everybody has the choice to pass evil on or to "transmute … it into pure suffering," this cannot happen through mere willpower; it requires contact with "an unalterable purity placed outside, out of any reach," God Himself (OC VI, 3 353). Patience (coming from the Latin *pati*, "to bear," "suffer"), however, is of the essence, for it "consists of not transforming suffering into crime" (OC VI, 3 353). Bearing the suffering rather than transmuting it into evil is key to the moral and spiritual life and lets us participate in Christ's suffering, centering our restless souls: "The scales are agitated in all directions. A nail fixes the center. Henceforth they show correctly. The nail does not show any number, but because of the nail the pointer shows correctly" (OC VI, 4 195).

Embracing the Cross is not an excuse for failing to combat injustice, but it is the answer when injustices cannot be prevented or resolved. It becomes the right response to totalitarian regimes, when resistance has failed—dissidents like the members of the White Rose, Stauffenberg, or Solzhenitsyn suffered for resisting the regime, some paying with their lives. Furthermore, rejecting ideological idols and instead suffering through the dark night of the soul until the only absolute good, God, reveals Himself can prevent totalitarianism from arising in the first place,

Where does this leave Arendt? Her answers are significant and have their place. Yes, thinking, judgment, political action, education, laws, and so on are important in preventing totalitarian regimes from arising, as Weil would agree. At the same time, I don't think they address the root of the problem, that is, that dimension of the human heart seeking to fulfill its hunger with the ideologies totalitarianism attempts to enact. Both thinkers' approaches demand a difficult personal choice, whether it is to think things through and engage in political action or to withstand idolatry—though the latter is more radical. Neither suggests an easy fix. I wish I could give a more comforting answer.

But ending on a note of hope: *force* is limited; totalitarian regimes come to an end eventually, even imploding like the USSR did. And from a supernatural perspective: seemingly overwhelming evil can become the vehicle for the victory of the good. This is not morbid masochism, but an empowering realization: evil can be turned around from the inside, though it might be at the cost of one's life. The victims turn out to be the winners, even if appearances say otherwise. "*In hoc signo vinces*," to quote Constantine, takes on a radically different meaning here. The Cross overcomes evil by turning it through love into suffering. It is the ultimate answer to the totalitarian worship of *force*.

Notes

1 Some parts of this chapter appeared in chapter 1 of my book *Brücken zum Übernatürlichen: Simone Weil über das Böse, den Krieg und die Religion* (Mainz: Bernardus, 2018), as well as in *Cahiers Simone Weil* under the title "Le mal, est-il mystérieux ou banal?" (*CSW* 35, no. 2 (2012): 255–78), and are kindly reprinted here with permission of the publishers.
2 Emmanuel Gabellieri, *Être et don: Simone Weil et la philosophie* (Leuven: Peeters, 2003), 209. All quotations by Weil and from secondary sources in a foreign language have been translated into English by me.
3 In her essay from 1939, "Quelques réflexions sur les origines de l'hitlérisme," Weil compares the methods used by the ancient Romans and Hitler: brazen lies, ruthless cruelty, calculated treachery, pretense of invincibility and so on (OC II, 3 181–2). Rome's cruel treatment of the colonies spread to its own citizens under Marius and Sulla, turning it, in Weil's eyes, into a totalitarian state (ibid. 204). The random cruelty, the terror, the manipulation of the masses, the army becoming the state party, and, most importantly, the state itself being worshiped are all features of a totalitarian regime (ibid., 206–7). Furthermore, she sees the French King Louis XIV's reign as totalitarian because of Richelieu. The main features of totalitarianism were present: terror, denunciations, propaganda, uprooting the provinces, and centralizing everything (ibid., 207–8). Simone Weil, however, is overstating her case, for these features' scope was limited. Society as a whole was not spying on each other; there were no concentration camps, no attempts to control every aspect of people's lives, and no random killings.
4 Simone Weil, *Écrits de Marseille (1940–1942)*, ed. Robert Chenavier et al. (Paris: Gallimard, 2008), 90. Henceforth OC IV, 1 parenthetically.
5 Examples of the archetypical Byronic hero (influenced by the Gothic novel and Satan in Milton's *Paradise Lost*) are Heathcliff in Emily Brontë's *Wuthering Heights* or Rochester in Charlotte Brontë's *Jane Eyre*.
6 Ursula Ludz and Thomas Wild (eds.), *Eichmann war von empörender Dummheit: Gespräche und Briefe* (München: Piper, 2011), 41, 44. See also RJ 94–5.
7 Simone Weil, *Cahiers (février 1942–juin 1942): La porte du transcendant*, ed. Alyette Degrâces et al. (Paris: Gallimard, 2002), 93. Henceforth OC VI, 3 parenthetically.
8 Simone Weil, *Cahiers (septembre 1941–février 1942)*, ed. Alyette Degrâces et al. (Paris: Gallimard, 1997), 253. Henceforth OC VI, 2 parenthetically.

9 Interestingly, its declining societal significance is one of the conditions for totalitarianism, according to Arendt (RJ 61; OT 299).
10 Stephan Kampowski, *Arendt, Augustine, and the New Beginning: The Action Theory and Moral Thought of Hannah Arendt in the Light of Her Dissertation on St. Augustine* (Grand Rapids, MI: Eerdmans, 2008), 105.
11 This does not mean that Arendt eliminates moral considerations from her thought, but that they are not based on the Natural Moral Law. The act of thinking and that of judging are morally significant; when engaged in, they prevent people from committing the "infinite evil" of people like Eichmann (RJ 188). Conscience arises from this dialogue with self.
12 As Claudia Bozzaro points out in *Hannah Arendt und die Banalität des Bösen* (Freiburg: Fördergemeinschaft wissenschaftlicher Publikationen von Frauen, 2007), 96.
13 Barry Sharpe, *Modesty and Arrogance of Judgment: Hannah Arendt's "Eichmann in Jerusalem"* (Westport, CT: Praeger, 1999), 2.
14 Bettina Stangneth, *Eichmann before Jerusalem: The Unexamined Life of a Mass Murderer*, trans. Ruth Martin (New York: Knopf, 2014), XXIV, 303–4.
15 Though Arendt fell for Eichmann's game, this doesn't mean, however, that her idea of the banality of evil is invalid. As Christopher R. Browning states, Arendt was fooled by Eichmann "because there were so many perpetrators of the kind he was pretending to be" ("Revisiting the Holocaust Perpetrators," quoted by Richard Bernstein in "Are Arendt's Reflections on Evil Still Relevant?" in *Politics in Dark Times: Encounters with Hannah Arendt*, ed. Seyla Benhabib (New York: Cambridge, 2010), 293–304, 301).
16 Raphael Gross, *Anständig Geblieben: Nationalsozialistische Moral* (Frankfurt aM: Fischer Verlag, 2010), 8, 174–5, 180, 199.
17 Claudia Koonz, *The Nazi Conscience* (Cambridge, MA: Belknap Press, 2003), 7.
18 Harald Welzer, *Täter: Wie aus ganz normalen Menschen Massenmörder werden* (Frankfurt aM: Fischer, 2005), 23, 40.
19 Koonz, *Conscience*, 128, 190–2.
20 Simone Weil, *Écrits de New York et de Londres (1942–43): Questions politiques et religieuses*, ed. Robert Chenavier et al. (Paris: Gallimard, 2019), 251. Henceforth OC V, 1 parenthetically.
21 Simone Weil, *Écrits de Marseille (1941–1942)*, ed. Anisse Castel-Bouchouchi and Florence de Lussy (Paris: Gallimard, 2009), 87, 96. Henceforth OC IV, 2 parenthetically.
22 Christopher R. Browning, *Ordinary Men: Reserve Police Battalion 101 and the Final Solution in Poland* (New York: Harper, rev. edn, 2017), 1, 68, 71–2, 85.
23 Stangneth, *Eichmann*, 268.
24 Peter Baehr explains Arendt's position in the following way in *Hannah Arendt, Totalitarianism, and the Social Sciences*: "The real world is a colorful, cacophonous place. Ideology is monochronic and tone-deaf" (Stanford: Stanford University Press, 2010), 13.
25 Ultimately, totalitarianism wants subjects thoughtless to the point of not distinguishing between fact and fiction (OT 474).
26 Interestingly, Arendt changed her mind on ideology's role in totalitarian evil at various points. In her first version of the *Origins of Totalitarianism* from 1951 and her last version from 1966, she recognized its importance. But she underestimated it in Eichmann's case.

27 For an analysis of Weil's ideas on barbarism, see Emmanuel Gabellieri's article "Psychologie du gros animal et philosophie de la barbarie chez S. Weil," *Cahiers Simone Weil* 9, no. 3 (1986): 260–85.
28 Simone Weil, *Écrits historiques et politiques: vers la guerre (1937–1940)*, ed. Simone Fraisse (Paris: Gallimard, 1989), 223. Henceforth OC II, 3 parenthetically.
29 But it creates the space for God to enter: "The only choice man has is to attach his love to something in this world or not." If he does not and waits, then God will descend (OC IV, 1 278).
30 Simone Weil, *Cahiers (juillet 1942–juillet 1943): La connaissance surnaturelle (Cahiers de New York et de Londres)*, ed. Marie-Annette Fourneyron et al. (Paris: Gallimard, 2006), 181. Henceforth OC VI, 4 parenthetically.
31 René Girard, *I See Satan Fall Like Lightning*, trans. James G. Williams (Maryknoll, NY: Orbis, 2001), 11.
32 This requires further explanations that I cannot give for lack of space.
33 Stangneth, *Eichmann*, 41.
34 Simone Weil, *Écrits de New York et de Londres (1943): L'Enracinement: Prélude à une déclaration des devoirs envers l'être humain*, ed. Robert Chenavier and Patrice Rolland (Paris: Gallimard, 2013), 289. Henceforth OC V, 2 parenthetically.
35 Prima facie, Arendt's concept of "thinking" might seem quite similar to Weil's "attention," but they are not. The latter is a contemplation and intense focus on, for example, truth, the good, beauty, the supernatural moral law, opaque situations, as well as paradoxes. Arendt's concept of thinking, however, is about dialoguing with oneself and realizing one couldn't live with oneself if one committed a horrific crime. The gaze is therefore inward, while it is outward in Weil's case.
36 Forgiveness and heroism are examples of actions, for revenge would be the expected consequence when experiencing evil while saving one's own skin the probable reaction to danger (HC 241).
37 "Arendt on Thinking," in *The Cambridge Companion to Hannah Arendt*, ed. Dana Villa (Cambridge: Cambridge University Press, 2000), 277–92, 279.
38 See references in note 1. Other worthwhile aspects on a more general level would have been her focus on reconnecting people to their roots, transmitting truth and beauty through education, finding inspiration in the past, designing a new constitution for France based on human needs rather than human rights, and so on.
39 Simone Weil does not seem to acknowledge, however, the natural limits of a person's energy. She accuses herself in an undated letter to Maurice Schumann of lacking strength because of a lack of faith. In the saints, she claims, the supernatural life supplies them with unlimited energy (EL 210). She fails to realize that the saints too broke down under too much strain, including St. John Bosco, St. John Vianney, and others.

Bibliography

Baehr, Peter. *Hannah Arendt, Totalitarianism, and the Social Sciences*. Stanford: Stanford University Press, 2010.

Bernstein, Richard J. "Arendt on Thinking." In *The Cambridge Companion to Hannah Arendt*. Edited by Dana Villa. Cambridge: Cambridge University Press, 2000, pp. 277–92.

Bernstein, Richard J. "Are Arendt's Reflections on Evil Still Relevant?" In *Politics in Dark Times: Encounters with Hannah Arendt*. Edited by Seyla Benhabib. New York: Cambridge, 2010, pp. 293–304.

Bozzaro, Claudia. *Hannah Arendt und die Banalität des Bösen*. Freiburg: Fördergemeinschaft wissenschaftlicher Publikationen von Frauen, 2007.

Browning, Christopher R. *Ordinary Men: Reserve Police Battalion 101 and the Final Solution in Poland*. New York: Harper, rev. edn, 2017.

Cabaud Meaney, Marie. "Le mal, est-il mystérieux ou banal?" *Cahiers Simone Weil* 35, no. 2 (2012): 255–78.

Cabaud Meaney, Marie. *Brücken zum Übernatürlichen: Simone Weil über das Böse, den Krieg und die Religion*. Mainz: Bernardus, 2018.

Gabellieri, Emmanuel. "Psychologie du gros animal et philosophie de la barbarie chez S. Weil." *Cahiers Simone Weil* 9, no. 3 (1986): 260–85.

Gabellieri, Emmanuel. *Être et don: Simone Weil et la philosophie*. Leuven: Peeters, 2003.

Girard, René. *I See Satan Fall Like Lightning*. Translated by James G. Williams. Maryknoll, NY: Orbis, 2001.

Gross, Raphael. *Anständig Geblieben: Nationalsozialistische Moral*. Frankfurt aM: Fischer Verlag, 2010.

Kampowski, Stephan. *Arendt, Augustine, and the New Beginning: The Action Theory and Moral Thought of Hannah Arendt in the Light of Her Dissertation on St. Augustine*. Grand Rapids, MI: Eerdmans, 2008.

Koonz, Claudia. *The Nazi Conscience*. Cambridge, MA: Belknap Press, 2003.

Ludz, Ursula, and Thomas Wild (eds.). *Eichmann war von empörender Dummheit: Gespräche und Briefe*. München: Piper, 2011.

Sharpe, Barry. *Modesty and Arrogance of Judgment: Hannah Arendt's "Eichmann in Jerusalem."* Westport, CT: Praeger, 1999.

Stangneth, Bettina. *Eichmann before Jerusalem: The Unexamined Life of a Mass Murderer*. Translated by Ruth Martin. New York: Knopf, 2014.

Weil, Simone. *Œuvres complètes*. Paris: Gallimard, 1988–2012.

Weil, Simone. *Écrits historiques et politiques: vers la guerre (1937–1940)*. Edited by Simone Fraisse. Paris: Gallimard, 1989.

Weil, Simone. *Cahiers (septembre 1941–février 1942)*. Edited by Alyette Degrâces et al. Paris: Gallimard, 1997.

Weil, Simone. *Cahiers (février 1942–juin 1942): La porte du transcendant*. Edited by Alyette Degrâces et al. Paris: Gallimard, 2002.

Weil, Simone. *Cahiers (juillet 1942–juillet 1943): La connaissance surnaturelle (Cahiers de New York et de Londres)*. Edited by Marie-Annette Fourneyron et al. Paris: Gallimard, 2006.

Weil, Simone. *Écrits de Marseille (1940–1942)*. Edited by Robert Chenavier et al. Paris: Gallimard, 2008.

Weil, Simone. *Écrits de Marseille (1941–1942)*. Edited by Anisse Castel-Bouchouchi and Florence de Lussy. Paris: Gallimard, 2009.

Weil, Simone. *Écrits de New York et de Londres (1943): L'Enracinement: Prélude à une déclaration des devoirs envers l'être humain*. Edited by Robert Chenavier and Patrice Rolland. Paris: Gallimard, 2013.

Weil, Simone. *Écrits de New York et de Londres (1942–43): Questions politiques et religieuses*. Edited by Robert Chenavier et al. Paris: Gallimard, 2019.

Chapter 4

POLITICAL VIOLENCE: A CONTRADICTION IN TERMS

Rose A. Owen

Introduction

At a panel on "The Legitimacy of Violence," where Hannah Arendt gave the germinal talk that would become *On Violence*, Susan Sontag posed the question of the hour: "It is personally hard for me to understand how in December 1967 in New York the discussion has at no point turned actively to the question of whether we, in this room, and people we know are going to be engaged in violence."[1] "I'm very glad you brought up this question," Arendt responded, "[as it is] of course in the back of all our minds."[2] Today, the question of whether or when to engage in violence for the sake of politics receives little attention. As such, we tend to forget that Simone Weil and Hannah Arendt lived in different times, when the question of violence felt charged, alive with the possibility that anyone, at any moment, might resort to political violence. Writing before and during the Second World War, despite her early pacifism, Weil fought briefly in the Spanish Civil War and came to believe in the necessity of retaliation against Nazi Germany. During the Second World War, Arendt called for the formation of a Jewish army, but later on she grew wary of the use of violence by the American left. Responding to their political contexts, Weil and Arendt ask: What is violence? How is violence related to politics? And is the use of violence ever justified?

In contemporary political thought, violence is a contested, and sometimes vaguely defined, concept. Types of violence (epistemic, structural, symbolic, etc.) proliferate, but what unites them remains unclear, except for analogization with the physical blow.[3] Weil and Arendt offer remarkably complementary definitions of violence that reveal the family resemblance between these disparate types. I show that Weil defines violence as *the transformation of humans into things*, while Arendt defines it as *the removal of men from the common world* (IF and OV). In both cases, violence destroys politics. For Arendt, the function of violence is to remove people from public, political life. For Weil, violence threatens the very existence of the city, the space of politics. Political violence, I conclude, is a contradiction in terms because violence is definitionally, for both thinkers, the antithesis of politics.

The question of whether and when the use of violence is justifiable follows closely on the heels of the question, what is violence? A certain strain of liberal ideology can proffer nonviolence as the answer to every political problem.[4] Although Weil and Arendt recognize the opposition between violence and politics, they each acknowledge the necessity of using violence for politics: in the Spanish Civil War, during the Second World War, and in the aftermath of the Holocaust, to execute Adolf Eichmann. These are exemplary instances of political violence, when violence is required to defend politics itself. The second contradiction, then, is that politics sometimes requires its opposite, violence, for its preservation, according to both thinkers.

I am not the first to raise the questions of the definition and justification of violence in their work. Roberto Esposito locates the Trojan war as the origin of politics for both thinkers: politics, Esposito writes, "is born at the heart of a *polemos* whose outcome is the destruction of a *polis*."[5] Deborah Nelson contends that Weil and Arendt share a tough demeanor, a way of looking at suffering that denies the value of sentimentality.[6] In this chapter, I likewise read for the continuity between Weil and Arendt's thought. A mirrored set of contradictions, I show, structures each of their reflections on the relationship between politics and violence. We can imagine several explanations for this resonance between their work. Weil and Arendt occupy a similar subject position, as two Jewish women thinking through the problem of violence before, during, and after the Second World War. They obsessed over the same texts and authors: the *Iliad*, alongside other ancient Greek philosophy, as well as Karl Marx influenced each of them. Arendt read Weil and favorably cited her writing on labor in *The Human Condition*.[7] What unites the two of them though, in my view, is their approach to violence as an irresolvable problem for politics. Rather than attempt to philosophically square their accounts, I accept their invitation to inhabit this space of contradiction.

The Problem with Simone Weil

Scholars of Weil tend to treat her as a pacifist who rejected violence outright, or as a philosopher who obsessed over the most ethical ways to exercise violence. Mary Dietz takes up Weil straightforwardly as a pacifist opposed to any use of force. According to Dietz, Weil reads the epic, *The Iliad*, as "an example of what it means to be fully human and humane; it is, itself, an act of justice, and embodiment of truth, and a rejection of force."[8] On this account, Homer exemplifies justice in his impartial depiction of the Greeks and the Trojans, and truth in his unflinching account of the horrors of war. Homer invites the reader to protect the value of human life by refusing "the will to force."[9] Although Weil would willingly starve herself to death for the sake of France, Dietz contends, she would never engage in violence to save her country from Nazi occupation. While we might be tempted to agree with Dietz's portrait of Weil, I believe Dietz puts too strong an emphasis on Weil's rejection of violence.

E. Jane Doering and Eric Springsted do not treat Weil as a pacifist, but instead as a philosopher concerned with creating rules for the ethical use of force.

Tracking Weil's historical attachment to and then abandonment of pacifism, Doering contends that "the paradox of force being both necessary and debasing left [Weil] distraught."[10] Weil grew to recognize the need to use force as Adolf Hitler rose to power, but she also knew that, once unleashed, force tends to multiply and spread. Haunted by the self-perpetuating nature of force, Weil set out to determine "how to use force, yet keep it from spiraling out of control."[11] For that purpose, Weil laid out the appropriate aims for war—to obtain limited ends or to instill the desire for peace—and cautioned against a war that set out to crush the enemy, since it led most easily to never-ending conflict. Weil's journal entries also provided guidelines to follow if one must engage in killing.[12] Like Doering, Springsted believes that Weil searches for the possibility of moral clarity in war, which requires the acknowledgment of equality under force, and compassion for the other.[13]

Doering and Springsted are right to say that Weil allows for the use of force and refrains from taking a strictly pacifist stance. Rather than interpret Weil as a philosopher interested only in reconciling the paradox of violence, I take my cues from Dietz, who argues that we ought to read Weil as a *political thinker*. Weil was deeply engaged with the political debates of her time, including debates about whether to go to war with Germany. Instead of proposing a philosophical solution, Weil sought to investigate irresolvable problems that did not have simple answers.[14] As I will show in my reading of her essay "The Iliad, or the Poem of Force," an ethical disposition toward—or a set of rules that dictate when to use—violence would not resolve the problem of force precisely because of how Weil defines the term. Weil defines force as *that which turns human beings into things*—things without the capability of ethical reflection (IF 183).

If we look at Weil's biography, her fascination with violence belies her apparent pacifist aversion. In the late 1920s and early 1930s, Weil did hold strong pacifist beliefs; she petitioned to eliminate the military draft of graduate students and supported universal disarmament. As early as 1936, her political commitments wavered, when she traveled to Spain to defend the Republic. There, she joined the anarcho-syndicalist National Labor Confederation and learned the basics of gunmanship, though she was not particularly skilled with a weapon. She left without seeing combat after stepping in a vat of hot oil. Upon returning home, Weil reflected on the "intoxication" of war, writing in a letter that she felt the possibility within herself of committing horrible war crimes.[15] Despite her initial defense of negotiating with Hitler, Weil abandoned her pacifism entirely by 1943, insisting on the need for the French to violently resist German occupation.[16] This shift in thinking is evident in Weil's work, from "Reflections on War" written in 1933, to "The Power of Words" in 1937, and "Reflections on Barbarity" in 1939.

In "Reflections on War" and "The Power of Words," Weil's early pacifism becomes apparent. In the former, she denounces war as the internal oppression of workers by the state and, in the latter, as needless violence fought over empty words like capitalism, communism, and nationalism.[17] Weil's tone begins to change in "Reflections on Barbarism," wherein she cautions readers against thinking of themselves as civilized, and Hitler as barbaric, lest they engage in even more barbaric forms of violence. These essays and fragments prefigure Weil's language in "The Iliad, or the Poem of Force." Just as she does in her essay on *The Iliad*, Weil refers to soldiers as "passive matter" in "Reflections on War," invokes Helen as an example of empty categories over which we wage wars in "The Power of Words," and notes the "intoxication of power" in the same essay.[18] Replacing the term "power" with "force" in "Reflections on Barbarism," Weil writes that the "concept of force must be made central in any attempt to think clearly about human relations."[19] Over time, readers can observe the development of Weil's thought as she moved away from pacifism and toward an understanding of force as an inevitability. Her transformation into an advocate for violent resistance against the Germans culminates with her family's flight from France in 1939 and her publication of "The Iliad, or the Poem of Force" soon after.

Weil wrote "The Iliad, or the Poem of Force" as she and her parents fled Paris. Based on this fact, Robert Zaretsky draws the parallel between Troy and Paris: "The tragedy outside the walls of ancient Troy now seems little more than rehearsal for the tragedy unfolding outside the walls of modern Paris. Though several millennia separate the two tragedies, their subject matter is the same: the inexorability of force and what it does to human beings."[20] When Weil spoke of the destruction of a city, her message rang close to home. Weil was not just waxing philosophical about the perils of war. She was drawing on her own experience as a refugee from an occupied land. Weil, then, writes from the perspective of those subjected to force, and what she writes is a cautionary tale.[21] The Germans may think that they can take control of France, Weil warns, but they are experiencing the hubris of those who wield force. What they forget is that the French might take up arms, or that other European countries might come to their aid. In short, they forget that the Germans themselves will one day fall prey to force. Indeed, Weil expressed disappointment in the fact that the French did not defend themselves against German invasion and lamented that she could not play a bigger role in the French Resistance.[22]

In the following pages, I read "The Iliad, or the Poem of Force" along the lines of two animating contradictions, or what Weil would call problems. First, I show that Weil's definition of force renders the idea of "political violence" a contradiction in terms. Force at once turns people into things, which are unable to act politically, and when taken to its logical conclusion, force destroys the space of politics itself, the city. The second contradiction, however, is that force is sometimes necessary for the defense of politics. Once humans begin to use force, Weil reasons, even the perpetrators turn into things, unable to engage in ethical reflection. In these instances, the only possibility of stopping those who wield force is through its equal and opposing exercise. Forceful retaliation, Weil implies, would be the only way to liberate Paris.

In "The Iliad, or the Poem of Force," Weil identifies force as the true hero of the *Iliad*. Weil defines force as "that x that turns anybody who is subjected to it into a thing" (IF 183). Taken to the extreme, force turns man into a corpse. The threat of force also transforms those subjected to it, for all intents and purposes, into a thing while they are still alive. Weil tracks the language in the epic around death and slavery to show how the dead warrior, Hector, becomes a thing dragged behind a chariot and how disarmed soldiers suffer the same fate as they supplicate for their lives. The flesh of those subjected to force loses "that very important property which in the laboratory distinguishes living flesh from dead—the galvanic response" (IF 186). Out of fear, the supplicant cannot quiver or tremble; he must stay as still as inert matter. Although people initially feel disgust at the sight of this, they quickly begin to act as though the person-turned-thing is not there. The living corpse "imitate[s] nothingness" and becomes treated like nothingness (IF 187). A "compromise between a man and a corpse," the person-turned-thing is a "logical contradiction," an impossibility in logic that becomes true in life (IF 187). "This thing," Weil writes, "is constantly aspiring to be a man or a woman, and never achieving it—here, surely, is death but death strung over a whole lifetime" (IF 187). The thingified person cannot think or act and therefore becomes more like a corpse than a living human, despite the fact that she continues to breath.

In the context of ancient Greece, the utterly abject slave exemplifies Weil's notion of the living dead. Stripped of "curses, feelings of rebellion, comparisons, reflections on the future and the past" and even memory, the slave no longer enjoys the privilege of "fidelity to his city and his dead" (IF 189). The slave loses his political membership, according to Weil. The only emotion a slave may express is love for his master, the person who violently subjugates him. "To lose more than the slave does is impossible," according to Weil, "for he loses his whole inner life" (IF 190). Even the slave's emotions, thoughts, and desires bend to the will of his master.

At several moments, Weil spells out the political implications of her definition of violence.[23] Aside from noting that the slave loses his citizenship status, Weil observes that the "whole of the *Iliad* lies under the shadow of the greatest calamity the human race can experience—the destruction of a city" (IF 209). Weil worries that violence threatens to destroy the city, embodied in the figures of both ancient Troy and her lost modern home, Paris. Of course, a human-turned-thing cannot participate in community or take political action. Weil suggests, though, that the stakes extend beyond the experience of the enslaved individual, to the very erasure of collectivity as such. This sense of loss echoes through her last finished work, *The Need for Roots*, written in a state of rootlessness, after Weil was exiled from her Parisian home. Weil thus identifies a deep, abiding contradiction between politics, emblematized in the space of the city, and violence, which destroys the city.

It would be easy to conclude from the contradiction between violence and politics that Weil disavows the use of force. Weil certainly imagined engaging in an individual nonviolent response to German occupation. During her period of illness, Weil dreamed of returning to the frontlines of battle, this time as a nurse.[24] She believed that nurses serving and dying alongside allied soldiers would provide inspiration, demonstrating the superiority of the allies' reasons for waging war. Weil's hope to join the fray, however, reveals a more complicated relationship to violence. Although the role of nurse is nonviolent, it is parasitic on the efforts of soldiers who engage in violence. Weil's support for the allied soldiers suggests a deep ambivalence about violence that stems from a second contradiction, or problem, underlying the first: that politics inevitably requires its opposite. The city depends on violence for its survival.

To some extent, Weil treats the inevitability of violence in politics as a rule akin to the laws of physics. She does, after all, compare force to mathematics in "Reflections on Barbarism" (SE 143). For every exercise of force, Weil suggests, there exists an equal and opposing response. In "The Power of Words," Weil refers to force as an equilibrium and states that "balance nullifies force."[25] Weil notes that "a spirit of revolt, whether loud or silent, aggressive or despairing, is always present wherever life is physically or morally oppressive."[26] While Weil's theorization of force may seem to leave no possibility for resistance, given the thingification of the oppressed, she always expects force to be returned in kind. Because those who use force also transform into objects, they cannot engage in the ethical reflection that would stay their hand. They become the embodiment of force, operating on the inert matter of those they subjugate. The only way to stop them is for the inevitable to happen. Force will change hands, and those who once wielded it will be subjected to it.[27]

The status of master and slave is not fixed, Weil tells us, since no one owns the use of force: "The truth is, nobody really possesses [force]. The human race is not divided up in the *Iliad*, into conquered persons, slaves, and suppliants on the one hand, and conquerors and chiefs on the other. In this poem there is not a single man who does not at one time or another have to bow his neck to force" (IF 191). *The Iliad* opens with the hero, Achilles, humiliated by the loss of his concubine, and except for Achilles, every man experiences defeat on the battlefield. Force may easily change sides. The victor of one battle will be defeated in another. The master could become the slave. The division between conquered and conqueror, slave and master, can transform in the blink of an eye. In fact, Weil believes, the roles will almost certainly reverse, because "all men, by the very act of being born, are destined to suffer violence" (IF 193). The strong and the weak "have in common a refusal to believe that they both belong to the same species: the weak see no relation between themselves and the strong, and vice versa" (IF 193). If all men recognized their shared humanity, Weil contends, they would see that their control of force is only temporary.

The strong fail to see the precarity of their situation because of their hubris. As if intoxicated, "the man who is the possessor of force seems to walk through a non-resistant element; in the human substance that surrounds him nothing has the power to interpose, between the impulse and the act, the tiny interval that is reflection" (IF 193). Unhindered by the interference of others, the man using force need not stop for reflection and, therefore, often acts without justice or prudence. He becomes overly confident. He starts to use force in ways that will ultimately destroy him by turning him back into the conquered, the supplicant, the slave. He "exceed[s] the measure of the force that is actually at [his] disposal. Inevitably, [he exceeds] it, since [he] is not aware that it is limited" (IF 194). Once he has overextended his use of force, he is at the mercy of fate, which sometimes lets him off easily, but usually spells his defeat. "Thus," Weil writes, "it happens that those who have force on loan from fate count on it too much and are destroyed"

(IF 194). Weil narrates the familiar Greek story of hubris, wherein the arrogant hero produces his own demise precisely because he overestimates his abilities—in Weil's analysis, because he believes he will possess force forever, rather than recognizing its fleeting nature.

Just as violence turns the victim into a thing, Weil argues, it also transfigures the perpetrator. Like the slave, the conquering soldier "becomes a thing, though his manner of doing so is different—over him too, words are as powerless as over matter itself. And both, at the touch of force, experience its inevitable effects: they become deaf and dumb" (IF 204). Weil creates a metaphysical split between matter and force. With no recourse to force, the victim cannot act. He is "inert matter, pure passivity" (IF 205). The perpetrator of violence, on the other hand, is "blind force, which is pure momentum" (IF 205). He acts unthinkingly, without the reflection that characterizes ethical human behavior. Homer brilliantly reveals this fate in the *Iliad*'s similes, "which liken warriors either to fire, flood, wind, wild beasts, or God knows what blind cause of disaster, or else to frightened animals, trees, water, sand, to anything in nature that is set in motion by the violence of external forces" (IF 205). Weil relies on these similes throughout the essay, taking Homer's literary language seriously as an expression of the thingification of both humans who use force, and humans subjected to force.

Homer gives voice to a larger ethical trend in the ancient Greeks, according to Weil. Homer offers a realistic portrayal of war: "Whatever is not war, whatever war destroys or threatens, the Iliad wraps in poetry; the realities of war, never" (IF 210). Through the *Iliad*'s depiction, the reader does not feel admiration of the warrior, or appreciation of the glory supposedly found in war, but instead regrets at the transformation of men into things. Weil labels the poem "a miracle" because its "bitterness is the only justifiable bitterness, for it springs from the subjections of the human spirit to force" (IF 211). For Weil, it is a fundamental truth that all humans suffer subjection at some point in their lives. The *Iliad* poses the ultimate ethical problem that "he who does not realize to what extent shifting fortune and necessity hold in subjection every human spirit, cannot regard as fellow-creatures nor love as he loves himself those separated from him by an abyss" (IF 28). Rejecting the Romans and Hebrews, who believe themselves exempt from misery, and even the Christians, who find joy in martyrdom, Weil urges us to return to the lucidity of the Greeks, who saw the suffering of violence as a common human experience.[28]

One way to read Weil's essay is as a caution against the use of violence, and certainly that thread persists in her writing. Yet even Homer's understanding of the equal subjection of all under force underlines the inevitability of force. In light of the context of Weil's authorship, I argue that her essay "The Iliad, or the Poem of Force" offers a subtle warning, or even a threat, to the Germans occupying France. Though they may feel confident in their position now, Weil predicts that that very hubris, fueled by the intoxication of force, will seal their fate. Of course, Weil was right to forecast the defeat of Germany, in part due to the very dynamics she describes—the overextension of the German army, and the failure to foresee the strength amassing among allied powers. Sadly, Weil would not live to see her premonition come to pass.

I have argued that Weil sees violence as deeply destructive of politics, and yet she does not completely reject the use of violence for politics. In the next section, I contend that Arendt's thought on violence follows the same arc, acknowledging at once the antipolitical nature of violence and the role of violence in politics as prepolitical foundation and, occasionally, as political justification for further violence. Arendt occasionally references Weil's work, but I am less concerned with her direct uptake of Weil and more interested in the theoretical resonances between their writings on violence. Reading the two together creates a new conception of political violence, as the inherently contradictory use of violence to defend politics itself.

Hannah Arendt's Inconsistencies

A disagreement has recently developed in scholarship on violence in Arendt's thought. Elizabeth Frazer and Kimberly Hutchings typify the more conventional view that Arendt treats politics and violence as opposites. For Arendt, Frazer and Hutchings write, "the phrase 'political violence' is a contradiction in terms."[29] Unlike political power, which never aims at particular ends, violence always operates on a means–ends logic. Moreover, violence may seek political goals or have political effects, but it always threatens to destroy political life, "by distrust, by policing, by the polarization" that deter political action.[30] Because of the antipolitical nature of violence, Frazer and Hutchings reach the Arendtian conclusion that "there can never be a political justification for political violence."[31]

Challenging this interpretation, Caroline Ashcroft argues that Arendt conceptualizes certain types of violence as "political violence." "Violence may be political," Ashcroft writes, "if paired with power and if aimed at creating or maintaining the public political space of action."[32] Ashcroft emphasizes the necessity of publicity for political violence and the role of violence in constructing spaces for politics. For Ashcroft, Arendt's early call for a Jewish army to fight the Nazis in the Second World War provides the perfect example; the political nature of the Jewish army "can be understood in terms of making a people."[33] The Roman expansionist war and the American Revolution also fall into Ashcroft's category of political violence. Ashcroft does acknowledge the forms of violence that Arendt characterizes as prepolitical, such as the violence Arendt describes in the ancient Greek polis, and antipolitical, including the violence of the French Revolutionaries, but these types stand in contrast to political violence.

Frazer and Hutchings, alongside Ashcroft, each identify a contradiction within Arendt's thought on violence. They are right to say, on the one hand, that politics and violence conflict and, on the other, that Arendt still acknowledges the possible uses of violence for politics. And yet while Frazer and Hutchings are too quick to dismiss political violence, Ashcroft papers over the contradiction that inheres in the term. What allows Ashcroft to make the argument for a logically consistent Arendtian concept of political violence, I believe, is her definition of violence. Following Arendt, Ashcroft defines violence as "an action of command over others via the use of instruments of force, and which is pointedly contrasted by her with what she terms power."[34] Command and the difference from power are two important facets of Arendt's definition of violence, but the key to Arendt's definition of violence, which I highlight, is that it *removes people from public, political life*. Once we accept that as the defining feature of violence for Arendt, the contradiction between politics and violence comes into sharp relief.

In my reading of Arendt, as in my earlier reading of Weil, I track the double movement of contradictions in Arendt's work. Much like Weil, Arendt sees violence and politics as opposites, such that the notion of political violence, as Frazer and Hutchings write, becomes a contradiction in terms. Still, as Arendt shows in *The Human Condition*, violence often underwrites political action. In the ancient Greek case, it does so by relegating slaves and women to labor in the home. Further, Arendt's definition of violence creates a particular political justification for the use of violence, which she explores in *Eichmann in Jerusalem*. This, then, is the second contradiction. Even as violence and politics stand in opposition, violence provides a prepolitical foundation for politics and becomes politically justifiable under certain circumstances, as in the trial of Adolf Eichmann.

Arendt's disbelief in political violence sits comfortably with her strong endorsement of nonviolent political action. In *On Violence*, Arendt responds to student protests against the Vietnam War and for racial justice. Asked about the Vietnam War for a survey, Arendt answered that she was "against the intervention of the United States in the civil war in Vietnam" and emphasized that "the way to resolve an armed conflict is always the same: cease fire—armistice—peace negotiations—and, hopefully, peace treaty."[35] Initially, Arendt supported the antiwar protests at Columbia University, a view in keeping with her endorsement of French student demonstrations, and earlier protests against the draft at the University of Chicago. She later changed her mind about Columbia, condemning in particular the tactics and aims of the Black Power movement. "As for riots helping effect social change," Arendt stated at the "Legitimacy of Violence" panel, "riots have, of course, occurred throughout history, and they have never led to anything; nothing blows away so quickly, and leaves so little trace."[36] In this quote, we hear the echoes of Arendt's condemnation of the French Revolution.

Written in the context of the late 1960s, Arendt's *On Violence* diagnoses and critiques an increasing "glorification of violence" by the New Left, especially student protesters in the United States and France (OV 14). Despite a rhetorical appeal to violence, violence remained a "matter of theory and rhetoric," a declamatory slogan that belied the nonviolence of most student protests (OV 18). Violence only became a tool of the New Left, Arendt believes, with the explicitly militant Black Power movement. Arendt diagnoses the contemporary turn to violence as symptomatic of the frustration of the faculty of action in modernity. By acting in concert, men bring something new into the world and interrupt processes that produce predictable outcomes. Due to the disintegration of public services and the centralization of power, among other causes, people turn away from seemingly ineffective nonviolent forms of political action.

This New Left glorification of violence represents a much older trend in political theory of taking violence for granted as "the continuation of politics by other means," in Carl von Clausewitz's words (OV 8). According to Arendt, political theorists refrain from studying violence because they see it as an inevitable part of political life. Friedrich Engels views violence as a way of accelerating economic development, while Karl Marx grants it secondary status in bringing about a communist society through class struggle. In his introduction to Frantz Fanon's *Wretched of the Earth*, Jean-Paul Sartre takes an even stronger stance, writing that violence "is man reconstructing himself."[37] Although Fanon himself glorifies violence, Arendt praises him for at least hewing closer to reality than his commentator.

When political theorists do discuss violence, they treat violence as a creative force. Fanon conjures the familiar figuration of "brotherhood on the battlefield" to argue that violence fosters group coherence (OV 67). To this, Arendt responds that,

> No body politic I know of was ever founded on equality before death and its actualization in violence ... The hope is an illusion for the simple reason that no human relationship is more transitory than this kind of brotherhood, which can be actualized only under conditions of immediate danger to life and limb. (OV 69)

The group coherence that emerges from violence, Arendt argues, is too short-lasting to found a political community. Arendt also denounces the Nietzschean characterization of violence as a life-promoting force. Contra Sartre, Fanon, and Nietzsche, who believe man creates himself through violence, Arendt writes that "all notions of man creating himself have in common a rebellion against the very factuality of the human condition—nothing is more obvious than that man, whether as member of the species or as an individual, does *not* owe his existence to himself" (OV 13). Arendt here refers to the fact of natality, that man is born into the world, rather than creating himself. It is particularly problematic to Arendt that theorists see the activity of violence as generative, as opposed to thought or labor, for example, given that violence destroys both individual life and political community.

Arendt condemns scientists, alongside the New Left and political theorists, for naturalizing violence. Citing "many recent discoveries of an inborn instinct of domination and an innate aggressiveness in the human animal," Arendt questions the validity of studies that compare human and animal behavior (OV 39). Even if man qualifies as an animal, other species' behavior should not set the standard for our own. With these comparisons, science merely makes violence appear natural, justifying and perpetuating the aggressive instincts scientists claim are innate. Not rage and violence but their absence, according to Arendt, signals dehumanization. Critiquing everyone from activists and theorists to scientists, Arendt proposes a new definition of violence, which includes five components that I will outline in the following pages: (1) violence needs implements, (2) violence is instrumental, (3) violence is the opposite of power, (4) violence pits "One against All," and

(5) violence leads to death. Taken together, I argue, these components of violence show that violence *definitionally removes people from public, political life.*

(1) *Violence needs implements.* Arendt believes that the revolution of technology is especially pronounced in warfare, where states must engage in an arms race to continually develop better weapons. These implements of violence multiply strength, the natural property of an individual. Because of the importance of weapons, it is tempting to think that the government could easily suppress any resistance by the people. Yet Arendt emphasizes that the superiority of the state "lasts only as long as the power structure of the government is intact—that is, as long as commands are obeyed and the army or police forces are prepared to use their weapons" (OV 48). Once the opinion of the people turns against the government, the state loses its power. Weapons, Arendt observes, echoing Weil, can easily change hands.

(2) *Violence is instrumental.* According to Arendt, "The very substance of violent action is ruled by the means-end category, whose chief characteristic, if applied to human affairs, has always been that the end is in danger of being overwhelmed by the means which it justifies and which are needed to reach it" (OV 4). The unpredictability of the end of human action often renders the means of action more important than the ends. Violence, Arendt explains, is particularly arbitrary, with highly unpredictable results. Despite this arbitrariness, it is likely that violence will produce more violence: "The practice of violence, like all action, changes the world, but the most probable change is to a more violent world" (OV 80).

While violence leads to violence, it is not an end in itself, since peace or victory represents the end of war. Unlike peace, power, and government, which Arendt describes as ends in themselves, violence finds its justification in the ends at which it aims. "Being instrumental by nature," Arendt writes, violence "is rational to the extent that it is effective in reaching the end that must justify it" (OV 79). Violence must therefore pursue short-term goals, which are easier to predict and achieve. For this reason, Arendt counterintuitively labels violence a tool of reform rather than revolution. Violence cannot find justification in the open-endedness of revolution.

(3) *Violence is the opposite of power.* Arendt defines power as "the human ability not just to act but to act in concert" (OV 44). Power belongs to a group, not an individual, and disappears the moment the collective dissolves. We might conflate power and violence because they tend to appear in combination, but "everything depends on the power behind the violence. The sudden dramatic breakdown of power that ushers in revolutions reveals in a flash how civil obedience—to laws, to rulers, to institutions—is but the outward manifestation of support and consent" (OV 49). Violence requires power to succeed. When a government loses the support of the people, it may turn to greater violence to enforce its rule. This display of heightened violence,

though, reveals a loss of power. As Arendt says, "impotence breeds violence," both psychologically and politically speaking (OV 54).

Violence and power are not opposites that produce one another. In fact, Arendt believes that "violence can always destroy power; out of the barrel of a gun grows the most effective command, resulting in the most instant and perfect obedience. What never can grow out of it is power" (OV 53). Increasingly desperate without the support of the people, a government may need to turn to violence to maintain its rule, but in doing so, the government sacrifices whatever power remains. The end of such a struggle, Arendt concludes, "is the destruction of all power" (OV 54). That is why rule by absolute violence, which Arendt dubs "terror," "turns not only against its enemies but against its friends and supporters as well, being afraid of all power, even the power of its friends" (OV 55).

(4) *Violence pits "One against All."* By another name, terror is the rule over "All by One." "The extreme form of power is All against One," Arendt writes, and "the extreme form of violence is One against All. The latter is never possible without instruments" (OV 42). One person requires the intensification of their strength through weaponry to rule over the masses. Even then, it is difficult for one to rule without the support of at least a small group of people to wield arms. Arendt warns against treating the silent consent of the majority in the instance of minority violence as a moment of One exerting violence against All. Offering the example of a student disrupting a lecture hall, Arendt shows that the majority of students who do not take action to overpower the dissenter ally themselves with the minority. This is different, Arendt cautions, than the minority exercising violence to coerce the majority into accepting their rule.

(5) *Violence leads to death.* Those who see death as an equalizer that forges brotherhood on the battlefield, including Fanon, miss the reality that "death, whether faced in actual dying or in the inner awareness of one's own mortality, is perhaps the most antipolitical experience there is" (OV 67). Death cannot foster group coherence or found political community, because "it signifies that we shall disappear from the world of appearances and shall leave the company of our fellow-men, which are the conditions of all politics" (OV 67–8). To Arendt, politics depends on plurality, "the fact that men, not Man, live on this earth" (HC 7). Through death, violence erases men from the common world, and therefore from politics. Men might pursue immortality in violent battles, as the ancient Greeks did, but they pursue individual glory precisely because they fear of equality in death.

Like Weil, Arendt turns to the ancient Greeks to understand violence. In *On Violence*, Arendt writes that the express purpose of slavery "was to liberate citizens from the burden of household affairs and to permit them to enter the public life of the community, where all were equals; if it were true that nothing is sweeter than to give commands and to rule others, the master would never have left his household" (OV 40). Arendt uses ancient Greek life to once again refute the notion that men naturally take pleasure in the violence of mastery. Men's desire to participate freely and equally in the nonviolent democratic politics of ancient Greece proves that they do not only aim to violently master others. The example of ancient Greece underlines what Arendt says in other texts, like *The Human Condition*: that the private realm is a space of violence.

Arendt's claim from *On Violence* draws directly from her work in *The Human Condition*, published a decade earlier. There, Arendt writes:

> What all Greek philosophers, no matter how opposed to *polis* life, took for granted is that freedom is exclusively located in the political realm, that necessity is primarily a prepolitical phenomenon, characteristic of the private household organization, and that force and violence are justified in this sphere because they are the only means to master necessity—for instance, by ruling over slaves— and to become free. Because all human beings are subject to necessity, they are entitled to violence toward others; violence is the prepolitical act of liberating oneself from the necessity of life for the freedom of the world. (HC 31)

Describing the organization of ancient Greek life, Arendt labels the political realm a space of freedom, and the private realm a space of violence. Violence in the private realm liberated Athenian citizens to exercise freedom through participation in democratic political life. To be a slave, Arendt concludes, "meant to be subject ... to man-made violence" (HC 31). Slaves were systematically excluded from political life so that they could labor to fulfill the bodily needs of citizens.

Arendt reveals the role violence plays in constructing the boundaries between private and public spaces. The private realm, in the ancient Greek model, existed as a space in which slaves and women labored to provide for male citizens. The exercise of violence forced these laborers to remain in the prepolitical home carrying out their duties and precluded them from participating in public, political life. Arendt calls death the most "antipolitical experience" because it erases men from the common world. Her arguments in *On Violence* and *The Human Condition* expose the ways in which violence forces some—in the ancient Greek context, women and slaves—out of the common world as well, by relegating them to the prepolitical private sphere to labor for others. Arendt thus shows that *violence removes people from public, political life* not just through death but also through entrapment in the private space of the home.[38]

Although contemporary scholars, feminist and otherwise, worry about the distinctions Arendt draws between public and private realms, I read Arendt as diagnosing a political problem—that the separation between public and private often requires violence—rather than providing a normative defense of that violence.[39] Keith Breen, for example, argues that "Arendt legitimate[s] a violent instrumentalism in vast spheres of human existence."[40] However, as Annabel Herzog points out, Arendt labels violence in private justifiable, rather than legitimate. On a conceptual level, Herzog contends, Arendt's understanding of violence allows her to create the categories of public and private.[41] Like Plato's *khora* in the *Timaeus*, violence functions as the abyss between public and private, a third space that makes the other two possible. I agree with Herzog on this point, but I also take it a step farther, underlining the fact that, for Arendt, violence quite literally functions to police the boundaries between private and public spheres.

When Arendt does defend the use of violence, it is in response to the mass violence of the Holocaust. In *Eichmann in Jerusalem*, Arendt famously concurs with the court's decision to execute Eichmann, although she provides an alternate rationale for her judgment. Addressing her decision to Eichmann, Arendt writes:

> Just as you supported and carried out a policy of not wanting to share the earth with the Jewish people and the people of a number of other nations—as though you and your superiors had any right to determine who should and who should not inhabit the world—we find that no one, that is, no member of the human race, can be expected to want to share the earth with you. (EJ 279)

Taking a paradoxical stance, Arendt favors the execution of Eichmann as punishment for his participation in the genocidal Final Solution. Arendt finds a political justification for violence in her definition of violence as antipolitical; because Eichmann, as part of the Nazi bureaucracy, attempted to remove people from the shared political world, Arendt passes judgment to remove him. Jennifer Culbert labels Eichmann's transgression a "formal crime," because he threatened to alter the human condition of plurality by destroying the space of appearances.[42] The structuring contradiction between violence and politics, therefore, leads to the further contradiction of a political justification for violence.

In her intellectual history of Arendt's thought, Ashcroft seeks a consistent Arendt, but Arendt's beliefs about violence appear to shift over time. Just as Weil comes to advocate for violence to defeat the Nazis, Arendt initially favors the formation of a Jewish army during the Second World War. By the 1960s, though, Arendt grows to support nonviolent action within the United States and abroad. Ashcroft's search for consistency threatens to obscure the change in Arendt's disposition toward violence over time and the contradictions that structure Arendt's thoughts on violence. Violence is antipolitical, and yet it provides a prepolitical foundation for democratic life. Violence removes people from the earth, and yet that very action might justify the use of retributive violence in certain cases. Rather than reconcile these apparent contradictions, Arendt—much like her predecessor, Weil—invites us to sit with her ambivalence toward violence as an irreconcilable political problem.

Conclusion

Weil and Arendt remind us that violence is always destructive of politics, but they are not pacifists; they do not prescribe against the use of violence under any circumstances. In fact, there is a particular set of circumstances that calls for the use of violence, according to both thinkers. For Weil, the protection of the city—Troy and her home, Paris—inspires dreams of French rebellion, and Arendt justifies the execution of Eichmann with his desire to erase the Jewish people. Political violence, then, refers to those instances in which violence comes to the defense of politics, to preserve the very existence of what Arendt calls the "space of appearances." The destruction of a city, or a people, precludes the plurality constitutive of politics. The difficulty lies in holding together this set of contradictions: that violence destroys politics, and that violence may also be necessary to protect politics itself.

Notes

1 Elizabeth Young-Bruehl, *Hannah Arendt: For the Love of the World* (New Haven, CT: Yale University Press), 414.
2 Ibid.
3 Kevin Duong, "Violence: Introduction to the Special Issue," *New Political Science* 44, no. 1 (2022), 2; for examples of this practice, see Judith Butler, *The Force of Nonviolence: An Ethico-Political Bind* (New York: Verso, 2020); Elizabeth Frazer and Kimberly Hutchings, *Violence and Political Theory* (Cambridge: Polity Press, 2020).
4 Duong, "Introduction," 3.
5 Roberto Esposito, *The Origin of the Political: Hannah Arendt or Simone Weil?* (New York: Fordham University Press, 2017), 13.
6 Deborah Nelson, *Tough Enough: Arbus, Arendt, Didion, McCarthy, Sontag, Weil* (Chicago: University of Chicago Press, 2017).
7 In *The Human Condition*, Arendt cites Weil's *La condition ouvrière* as "the only book in the huge literature on the labor question which deals with the problem without prejudice and sentimentality" (HC 131). Weil's diary, Arendt continues, includes a quote from Homer that impresses upon us the inescapability of necessity: "Much against your own will, since necessity lies more mightily upon you" (HC 131). Although it is beyond the scope of this chapter, one could make the case that Weil and Arendt theorize an important connection between violence and labor. Weil writes about the transformation of workers into things in the factory, alluding to the presence of force under capitalist production. As I demonstrate, Arendt contends that violence polices the boundary between public and private spheres, relegating some to the private sphere to perform labor. For both thinkers, necessity and labor are not equivalent to violence. Quite the opposite, Weil and Arendt understand that necessity is a natural part of life. It is when people try to escape necessity, by making others labor for them, that violence enters the equation.
8 Mary Dietz, *Between the Human and the Divine: The Political Thought of Simone Weil* (Totowa, NJ: Rowman and Littlefield, 1988), 94.
9 Ibid., 95.
10 E. Jane Doering, *Simone Weil and the Specter of Self-perpetuating Force* (Notre Dame, IN: University of Notre Dame, 2010), 2.
11 Ibid., 40.
12 "(1) keep one's courage devoid of cruelty, (2) retain intact an inner love of life, and (3) not inflict death without accepting it for oneself." Doering, *Simone Weil*, 66.
13 Eric Springsted, *Simone Weil for the Twenty-First Century* (Notre Dame, IN: University of Notre Dame Press, 2021), 219.

14 As Zaretsky notes, "Reflecting on a problem, rather than solving it, was Weil's goal." Robert Zaretsky, *The Subversive Simone Weil: A Life in Five Ideas* (Chicago: University of Chicago Press, 2021), 43.
15 Weil states elsewhere that soldiers must be brutal, violent, and inhuman in war. Zaretsky, *The Subversive Simone Weil*, 60–3, 81, 83.
16 Weil even says she would allow Germans to subordinate the Jews and communists within their country to prevent war. Doering, *Simone Weil*, 22, 37; Zaretsky, *The Subversive Simone Weil*, 117.
17 Simone Weil, "Reflections on War," *Politics* (February 1945), 51–6.
18 Simone Weil, *The Power of Words* (London: Penguin Random House, 2020), 14, 24.
19 Weil, "Reflections on Barbarism," SE 143.
20 Zaretsky, *The Subversive Simone Weil*, 28.
21 For more on how Weil thought about colonialism, see Benjamin Davis, "The Colonial Frame: Judith Butler and Simone Weil on Force and Grief," in *Simone Weil, Beyond Ideology?* (London: Palgrave Macmillan, 2020), 125–42.
22 Zaretsky, *The Subversive Simone Weil*, 117.
23 My interpretation of what Weil calls "la force" as violence is somewhat controversial. In "What Is *la force* in Simone Weil's *Iliad*," D. K. Levy argues for a distinction between might and violence. For Levy, *la force* is best understood as might, the equally distributed capacity to exercise violence. Violence, on the other hand, is applied force: "Swords swung, cleave limbs. Bullets fired, deform and destroy bodies. Bombs fall to their targets exploding with expansive forces on anything proximate." The supplicant who turns into a thing is subject only to might, not force *qua* violence, on Levy's account. While Levy's argument is compelling, I find the difference between might and violence in Weil too slippery to draw such a sharp distinction between the two; the threat of violence easily slides into the exercise of violence. On my reading, Weil's *la force* encompasses the capacity to both commit violence and its exercise. D. K. Levy, "What Is *la force* in Simone Weil's *Iliad*?" *Philosophical Investigations* 43, no. 1 (January–April 2020).
24 Weil writes, "Women would need to have a good deal of courage. They would need to offer their lives as a sacrifice … ready to be always at the most dangerous places and to face as much if not more danger than the soldiers who are facing the most." Zaretsky, *The Subversive Simone Weil*, 153.
25 Weil, *The Power of Words*, 24; Doering, *Simone Weil*, 29.
26 Weil, *The Power of Words*, 20.
27 Simone Weil imagined the possibility of conquering forces refraining from violence in her unfinished play, *Venise Sauvée*, written alongside "The Iliad, or the Poem of Force." Of course, Nazi Germany ultimately did not ethically abstain from violence during the Second World War.
28 Weil, "The Iliad," 29–30.
29 Elizabeth Frazer and Kimberly Hutchings, *Can Political Violence Ever Be Justified?* (Cambridge: Polity Press, 2019), 80; Richard Bernstein similarly says that "the very idea of 'political violence' is self-contradictory." Bernstein, *Violence: Thinking without Banisters* (Cambridge: Polity Press, 2013), 84.
30 Frazer and Hutchings, *Political Violence*, 85.
31 Ibid., 84; John McGowan goes even further, claiming that, for Arendt the political is "a utopian space characterized by the absence of violence." McGowan, "Must Politics Be Violent? Arendt's Utopian Vision," in Hannah Arendt and the Meaning of Politics,

ed. Craig Calhoun and John McGowan (Minneapolis: University of Minnesota Press, 1997), 263.
32 Caroline Ashcroft, *Violence and Power in the Thought of Hannah Arendt* (Philadelphia: University of Pennsylvania Press, 2021), 158.
33 Ibid., 68.
34 Ibid., 15.
35 Young-Bruehl, *Hannah Arendt*, 384.
36 Ibid., 415.
37 Jean-Paul Sartre, "Preface," in *The Wretched of the Earth* (New York: Grove Press, 1961), lv.
38 Jacqueline Rose's feminist appropriation of Hannah Arendt's thought in *On Violence and on Violence against Women* resonates with my interpretation. Jacqueline Rose, *On Violence and on Violence against Women* (New York: Farrar, Straus and Giroux, 2021), 177–8.
39 Much of the 1990s feminist uptake of Arendt revolved around the public/private distinction in her work. See Linda Zerilli, "The Arendtian Body"; Honig, "Toward an Agonistic Feminism: Hannah Arendt and the Politics of Identity"; Mary Dietz, "Feminist Receptions of Hannah Arendt," in *Feminist Interpretations of Hannah Arendt*, ed. Bonnie Honig (Philadelphia: Pennsylvania State University Press, 1995); and Seyla Benhabib, "Feminist Theory and Hannah Arendt's Concept of Public Space," *History of the Human Science* 6, no. 2 (1993), 97–114.
40 Keith Breen, "Violence and Power: A Critique of Hannah Arendt on 'the Political,'" *Philosophy & Social Criticism* 33, no. 3 (2007), 355.
41 Annabel Herzog, "The Concept of Violence in the Work of Hannah Arendt," *Continental Philosophy Review* 50 (2017), 165–9.
42 Karl Jaspers, with whom Arendt was in conversation, accuses Eichmann of a "crime against mankind"; Jennifer Culbert, "The Banality of Death in Eichmann in Jerusalem," *Theory & Event* 6, no. 1 (2002).

Bibliography

Ashcroft, Caroline. *Violence and Power in the Thought of Hannah Arendt.* Philadelphia: University of Pennsylvania Press, 2021.
Benhabib, Seyla. "Feminist Theory and Hannah Arendt's Concept of Public Space." *History of the Human Science* 6, no. 2 (1993): 97–114.
Bernstein, Richard. *Violence: Thinking without Banisters.* Cambridge, MA: Polity Press, 2013.
Butler, Judith. *The Force of Nonviolence: An Ethico-Political Bind.* New York: Verso, 2020.
Culbert, Jennifer. "The Banality of Death in Eichmann in Jerusalem." *Theory & Event* 6, no. 1 (2002).
Davis, Benjamin. "The Colonial Frame: Judith Butler and Simone Weil on Force and Grief." In *Simone Weil, Beyond Ideology?* London: Palgrave Macmillan, 2020, pp. 125–42.
Dietz, Mary. "Feminist Receptions of Hannah Arendt." In *Feminist Interpretations of Hannah Arendt.* Edited by Bonnie Honig. Philadelphia: Pennsylvania State University Press, 1995, pp. 17–50.

Doering, E. Jane. *Simone Weil and the Specter of Self-perpetuating Force*. Notre Dame, IN: University of Notre Dame Press, 2010.

Duong, Kevin. "Violence: Introduction to the Special Issue." *New Political Science* 44, no. 1 (2022): 27–41.

Esposito, Roberto. *The Origin of the Political: Hannah Arendt or Simone Weil?* New York: Fordham University Press, 2017.

Frazer, Elizabeth, and Kimberly Hutchings. *Can Political Violence Ever Be Justified?* Cambridge: Polity Press, 2019.

Herzog, Annabel. "The Concept of Violence in the Work of Hannah Arendt." *Continental Philosophy Review* 50 (2017): 165–9.

Honig, Bonnie. "Toward an Agonistic Feminism: Hannah Arendt and the Politics of Identity." In *Feminists Theorize the Political*. Edited by Judith Butler and Joan Wallach Scott. Oxfordshire: Routledge, 1992, pp. 215–35.

Levy, D. K. "What Is *la force* in Simone Weil's *Iliad*?" *Philosophical Investigations* 43, no. 1 (January–April 2020): 19–39.

McGowan, John. "Must Politics Be Violent? Arendt's Utopian Vision." In *Hannah Arendt and the Meaning of Politics*. Edited by Craig Calhoun and John McGowan. Minneapolis: University of Minnesota Press, 1997, pp. 263–96.

Nelson, Deborah. *Tough Enough: Arbus, Arendt, Didion, McCarthy, Sontag, Weil*. Chicago: University of Chicago Press, 2017.

Rose, Jacqueline. *On Violence and on Violence against Women*. New York: Farrar, Straus and Giroux, 2021.

Springsted, Eric. *Simone Weil for the Twenty-First Century*. Notre Dame, IN: University of Notre Dame Press, 2021.

Weil, Simone. "Reflections on War." *Politics* (February 1945): 51–6.

Weil, Simone. *The Power of Words*. London: Penguin Random House, 2020.

Young-Bruehl, Elizabeth. *Hannah Arendt: For the Love of the World*. New Haven, CT: Yale University Press.

Zaretsky, Robert. *The Subversive Simone Weil: A Life in Five Ideas*. Chicago: University of Chicago Press, 2021.

Zerilli, Linda. "The Arendtian Body." In *Feminist Perspectives on Hannah Arendt.*. Edited by Bonnie Honig. University Park: Pennsylvania State University Press, 1995, pp. 167–94.

Part II

SOCIETY, WORLD, AND THE NEED FOR POLITICAL ROOTS

Chapter 5

WE COME AND GO: THE WORLD IS HERE TO STAY— HANNAH ARENDT AND THE WORLD AS COMMON

Elvira Roncalli

A Heap of Broken Ruins

Hannah Arendt's thought is deeply political, but not in the traditional sense of the term. Her body of work emerges out of a lifelong interrogation and exploration of the horrific events of the twentieth century. Each one of her texts marks a renewed effort to understand why and how these events came about. At the end of the Second World War, after massacres, genocides, fire bombings, and atomic bombs, which left millions dead, only ruins remained. The world Arendt had come to know in her youth lay in pieces for everyone to see. In those ruins, Arendt saw not just the end of the war and its destruction but also the end of a world as it had been conceived, thought, and understood by the Western European tradition of philosophical thinking.

The events that marked the first half of the twentieth century "exploded," as Arendt put it, the conceptual framework handed down by tradition. The magnitude and the monstrosity of those events so defied comprehension that this framework of concepts and ideas, which had up until then provided so many with a way of making sense of the world, suddenly collapsed into shambles. Arendt took as her task, therefore, the challenges of finding a way to understand what took place without explaining it away, of reconciling with a world where atrocities had taken place without condoning such atrocities, and of coming to grips with what happened so as to prevent it from ever happening again.

Of course, however regrettable the loss of tradition was, Arendt also saw it as liberating. One could look at the events of the present without having to rely on a pregiven conceptual thread, and in this, Arendt saw the possibility of thinking anew. We could say that her work, from the *Origins of Totalitarianism* to *The Life of the Mind*, exemplifies this novel way of thinking that is always in a state of tension, between a present that defies our understanding and a past bereft of a conceptual framework, or "banister," as she called it. Her thinking is bold and original precisely because it does not assume an unbroken continuum between the past and the present; the past does not already contain the present, but rather the present illuminates the past. Thinking politically is, oddly enough, what makes Arendt's thought both timely and timeless, deeply contextual and detached; it illuminates political experiences happening in different places and at different times.

Many of Arendt's critics find her understanding of politics enlightening yet deeply problematic. Arendt, they claim (and I am simplifying here for the sake of brevity), is attached to a classical notion of the political, which rests on the separation between a public and a private sphere of life. Not only does it overlook the exclusionary power enforced historically through such division, it also leaves the embodied dimension of our existence, its intrinsic vulnerabilities and dependencies, out of the political sphere entirely. Judith Butler, to name just one well-known philosopher, both an admirer and a critic of Arendt's work, expresses her concerns in the following way: "Significantly, it is precisely this operation of power—the foreclosure and differential allocation of whether and how the body may appear—that is excluded from Arendt's explicit account of the political. Indeed, her explicit account of the political depends upon that very operation of power that it fails to consider as part of politics itself."[1]

Critiques such as these raise important questions about Arendt's understanding of what the political is about and cannot be dismissed lightly. They go directly to the heart of her conception of politics. And yet they seem to arise from a philosophical position that places the subject as the starting point for thinking politically, whether it is conceived as embodied and vulnerable or as independent and self-sufficient. In this essay, I intend to show that it is the world—and not the isolated subject, conceived abstractly or reductively, or the self, conceived as an ethereal substance—that is central in Arendt's conception of the political. This is not to say that there is no self or that the subject is a mere artificial construction that needs being undone, as postmodern thought maintains. Arendt is no postmodern thinker. Her thought escapes every attempt of classification, even as she herself admits of belonging among those who dismantle metaphysics. To put it simply, for Arendt, politics always entails a plurality of unique individuals, acting in concert with others, whose words and deeds appear within the world and whose primary concern is for the world.

In her well-known 1964 interview with Günter Gaus, Arendt identifies the "world" as the "space for politics" (EU 1–23, 17). In responding to Gaus's question about the "world as the space where politics can originate," she states: "I comprehend it now in a much larger sense, as *the space in which things become public*, as *the space in which one lives* and which must look presentable. In which art appears of course. *In which all kinds of things appear*" (EU 20).[2] Thus, world and politics are deeply connected by their appearing quality, "appearingness" she calls it, and, I argue, it is this relation between world and politics that is central to Arendt's thought. Therefore, if we want to understand Arendt's political thought, we need to start by looking at what she means by "world," something that is both all too obvious yet elusive. "World" in Arendt's thought is a complex and encompassing notion that is easily overlooked. Is it not obvious that politics is concerned with the world? Without a world there is no political sphere, and therefore no politics; that much is clear. Just what Arendt means by "world," however, is far from being immediately clear. As she suggests in her response to Gaus, her understanding of "world" is not univocal, not rigid, and not static.

Within the limits of this essay, I examine the relationship between politics and the world in Arendt's thought. It is my contention that bringing such a relationship into the foreground will prove helpful in thinking through some of the issues raised by Arendt's critics. It will also, hopefully, make apparent that the relationship between world and politics is paradoxically ubiquitous and frail at the same time.

This essay is divided into three parts or "scenes," as I call them.[3] The first scene focuses on the relationship between the world and the political as crucial for there to be a world as common. Arendt speaks of "worldliness" to highlight such a relation, which itself is polyvalent. The second scene explores the phenomenon of worldlessness, which occurs as the absence or lack of a common world. Lastly, the third and final scene looks to the experience of women in the Italian Resistance as a way of concretely illustrating the political in the Arendtian sense.

Scene One: Worldliness

In *The Human Condition*, Arendt tells us that "worldliness" is one of the conditions under which human life is given on earth, and that "worldliness" is specifically related to the activity of fabrication, the activity of producing things and objects that endure, conferring stability and solidity to life. In contrast with the "labor of our body" that is caught in an endless cycle of life's needs, "the work of our hands" builds objects that outlast the lifecycle of living organisms. Thus, she writes: "Without a world into which men are born and from which they die, there would be nothing, but changeless eternal recurrence of the same" (HC 97).

The world provides a stable and a permanent dwelling to humans, but this is not all. She writes: "In order to be what the world is always meant to be, a home for men during their life on earth, *the human artifice must be a place fit for action and speech*, for activities not entirely useless for the necessities of life, but of an entirely different nature from the manifold activities of fabrication by which the world itself and all things in it are produced" (HC 173-4).[4] In other words, the world as an enduring dwelling place is essential to the living together of people, but that does not mean that such a lasting place is also "a place fit for action and speech." Thus, "world" refers to the physical dwelling space that endures and provides stability, as well as to "a place fit for action and speech." These two notions of the world are clearly intertwined: human cohabitation—how living space is structured—makes possible, or not, that a space, or spaces, "fit for action and speech" open up. But the world as an enduring dwelling place and the world as "a place fit for action and speech" are not the same.

If politics concerns the living together of people, the *inter homine esse*, then how they live "together," how they interact with each other is crucial. An enduring dwelling place by itself is not sufficient for the political space to come into being; there needs to be the possibility of interacting together in a public, or an open space, for there to be politics. Arendt tells us that both a plurality of people and a public space are key in making visible, in allowing for appearing and perceiving. They are in fact two sides of the same phenomenon. Only when people come together as a plurality does there arise a public space, and it is in this public space that things appear and become visible.

Arendt writes that "human plurality" is "the basic condition of both action and speech" and that it "has the twofold quality of equality and distinction" (HC 175). Thanks to their equality, human beings are able to understand each other, and if they were not distinct, that is, distinguished from one another, "they would need neither speech, nor action to make themselves understood" (HC 175-6). Concerning action, Arendt writes: "Action, the only activity that goes on between men without the intermediary of things or matter, corresponds to the fact that men, not Man, live on the earth and inhabit the world … this plurality is specifically *the* condition—not only the *conditio sine qua non*, but the *conditio per quam*—of all political life" (HC 7). Plurality, publicness, words, and actions are interrelated and make visible what otherwise would remain hidden. Plurality is not an undistinguished mass, nor a homogenous collective group where all look the same. There is no plurality unless the distinctness of each, "who" one is, appears and becomes visible to everyone.

That plurality is intertwined with publicness may be evident enough, but something else perhaps not as obvious yet enormously important for Arendt's notion of the political is also at play, namely that such a public space is where human beings come together and interact not in function of their position or location in society. This is why I refer to the "public" dimension as being "open," by which I mean that it is not preshaped or prestructured in any way. In other words, people appear before each other, and in that interaction, "who" one *is* becomes visible precisely because they, together, act and speak "anew." Even if they have been "together" in some fashion before, they have not been together in this way, that is, by relating to one another through words and deeds as "they are," and it is because of this that "who" someone is transpires and comes through. Arendt writes that "the revelatory quality of speech and action comes to the fore when people are with others and neither for or against them—that is in *sheer togetherness*" (HC 180).[5] They appear to one another insofar as there is enough space between them so that "who" one is can indeed come into relief and be seen.

To bring to light the full import of the "world" in Arendt's thought, it is worthwhile to turn to *The Life of the Mind*, the last and least explicitly political of all her works, insofar as it examines the mental faculties of thinking, willing, and judging, all of which presuppose the withdrawal from the world. In the very first sections of the volume on "Thinking," Arendt highlights the continuity between the natural world and the human world, something that may surprise us since in *The Human Condition*, the stability of the human artifice is set up against the background of the cyclical repetition of the same found in nature. She writes that the natural world and the human world are anchored in the same "law of the earth," namely "diverseness" when considered from the perspective of the natural world, and "plurality" when viewed from the side of the human world.

In the first section, titled "the world's phenomenal nature," Arendt speaks of "worldliness," as inherent in all living creatures and characteristic of all life on earth, and thus not strictly limited to the human capacity for building things. The natural world, she writes, is characterized by "an infinite diversity of appearances," "views, sounds, and smells" matched by "an equally astounding diverseness of sense organs" so that what appears appears differently to different species. By "phenomenal" character of the world, Arendt means that there is no being beyond appearances. For her, "being and appearing coincide," what appears, is, and what appears does so on the basis that it is seen, heard, and perceived. All living creatures have an urge to appear, as if appearing on a stage, where the stage "is common but *seems* different to each species" and to "each individual specimen" (LM 19–23).

Thus, "world" is to be understood not solely as the product of human making, the solid human artifice built to provide a stable dwelling place, but also in relation to nature, specifically with regard to the stunning diversity of living creatures, which appear and are perceived in an ongoing playful spectacle of sounds, colors, smells, and views. "Worldliness" is not limited to the human world, and it does not refer to enduring stability only. It describes something more fundamental that encompasses all living creatures, human and nonhuman, namely the condition of being a member "of the world," which entails appearing and perceiving. Everything appears in a variety of ways, is perceived by a variety of organs, and through this interactive play, the fabric of the world comes to the fore.[6]

Plurality and diverseness become manifest in and through the interplay of appearing and perceiving. Specific to human plurality, the distinctness of each person appears to others in and through that person's words and deeds, and in this interaction, the "inter" or "*infra*," as Arendt often calls it, that which lies between people, is disclosed as well. It is precisely through this plural interplay of words and deeds in an open space that *the world as common* comes to the fore. Without this ongoing interplay, there is neither a "who" nor a common world.[7]

A passage from *The Life of the Mind* is particularly illuminating in this regard: "Seeming—the it-seems-to-me, *dokei moi*—is the mode, perhaps the only possible one, in which an *appearing world is acknowledged and perceived*" (LM 21).[8] In another passage found in her *Diaries*, Arendt states very clearly that such an interplay of appearing and perceiving, a play of plurality and distinctness, through words and deeds is what discloses not just "who" one is but also a *world as common*:

> The common in-between shows itself to everyone in a different way; *dokei moi* = *doxa*. In the word (only in it) do I *reveal* my *doxa*. This is my part of the world as well the way the entire world appears from my point of view. In listening, I experience the world, that is to say of how the world appears from other points of view. In every *doxa* the world manifests itself. It is not simply an opinion. And the world manifests itself only in the *doxa*.[9] (emphasis added)

This passage makes explicit the significance of relating to the world: it is through the plural exchange of opinions that the world appears. Without such a relation to the world, there is no plurality and no *world as common*. Relating to the world means relating to others whose relation to the world is different than my own, and it also means seeing the world from the other's point of view; it entails shifting perspectives; it implies a sort of flexibility. As Arendt writes: "*To understand*, in politics, does not mean to understand the other (only love, deprived of a world, 'comprehends' the other), rather to understand the common world as it appears to the other"[10] (emphasis added); therefore, before the I or the other, it is the world, what lies between people, that politics is about.

To sum up: in the world as our enduring dwelling place lies the possibility for "a space fit for actions and speech" that opens up when humans come together to disclose both their distinctness and the space that lies between them. However, such a space is not to be understood as a given. The political dimension of living together, even though vital, is not there just because people speak and act. There need to be spaces where words and actions can indeed appear. Even when this happens, when words and deeds do appear, they are fleeting, disappearing as soon as they have appeared, thereby rendering the perdurance of a *common world* uncertain.

Returning to the question raised at the beginning of this section—"to what extent does the living together of people allow for a manner of coming together and interacting through words and deeds that makes visible plural distinctness as well as a world as common?"—we find that the answer is as simple as it is challenging. "A place fit for actions and words"[11] is potentially there whenever people come together. Politics, in this sense, is somewhat ubiquitous. That said, not only are words and actions quick to fade and their endurance uncertain, but the possibility of "spaces fit for actions and words" has rarified in modern society. What has affirmed itself instead, according to Arendt, is "private life" that is a life deprived of "the reality that comes from being seen and heard by others ... The privation of privacy lies in the absence of others; as far as they are concerned private man does not appear, and therefore it is as though he did not exist" (HC 58).

The possibility of human distinctness and the possibility of a common world are deeply intertwined in Arendt's notion of politics; there is not one without the other, so much so that human life is "dead to the world" if it does not appear (HC 176). To be clear, politics as "a space fit for action and words," which is public and visible, does not mean that it is available only to a select few at the exclusion of others. While, historically speaking, this may have been the case, Arendt does not conceive the public sphere as circumscribed to some privileged groups. The very notion of plurality, as the appearance of many distinct individuals, is inherently upsetting to domineering and exclusionary structures. Arendt makes this clear, for example, when she distinguishes power from domination; power arises when people come together and act in concert, whereas dominance requires violent means to be established (OV 35–56). Arendt argues that visibility and publicness are inherent to politics, that politics relies on the acknowledgment of the many who, together, in their distinctness reveal what lies in common. As she writes: "Under the conditions of a common world, reality is not guaranteed primarily by the 'common nature' of all men who constitute it, but rather by the fact that, differences of positions and the resulting variety of perspectives notwithstanding, everybody is concerned with the same object" (HC 58). Hence, not only a life that does not appear is "dead to the world," without the plural and manifest interplay of many, there is no common world as such either.

Scene Two: Worldlessness

In *The Human Condition*, Arendt considers some specific modern events that, in her assessment, led to the contemporary condition of "world alienation." Among these are industrialization, global exploration, the reformation, the invention of the telescope, the rise of a new science and a new philosophy. World alienation, or worldlessness as she often calls it, refers to the loss of a common world, the ensuing reduction of "all experiences with the world and with other human beings, to experiences between man and himself" (HC 254). The rise of modern society, Arendt argues, occurs at the expense of the public world, which shrinks to the point of disappearance; the private sphere declines as well, even as the laboring activities devoted to life sustenance expand into the public sphere.

World alienation exemplifies a way of living together where people are at once disconnected from each other and from the world. Arendt describes this alienation as "a twofold flight from the earth into the universe, and from the world into the self," something that comes about through the rise of the human activities of "work" and "labor," throughout the modern age (HC 6). Arendt argues that while "labor" is indispensable to life's sustenance and "work" necessary to the world's enduring stability, in their respective different modalities, they are alike in that they both presuppose turning away from the world. As "work" and "labor" impose themselves in modern life, the relationship with the world, as public and plural, wanes.

Labor is the activity by which humans sustain life and attend to biological needs. Through this activity, humans interact with their environment in a way described by Marx as "metabolism with nature," which aptly illustrates the complete absorption into life processes that leave nothing behind. Insofar as we labor, insofar as we are *animal laborans*, we are no different than other living creatures, we submit to the cycle of life necessities, we are thrown back onto ourselves, and even though we are not isolated from others, we do not appear before one another. The dimension of life's sustenance is characterized by being secluded, withdrawn, and by the sameness of repetitive gestures and movements that make us all look alike. When Arendt describes the activity of *animal laborans* as the flight from the world into the self, she is describing the movement of life that turns everyone, necessarily, to one's needs and wants and, because of that, becomes "absorbed" by it.

This does not mean, however, that this sphere of life is irrelevant. On the contrary, Arendt writes: "We shall see that there are very many relevant matters which can survive only in the realm of the private. For instance, love, in distinction from friendship, is killed, or rather extinguished the moment it is displayed in public" (HC 51). Like love, there are aspects of human existence that require protection from the light of the public. At the same time, love is like a fire that burns the distance between the two lovers, and it is precisely for this reason that it is fatal to the world. "Love, by reason of its passion, destroys the in-between which relates to us and separates us from others" (HC 242). The intimacy and necessity of the private sphere does not allow for a space that lies between people, a space where words and deeds can properly stand out; the closeness that life's sustenance demands does not afford the distance, the in-between, where one can reveal "who" he or she is. In this modality of being together, there is no proper space in between, and without that, there is no possibility of a common world. If human beings remain bound to the sustenance of life needs without the possibility of emerging from that modality of interacting with one another, they are, and will remain, worldless. There is no *inter esse*, properly speaking, and no "distinct who," because there is no space in between. Sameness and repetition, not plurality, characterize life's never-ending cycle, and a *common* world is not disclosed.

Work is the human activity that produces things, the activity of *"homo faber,"* and as already pointed out, this activity is indispensable for building an enduring and permanent world. Arendt writes: "The products of work—not the products of labor—guarantee the permanence and durability without which a world would not be possible at all" (HC 94). Strangely, however, Arendt implicates this activity in the process of world alienation because of its specifically secluded modality, which rests on turning away from the world. The activity of fabrication proceeds from an image of an object and dictates, step by step, the materials and the instruments needed for that specific object to be produced. There is no repetitive cycle here, but a linear procedure, with a clear beginning and a clear end. While labor as metabolism with nature leaves nothing behind, work or fabrication produces things, but distances itself from the world so as to be able to better measure it and fit the object properly within it. Its inherent instrumentality, by which everything becomes a means to an end, and the violence intrinsic in this activity—to make a table we have to cut down a tree—are destructive of the political as the space where people come together by way of words and deeds. Isolation, instrumentality, and violence destroy, rather than establish, our relation to the world. In asserting itself throughout the modern age, instrumentality and justification of violence have prevailed as well. Surely, politics has been understood in instrumental terms, and violence has been considered an integral part of politics, but this is not politics in the Arendtian sense, even if such a notion of politics continues to prevail.

When Arendt states that "world alienation, and not self-alienation" "has been the hallmark of the modern age" (HC 254), she is not just referring to a transitory phenomenon or an isolated event. Rather, she is talking about something that has profoundly altered our living together, one where production, consumption, and an increasingly sophisticated technology govern our daily lives and what we do. Arendt describes the glorification of labor and work in the modern age as the enlargement of the private: "This enlargement of the private, ... does not make it public, does not constitute a public realm, but it means only that a public realm has almost completely receded" (HC 52). The cyclical busyness of looking after life, the consumption of goods, even durable goods, at an increased pace defies the stability of the world. At the same time, the production of many more objects has insulated humans into a world of artifacts on which they have become increasingly dependent and in which they find themselves trapped. Labor and work are valuable human activities insofar as they respond to the specific human condition as it has been given to humans on earth. Their expansion to the point of taking over every dimension of the human condition deprives human beings of the possibility of a world as common, which Arendt sees as very dangerous, politically speaking.

Ultimately, worldlessness is a form of expropriation brought about by human activities themselves. As the Latin etymological origin of the term indicates, *ex proprius*, to be expropriated is to be deprived of one's own property, of what one owns, eventually also used to indicate what is most one's own—Marx, for instance, speaks of man's alienation with regard to capitalistic production, which, in his analysis, robs the worker of its labor force, the inherent capacity to produce things, therefore robbing the worker of his humanity. Just like the expropriation of large strata of populations at the beginning of the modern age made them expendable and turned them into a mass that could be exploited by the industrial revolution, in the same way other forms of expropriation have deprived humans of what is mostly their own, not property as such but of a relation to the world, of a place in the world. What is most one's own, what is *proprius*, is not found within oneself, but lies *in between* oneself and others; paradoxically, it lies in relating to the world in and through others.

Scene Three: Elsinki and the Italian Resistenza

Figure 5.1[12] shows Elsa Oliva with her partisans' companions.[13] It was taken between 1944 and 1945, in Italy, during the time known as the Italian Resistance— *la Resistenza*—when many men and women mobilized to fight against the occupation of German fascist troops. The new Italian republic was, in many respects, forged out of the values that arose from that struggle.

Turning to the Italian *Resistenza* helps illuminate the significance of the relation between the political and the world in a concrete way. For one, the *Resistenza* is the coming together of many people to resist and fight against the German occupation and its puppet Fascist Regime, the Salò Republic. It entailed armed fighting, and not for nothing the *Resistenza* has been called a civil war, but what happened during those twenty months between September 1943 and April 1945 cannot be reduced to military fighting alone. When considered from the perspective of women who took part in it, the *Resistenza* is first and foremost political action in the Arendtian sense. Women, at this time in Italy, were not considered full citizens. They did not have the right to vote, and by law, they were under the full authority of a male figure, whether their father, brother, or husband. Essentially, they were invisible or, as Arendt puts it, "dead to the world."

The picture shows Elsa, or *Elsinki*, as she was known during the *Resistenza*, with a group of men. They are all young and smiling. They are all armed. The picture provokes many questions about the time, the place, and most especially about

Figure 5.1 Elsa Oliva with her partisans' companions. Permission has been granted to use this photo from Istoreto, Istituto Piemontese per la storia della Resistenza e della società contemporanea "Giorgio Agosti."

Elsinki. An armed woman with a group of men, at this time in Italy, strikes one as out of the ordinary, to say the least. The picture conveys a dissonance between what it shows and the world as it was. Elsinki is "out of place," somewhere else than where she would be expected to be.

Indeed. *Elsinki* has left the security of home and has left behind the kind of life laid out for her as a woman. She knows that she is putting her life in danger, but she also knows that she cannot simply watch and do nothing. From the start, she wants to fight, even though, as a woman; it is not immediately evident that she will be accepted in a partisan band. She may have left behind the life destined to her as a woman, like many other women have done at this time, but the expectation of such a life has not left her completely, and wherever she goes, she is seen and treated as a woman.

One particular event, recalled by Elsinki herself, details how she was able to alter her condition. Soon after joining the partisans, Elsinki asked to speak publicly to all of her companions. Once they were assembled, she explained to them why she was there: to fight like everyone else, to guard when it was her time to guard, to do her part no less and no differently than anyone else, and, she added, she was not there to find a boyfriend. She demanded that she be treated like every other member in the partisan band and vowed that she would treat everyone likewise. If they accepted these conditions and agreed to interact with her as they would with anyone else, and not treat her differently due to her being a woman, then she would stay, otherwise she would not.[14] She was direct and firm, but she knew that she risked losing precisely what she had wanted more than anything else, namely the ability to fight alongside the partisans. No one objected, and so Elsinki stayed with the partisans and fought as part of their unit till the very end. She even became the head of her formation for a time, and when the higher ups demanded that she be demoted since it is "not proper" for a woman to be in a commanding position, her companions stood by her.

This event may be considered irrelevant from the broader perspective of the *Resistenza* fighting, and, in fact, it is only one among many similar stories that have now been lost to history. However, I contend that events such as this capture the *Resistenza* in its manifold dimensions; more importantly, events such as this capture the truly political side of what is generally viewed as armed fighting, though their political significance emerges only when considered in light of Arendt's understanding of the political. Here is how. By addressing her companions publicly, Elsinki places herself on equal footing with everyone there and, in doing so, puts in disarray the preestablished order and whatever hierarchy is in place. Her speaking publicly to all makes visible her relationship to the world and makes it possible for others to do likewise, an act that, in turn, makes manifest the space between them. Even though they move in the same space as before, that space has now been altered. It is as if they are moving in a "new" world, as if they see each other in a new light. By speaking openly and publicly to all, Elsinki interrupts the established manner of relating to one another and redraws the dynamics of their interrelations. When we consider the fact that the speaker is a woman, traditionally viewed and treated as subaltern to man, and that she does so in the traditionally masculine setting of armed fighting, the subversiveness of this event emerges in its full force. It reconfigures the space in which they move by reconfiguring how they come together, that is, "freely" and not in conformity to some predetermined manner of engagement. It is such an interruption that opens up "a place fit for action and words," wherein "who" one is and what lies in between them can appear in and through speaking and acting together. It is important to underline the interplay of speaking and hearing, of seeing and being seen. Elsinki's words reveal her relation to the world and what lies between her and her companions. Without everyone hearing Elsinki's words and acknowledging them, that is, "understanding the world as it appears to her," there would not be a world in common and nothing new.

This is just one event that can be easily dismissed as insignificant. By itself it does not substantially change the history of the Italian *Resistenza*. However, if we consider that the *Resistenza* was characterized by many similarly disruptive events, where men and women came together "anew," moving in a space that allowed both their plural distinctness and their world in common to become visible, then a simple event becomes a political experience par excellence, putting into question the univocal narrative of the *Resistenza*, as being nothing but a military struggle. This aspect alone raises many questions about what is seen and what is not seen, how modalities of interaction that are subversive of the status quo are, in fact, seen, heard, and acknowledged. When new forms of relations arise out of the coming together of men and women, how are they sustained and furthered? Are they forgotten and let go for the sake of a stability and an order that limit and restrict precisely "spaces fit for actions and words"?

Elsinki's concrete example is revealing in a number of ways. For one, it brings to light that the structured ways of living together, even when they seem permanent and unchanging, do not completely eradicate the possibility for "places fit for actions and words" to open up. As already said, it is in fact possible wherever people come together. This exhibits Arendtian politics as truly democratic and empowering for all, wherever people are, as they come together through words and actions, thereby revealing "who" they are and what lies between them. Power so understood is embodied and visible; it does not depend on an operation of power that precludes the participation of many who are distinct individuals; rather than a "foreclosure," power manifests itself as a disclosure that opens new possibilities of relating with each other and living together. There is a plurality, and a common world only through public interaction; otherwise there would only be the privacy of one's subjective experience. The political is what makes the relation to the world of one visible to another in an interplay of seeing and perceiving, speaking and hearing, and illuminates what lies in between.

Thus, politics, in the sense of publicly disclosing distinctness and the world as common, does not leave behind gender, race, or other concrete "marks" of our embodied existence; rather, it brings them out into full light, not as separate and isolated aspects, not as part of "a common nature," but as integral to the distinctness of "who" one is as a particular individual, whose relation to the world becomes visible in interacting with others. In fact, it is precisely those who have been excluded from appearing, from speaking and acting together with others, whose words and deeds are most revealing in that they bring to light their "place" and their relation to the world that has remained hidden, unseen, thus dislodging the structures that have locked them out. Such appearing is inherently disruptive: it interrupts what are assumed to be given and unchanging ways of living together, thereby revealing that they are neither given nor unchanging. Arendt's critics who argue that her politics is dependent on a notion of power that is exclusionary fail to see the degree to which, on the contrary, Arendt's politics subverts exclusionary power and puts it out of order. Politics is not about how we are all alike in one way or another, but rather it is about making distinctness and plurality appear in and through how we come in relation with one another. Politics in this sense is defiant; it reveals the new; it demands courage, and because of that, it strikes us as rare. But what if it happens more often than not, only not acknowledged as such?

Politics Is Relating to the World

In this essay, I have tried to show that Arendt's notion of the political is grounded in a relation with the world, a relation that is not given but is disclosed through words and deeds that are heard and seen, and through which what lies in between comes to the fore as well. This relation is our only possibility for a *common* world. And, without a world that is common, we become isolated from each other, dispersed, thrown back onto ourselves, incapable of understanding the world "as it appears to the other," alienated and lost.

Relating to the world means interacting with each other through words and deeds. It means coming together "without the intermediary of things and matter," and not in function of a position, of a role, of an office that are preassigned, nor in the name of a nature presumably shared. The revelatory power of words and deeds and the interruption of acquired given ways of being together are simultaneous. Moreover, this interaction requires that we shift our perspective, that we are capable of seeing the world from the other person's position, that we can "move" around in a way that allows us to see what lies in between from different sides. This is why not the I, not the subject but the world as that which lies in between us is what politics is all about. As she writes: "In the end, politically speaking, it is not about ourselves. It is about the world."[15] The I imprisons and fixes us, while politics as relation to the world demands that we be free and flexible, capable of shifting positions as we move and interact with others.

Similarly, public and private are not to be understood rigidly as connected necessarily to a physical space that is given, already there. In Arendt's understanding of the political, they refer to different modalities of interaction whereby a world as common does appear or not. Such a distinction has everything to do with the extent to which "who" one is and the world as common are revealed, something that can happen wherever and whenever people are together. Thus, this possibility is everywhere. The political "space fit for actions and words" may arise in secluded spaces as it did, for example, during the Italian *Resistenza*, in private homes transformed into public political arenas.

It is true that words and deeds will last so long as there are people who remember them, and this is why Arendt's notion of politics is fragile. Human beings are born and die, and while they are in the world, they have the power to speak and act with one another, thus revealing the world as new. It seems that what is new is only so for a short while, but it is in that juncture, during that brief moment, that the world as that which lies in between comes to the fore. Still, that it continues to happen is what really matters. After all, we come and go. The world is here to stay.

It may be objected that Arendt's understanding of politics offers too little, and that it does not seem to go far enough. How does revealing the world as common even begin to address injustice in its many forms? How does it offer ways of undoing structured practices of exclusion such as systemic racism and sexism, for example? The short answer is that there is no world as common without plurality being visible. It is the visibility of plurality that has the power to shatter systemic modalities of interaction. If Arendt's understanding of the political may seem to offer too little or not enough, it is perhaps because we are still expecting politics to change the world, where change means remaking it. But for Arendt, politics is all about relating to the world, illuminating it through words and deeds, so that plurality and what lies in common do in fact appear. And that, for as little as it may sound, is radical.

Notes

1. Judith Butler, *Notes toward a Performative Theory of Assembly* (Cambridge: Harvard University Press, 2015), 88.
2. Emphasis added.
3. I deliberately use the term "scene" to underline the appearing dimension of the political in Arendt. A scene is about showing something, and through each scene, I draw your attention toward what I find to be significant in Arendt's politics.
4. Emphasis added.
5. Emphasis added.
6. Implicitly, Arendt seems to be suggesting that the natural world in its stunning diverseness can serve as a space that attunes us to the interplay of appearing and perceiving by sharpening our senses' ability to pick out its manifold and subtle manifestations.
7. It is worth pointing out that Arendt goes as far as writing that "the almost infinite diversity" of appearances, "the sheer entertainment value" of the world's "views, sounds, smells, … is hardly ever mentioned by the thinkers and the philosophers" (LM 20).
8. Emphasis added.
9. In Italian: "L'infra comune si mostra a ognuno in modo diverso; dokei moi = doxa. Nella parola (solo in essa) **rivelo** la mia **doxa**. Questa é sia la mia parte di mondo, sia il modo in cui il mondo intero appare dal mio punto di vista. Nell'ascolto, faccio esperienza del mondo, ovvero di come il mondo appaia da altri punti di vista. In ogni doxa si manifesta il mondo. Essa non é semplicemente opinione. E il mondo si manifesta soltanto nella doxa." Hannah Arendt, *Quaderni e Diari. 1950-1973* (Vicenza: Neri Pozza Editore, 2007), quaderno XVII, 4, 325. I am referencing the Italian edition of Arendt's "Diaries" as no English translation is available. The translation of these passages from Italian into English, throughout this essay, is mine. The original German edition, *Denktagebuch, 1950-1973*, was published by Piper Verlag GmbH (München, 2002).
10. In Italian: "Comprendere in politica non significa mai comprendere l'altro (solo l'amore privo di mondo 'comprende' l'altro,) bensí comprendere il mondo comune come esso appare all'altro." Arendt, *Quaderni e Diari, 1950-1973*, quaderno XIX, 2, 367.
11. I use "a space fit for actions and words" interchangeably with "a space fit for actions and speech."
12. The author thanks Istoreto, Istituto Piemontese per la storia della Resistenza e della società contemporanea "Giorgio Agosti" for kind permission to use the photo.
13. "Partisan" here is not to be taken in the current political use of the term, namely, "along party lines." Partisan is a fighter who took part in the liberation struggle in Italy during the Second World War—after the removal of Mussolini from office—and the occupation of the northern part of Italy by German forces.
14. Anna Maria Bruzzone and Rachele Farina, *La Resistenza Taciuta: Dodici vite di partigiane piemontesi* (Torino: Bollati Boringhieri, 2003), 140.

15 In Italian: "In fin dei conti, politicamente parlando, non si tratta di noi. Si tratta del mondo." Arendt, *Quaderni e Diari, 1950–1973*, quaderno XXIV, 21, 500.

Bibliography

Arendt, Hannah. *Quaderni e Diari. 1950–1973*. Vicenza: Neri Pozza Editore, 2007.

Bruzzone, Anna Maria, and Farina Rachele. *La Resistenza Taciuta: Dodici vite di partigiane piemontesi*. Torino: Bollati Boringhieri, 2003.

Butler, Judith. *Notes toward a Performative Theory of Assembly*. Cambridge: Harvard University Press, 2015.

Hill, Melvyn A. *Hannah Arendt: The Recovery of the Public World*. New York: St. Martin's Press, 1979.

Kohn, Jerome, ed. *Arendt: Essays in Understanding 1930–1954*. New York: Harcourt Brace, 1994.

Chapter 6

AN ETHICS OF GOD'S GRACE TO BALANCE A POLITICS OF WORLDLY AFFLICTION: A WEILIAN COMPANION TO RONCALLI ON ARENDT

Kathryn Lawson

"When Everything Is Lost"

Simone Weil's oeuvre, like that of Hannah Arendt, is deeply informed by the social political turmoil that was a nearly constant overtone of her short life from her birth in Paris, France, in February of 1909 to her death at a sanitarium in Ashford, UK, in August of 1943. As an ethnically Jewish woman in Europe at that time, Weil could not have escaped the political had she tried, but she had no desire to avoid the force of political life. Instead, she looked directly and unflinchingly at the hardship and affliction in Europe and across the world during her lifetime. Indeed, she went so far as to seek out and organize political dissidents to push back against the machinery of totalitarianism with both her words and her actions. But Weil's undeniably political thinking is perhaps even more unorthodox than Arendt's in that Weil's mature political thought is grounded in religion. All of Weil's philosophy in the last five years of her life is an attempt to reconcile the destructive force of wars, the cruel thoughtless mechanism of totalizing social structures, and the mundane evil of human existence with the beauty of the world, the delight of friendships, the love of one's neighbor, the elation of communal religious rites, and the possibility of divine grace. Weil experienced both force and grace, and as such, her work centers a political agonism that aims toward balancing these two seemingly contradictory poles. Rather than a sense of regret or bitterness for being born into such a tumultuous time and place, Weil saw this as the ultimate opportunity: "You could not have wished to be born at a better time than this when everything is lost" (FLN 47). In the affliction that war creates, Weil saw the possibility of newness, creation, divinity. She felt that such affliction laid bare a political system that did not serve the people but rather served only itself. This revelation brings with it the possibility of change.

For Weil, the true danger of politics is to forget that all political parties are always totalitarian (APP). The very nature of the political party is to demand allegiance from its members and to put the institution of the party above all else.

The selective amnesia that makes each citizen forget about her own country or, in particular, her own party within that country leads to a thoughtless destruction of outliers. The party takes care of itself and maintains its power at all costs. This does not necessarily happen with any particular ill intent by citizens or party members but is simply the mechanism of domination at work. The agonistic ethics that Weil offers as a way of pushing back against totalitarianism in all institutions involves a self-abnegation in the face of the other, which allows for a decentering of the self and an openness to the possibility of the world of the other human and the cultivation of an unbreachable, unknowable space between the other human and the self, which can only be filled by the divine. To allow for the other person to exist, one must leave space for the absolute mystery of our existence. For Weil, *I* cannot ever become *we*, because there must be a space left open for God (IC 176).

Alongside Roncalli's reflections on Arendt and world, I intend to show that our connection to the Good *through* the world and our relations *in* the world are the ethical foundation upon which Weil's conception of the political is built. This simultaneously notes perhaps the greatest differences and similarities between these two figures: while Weil emphasizes God or the Platonic Good, Arendt emphasizes the shared world, but simultaneously, both thinkers emphasize the space in between as the site of the political. The political always entails a plurality, acting in concert with others whose words and deeds appear. For Weil, the ethical foundation of the political is God, who can only be accessed via the world and, in particular, through releasing one's small sense of the I in favor of an I that is interconnected with other people and the larger, divine desire in all things. Only from this place, in the cultivation of an ethical expansion of the self, can one begin to explore the political response to a world riddled with affliction. The process of releasing the small self and expanding the notion of the self to include one's relationship to other people is necessary for ethical action. For Weil, the most important aspect of this expansion is neither the I nor the other person, but the space in between. The space of the good, the divine, and/or the mystery is the space that allows for political action.

In a letter to Father Perrin concerning her refusal to be baptized, Weil states that "we must feel the reality and presence of God through all external things, without exception, as clearly as our hand feels the substance of paper through the penholder and the nib" (WG 4). Weil asserts that the only experience we may have of the divine is in the matter of the world. For Weil, there are four loves through which we can experience God: "religious ceremonies, the beauty of the world, and our neighbor … To these three loves friendship should perhaps be added; strictly speaking it is distinct from the love of our neighbor" (WG 83). The love of the neighbor is the same thing as justice, for Weil. It is a manifestation of that which is beautiful, good, and miraculous because injustice is not just possible but also probable. Justice seeks to find a balance between two things that are unequal: "The supernatural virtue of justice consists of behaving exactly as though there were equality when one is the stronger in an unequal relationship" (WG 87). Justice is a pause in the social political mechanization. It reflects on the possibility to do something other than gain power. Weil offers the example of the Good Samaritan, who changes a heap of flesh at the side of the road into a human being by paying attention to his affliction and acting accordingly. This action is a denial of the small sense of the self: "In denying oneself, one becomes capable under God of establishing someone else by a creative affirmation. One gives oneself in ransom for the other. It is a redemptive act" (WG 91). Thus, God and political motivation must be connected by one's own actions, and rather than marking two distinct arenas of Weil's thought, it is this relation between the ethical Good and existential political need that is central to Weil's thought. To recognize the matter of the world is to be able to experience God or the Good and thus to act politically.

Within the limits of this chapter, I examine the relationship between politics, God, and the world in Weil's thought. It is my belief that bringing such a relationship into the foreground will prove helpful in exploring why Arendt and Weil can and should be thought of together. Predominantly a companion to Roncalli's chapter on Arendt, this chapter seeks to bring Arendt and Weil into conversation on the link between world and politics and considers how this could be relevant for our own contemporary political world. This essay is divided into three brief scenes, which will correspond to Roncalli's meditation on Arendt and the world.[1] In the first scene, I will focus on the relationship between God and the political as crucial for there to be a world as common. In the second scene, I will consider Godlessness, or the inability to raise oneself from the lower void, and allowing force to dominate one's life. In the third scene, I will refer to the life and work of the late Sister Dianna Ortiz as a way to concretely illustrate the political in the Weilian sense.[2]

Scene One: "In the World but Not of the World"

The Weilian conception of the world is complicated by the relationship to the divine. In addition to the Arendtian triad of plurality, "who," and world discussed by Roncalli, Weil brings in the concept of God, or the desire for the Good. This addition is arguably something that makes Weil's thought less appealing to praxis-oriented political thought and certainly less traditional in the realm of political philosophy. A common critique is that Weil's use of the Good or God brings about a division that rejects matter and celebrates spirit.[3] Of course, this critique has also been commonly leveled against Plato, who is foundational to Weil's own philosophy. In clarifying her reading of Plato, Weil explains that God *is* the world, and as such, it is nonsensical to reject that world, which is our only access to the Good:

> The visible world is his [God's] body. That does not imply pantheism; he is not in the visible world just as our soul is not in our body. Plato says this explicitly elsewhere. The Soul of the world is infinitely more vast than matter, contains matter, and envelopes it from all parts (34b). (IC 92)

The world is the dark mirror through which we experience the divine and the love to and from other humans, as in 1 Corinthians 13: "For now we see in a mirror, darkly; but then face to face: now I know in part; but then shall I know fully even as also I was fully known. But now abideth faith, hope, love, these three; and the greatest of these is love." To smash the mirror is not to get closer to another human, or to the divine; it is to lose all contact. There is a gap, there is a lack of clarity, but there is also our closest possibility of divine love and human ethics. Weil argues that "Nothing in the world is the centre of the world, that the centre of the world is outside the world" (IC 174) and that "God, being outside the universe, is at the same time the center" (WG 99). The heart of all ethical communal political social action, the ultimate meaning of existence, is God. It is divine love. Rather than this diminishing the importance of political action, love imbues political action with a spiritual depth.

This addition of the divine removes the center of the world from the Arendtian *agora*, placing it outside of the human world. This gives us two distinct ontologies, which clarify Arendt's focus on working within the political system, and Weil's emphasis on working outside of the political system. For Weil, a philosopher should be an exile from every organization in order to avoid the groupthink that collectivity brings about for both Weil and Arendt. According to Roberto Esposito, in Weil's reading, a totalitarian regime is the natural outcome of the structure of democratic nation-states. Unlike Arendt, who sees totalitarianism as a breakdown in the system, Weil sees it as the inevitable outcome of systematizing politics.[4] The centralization of power and the structure of upholding the party line within political organizations leads the individual to blind spots in her thinking and black-versus-white ideologies that always put one's own party in the right and the opposition party in the wrong. Political parties do not make enough room for the discourse and flexibility that is necessary for democratic action.[5] As such, the role of the political philosopher is to stand outside the agora, taking note of those it rejects (for it will always reject some people). Further, the role of the political philosopher is to dismantle systematized power structures.

Yet, Weil's skepticism about political parties by no means makes her apolitical. Among her many political actions, Weil traveled to Germany in 1932 to work with Marxist activists, and to Spain to fight for the Republicans in the Spanish Civil War in 1936.[6] She holds open the desire to undo the political party system, *and* she tirelessly works within political parties to improve the conditions for those who are most vulnerable: soldiers and laborers, both of whom Weil saw suffering on the frontlines of war and industry, and both of whom she saw falling between the cracks of society. She holds open this suffering alongside the love she feels for those people to craft a political agonism. As Esposito argues: "Her intention is to forge the contradiction between unreconcilables to the point of reinforcing them precisely through their mutual conceptual and symbolic frictions" (OP 62). This pedagogy of dialectic thinking asserts an agonism that allows for both the suffering and the love that we experience.[7]

The human world is the space where it is possible and safe to engage in shared religious rites, the beauty of the earth, friendship, and love of the neighbor (WG

83). The world is a shared space that offers us one another and opens up a space that cannot be filled by anything herein, a space for the divine. It is our ethical duty to allow each person to live in a world in which they can discover and express that desire for the good, that divine love. In so discovering, one realizes that the center of the world is actually outside of the world. One remains very much in the world, in the here and now, working to build ethical communal spaces, but one also recognizes that the good they seek and which must be cherished in all other humans is not of the world but of God. For Weil, we are in the world but not of the world.

Scene Two: An Optimistic Realism

To consider Weil in Arendtian terms, we could read decreation as an attempt to overcome the distinction between private and public life in the sense that decreation involves recognizing the self as interconnected to others and the private as necessarily public or the inner life as entangled with external relations. A common critique of Weil is that decreation seems to suggest the disappearance of the self as a distinct *who*, which is the opposite of the appearance of the *who* in Arendt.[8] And in some senses, this is true: the self as center, egoistic, and master of the world *is* displaced in the process of decreation. But the thinking self is expanded and enriched. The private self is recognized as an interconnected part of a larger relational sense of self. As Roncalli notes in Arendt, the fabric of the world comes to the fore as a plurality, and this is also true for Weil's process of decreation. But for Weil, the *Who* that is revealed here is not the personality of the I; rather, it is the *Divine Who*. Through attentive creative ethical engagement with the world, I become a divine conduit, tuning into that core desire and love for the Good that exists at the center of all human beings. In this sense, it is not the world as common that is revealed, but God as common and our desire for God as the precious aspect at the center of all human beings. From the recognition of our common core, namely, the never-ending quest for the Good, we can begin to grow roots, form ethical communities, and practice genuine politics. Weil explains that "the beauty of the world is God's own beauty, as the beauty of the body of a human being is the beauty which belongs to that being .... But wisdom, righteousness and the rest cannot appear to us in the world but only in a human being who will be God" (IC 150). Ethical political action involves a recognition of God and our shared desire for the Good. Politics is fueled by divine love accessed through love of matter:

> In law, the love of God is first. But in fact, as among men all concrete thought has a real object, this renunciation necessarily operates while thought is applied either to things or to men. In the first case the love of God appears first as an adherence to the beauty of the world, the Stoic *amor fati*, the adherence to that indiscriminate distribution of the light and of the rain which here below expresses the perfection of our Heavenly father. In the second case, the love of God appears first as love for one's neighbour, and before all for the weak and

unfortunate neighbour, whom, according to the laws of nature, we do not even notice in passing him. (IC 175)

Weilian decreation is often unfairly charged with pessimism and self-annihilation. Contrarily, I read Weil as similar to Nietzsche when he is called a nihilist rather than the physician who diagnoses the nihilism and offers therapeutic solutions to live with it.[9] The balance and logic of Weil's ethics argues that there must be a recognition of *fati* in order to cultivate *amor*. This is a key decision in Weil: to look unflinchingly at our world, our fate in all its cruelty, and to choose love.[10] Weil's realism is infused with optimism in the movement from recognition of fate into ethical action. Decreation is necessarily followed by recreation. To explain this, Weil cites the end of the biblical *Book of Job*, in which revelation and love of God is born out of absolute affliction (IC 102). From affliction and love comes ethical possibilities and political action.

But Weil's unflinching look at the reality of our world with its absurdity, suffering, and absence comes with a terrifying risk. It is absolutely possible to become lost in nihilism, to sink into what Weil refers to as the lower void. Indeed, the fear of this nihilism can and does keep many people suspended in a thoughtless, *ersatz* existence. It is safer not to look cleanly at the reality of the world. But this is not an option for Weil in her quest for truth:

> The void that one grasps between the pincers of contradiction is indubitably the one which lies above, for the more one sharpens the natural faculties of intelligence, will and love the better one grasps it. The void which lies below is the one into which one falls by allowing the natural faculties to become atrophied. (NB 412)

In acknowledging the darkness and affliction of human life, Weil encourages also recognizing the lightness and the divine love. Weil suggests embodying that love through cultivating ethical action. In this way, there can be ethical good that comes from the pain. If one turns away completely from the light and is consumed utterly by the dark, one falls into the lower void and becomes the nihilistic or self-destructive person that Weil herself can be critiqued as embodying.[11] It is my contention that such a critique of Weil is unmerited in that it misses the spirit of her work and one half of her agonistic thought.

To avoid the lower void with its godlessness that leads to a worldlessness and a rootlessness, decreation must be understood not as a self-destruction but as a transformation of the self from solipsistic to interconnected:

> If we accept the coexistence with ourselves of beings and of things we shall not be avid for domination or for riches, since domination and riches have no other use than to cast a veil over this coexistence, diminishing the share of all that is other than ourselves. All crimes, all grave sins are particular forms of the refusal of this coexistence; a sufficiently close analysis shows this for each particular case. (IC 189)

By admitting to coexistence, we begin to live ethically, avoiding crime. We gain the possibility of crafting laws and political structures on this foundation of love for the world and our deep-seated interconnection to beings and things.

Despite her *amor fati* and recognition of universal interconnection, Weil nevertheless maintains the distinction between the supernatural spirit and the natural body. Thus, there remains a hierarchy of spirit over body (an ontological fact that is distasteful to much political thought) in Weil's ontology. Weil considers there to be two distinct realms: the natural (earthly body) and the supernatural (divine spirit). However, the hierarchy of supernatural spirit over natural body is not a violent domination but rather a conscious decision to choose love: "Once a certain threshold is crossed, the supernatural part of the soul reigns over the natural part not by violence but by persuasion, not by will but by desire" (IC 97). Weil explains this by considering Plato's allegory of the cave, which *can* be read as a rejection of the reality of the world but which, for Weil, is actually a deepening of one's capacity to love:

> The unreality of things, which Plato so powerfully depicts in the metaphor of the cave, has no connection with the thing as such; the things in themselves have the fullness of reality in that they exist. It is a question of things as the object for love. In this reference they are like shadows cast by puppets. (IC 134)

For Weil, the world is not rejected as an illusion when one turns away from the shadows on the cave wall and ascends to the light of the sun. The allegory is not a matter of rejecting existence. Instead, it is a matter of loving existence with a greater depth and awareness. To love God is to love the world more. Thus, Weil's philosophy produces optimistic realism that recognizes the affliction and suffering of existence and chooses to act in accordance with divine love. It requires traversing both of these poles, and it holds the danger of falling into despair and nihilism. The ethics of divine grace and love must be the impetus for a politics that recognizes the worldly necessity of affliction and human suffering. Politically, one must be grounded in the reality of existential suffering, and ethically one must respond with love. Weil admits that this is a painful path, and yet, there is no other ethical option than to leap into divine love. Only from there can one pursue political action.

Sister Dianna Ortiz: Living with God and Affliction

Speak, bear witness ... .
>> Between the hammer strokes
>>> The heart survives

>>> like the tongue
>>>> that between the teeth
>>>>> and in spite of everything

goes on praising.
—Rainer Maria Rilke, *The Duino Elegies*[12]

The incredible and inspirational life of Sister Dianne Ortiz is not a story any person would want to experience first hand. Indeed, even experiencing it second hand through reading her biography, *The Blindfold's Eyes: My Journey from Torture to Truth*, is not easy. She is pictured above around the time that she held a five-week hunger strike and "vigil for truth" in Washington, DC. Ortiz was kidnapped in 1989 while working as a missionary with Indigenous children in Guatemala. During the kidnapping, she was brutally raped and tortured. Citing left-wing sympathies, the Guatemalan military had long brutalized Indigenous populations in their country. Backed by the US government, the military strategically targeted those who aided the Indigenous, and this eventually included Ortiz. A common excuse the military used to justify their brutality was the claim that those aiding the Indigenous were supporting Marxist guerillas. Following her escape, Ortiz tirelessly worked to end government-supported practices of torture and advocate for those who had experienced torture. Ortiz spent her life in the service of God, justice, and other people who could not speak out or receive the attention that she, as an American, received. Filled with affliction, political action, community support, and God, Dianna Ortiz's struggle is certainly Weilian and offers an apt portrait of how we may conceive of Weilian politics playing out in the world.

Affliction, the translation of Weil's *malheur*, is a more intense word for a type of suffering that is physical but also psychological and spiritual. It is infused with

Figure 6.1 Sister Dianna Ortiz, 1996. Credit: Stephen Crowley.

loss, suffering, humiliation, impotence, pain, and an uprooting of one's entire life physically, socially, and politically. Weilian affliction crushes body and soul, making a person a slave (WG 67–82). For Weil, affliction is absolutely terrible and is never something that should be sought after. Richard Rees writes that Weil "believed suffering should be avoided, when legitimately possible, but she knew it was often unavoidable and she knew its potential value" (FLN viii). There is an important distinction in Weil between the suffering that is an inevitable aspect of human existence and seeking out or glorifying suffering. I begin with this as an acknowledgment of Dianna Ortiz's truly horrific affliction in the hours she spent being tortured and for the rest of her life through the memories seared into her mind and flesh, but also the affliction baked into the refusal to acknowledge or properly investigate her case by both the Guatemalan and the US governments. The affliction that Ortiz endured brought about an alienation in her from both God and the community of fellow humans. Weil says: "Affliction makes God appear to be absent for a time, more absent than a dead man, more absent than light in the utter darkness of a cell. A kind of horror submerges the whole soul. During this absence there is nothing to love" (WG 70). As such, God is not a solution or an escapist consolation for human affliction. Instead, God asks us to bear that affliction: "If we want to have a love which will protect the soul from wounds, we must love something other than God" (NB 497). This posture toward God demands ethical political action and does not allow us to use God's love as an escapism from our suffering. The affliction of Ortiz is a stark reminder of the ghastly and intentional suffering perpetrated in this world, and her subsequent political actions demonstrate the choice of divine love in spite of (and at times because of) that affliction.

Through Affliction to Social Justice and a New God

Unlike Weil, who moved from a political atheism into a religious politics, Ortiz describes her early life as being guided by a "religious naivete" that prompted her to refuse fastening her seatbelt in the car because of a belief that God would protect her.[13] Ortiz was moved by the ideas of Liberation theology, which involves a close tie between the church, social justice, and the work of equality and education for the poor. This commitment is what drew Ortiz to Guatemala and what prompted her to stay despite the death, rape, and torture threats she received against both her and her family. After her violent torture, Ortiz slipped into a state that she calls a paralysis or a living nightmare between the crucifixion and the resurrection.[14] From this state of paralysis, she could only see the narrative of a Christian God as a cruel hoax. However, over time and with immense therapeutic care, she began to conceive of a new possibility of the divine:

> I knew my old God had died, the God who was strong, powerful, a protector. The Good Shepherd, was no longer someone I believed in. If I were to see God in a new way, based on my experiences, God would have to be helpless, broken, tortured, but still alive and able to love … Wasn't it an act of resistance to refuse

to believe that God was dead, to reject the world they [her torturers] tried to make me believe in? Maybe my absence of belief in God was another blindfold the torturers had tried on, one I could now take off.[15]

Of course, Christianity is a religion in which God himself suffers horrific torture through Jesus's time on the Cross. And like Weil, Ortiz can imagine this suffering and the sense of being forsaken by the divine but struggles with the possibility of the resurrection and the return to love. Ortiz considers that in his moment of absolute affliction, Jesus forgets the suffering of the other men being crucified beside him. Affliction may make us forget the suffering of others, but the cure for affliction is to remember the suffering of others and to do our utmost to alleviate their affliction. By shifting her thoughts on affliction in this way, Ortiz suddenly transitions from continually reliving and rehearing her own screams to hearing the screams of the others who were simultaneously being tortured on that day. This shift sets her on a trajectory to stop the suffering of all people being tortured in Guatemala and the world over.

The divine layer of this healing process involves Ortiz finding God in others: "God, I saw, was not a shepherd watching over us, his sheep. This was a God of the same species."[16] This is the necessary link between God, politics, and the world. The only access to God available to humans is in and through the human plurality of a shared world. Ortiz recognizes the affliction of others and chooses to respond with divine love:

> I think God and the cries of the thousands of oppressed people of Guatemala are awakening within me this sleeping silence and are breathing courage within me, a courage that is allowing me to take control of my life and that is allowing me to free myself from the fear that seeks to paralyze me and to silence me. [17]

It is those she recalls being tortured alongside her and those who continue to be tortured that inspire divine love in Ortiz. In others and through God, she is driven to fight for the cessation of torture in Guatemala, as well as the revelation of the truth around the American government's involvement in that torture.

For Ortiz, this journey involved years of nonviolent protest, resistance, petitioning politicians, letter writing, reliving her atrocities for numerous governmental bodies in Guatemala and America, cofounding the Torture Abolition and Survivors Support Coalition, which became a global movement, and embarking on a vigil and hunger strike across from the White House seeking the declassification of all US government documents related to human rights abuses in Guatemala. When Ortiz's vigil succeeded, the files released were heavily redacted and did not reveal the identity of the American torturer (named only as Alejandro to Ortiz) or by what authority he had access to the scene of her torture. But Ortiz's case became part of a massive review of American foreign policy and eventually led to the revelation that an Indigenous genocide occurred in Guatemala and was supported by the American government out of fear of a communist uprising.

Eventually Ortiz begins to see God in the beauty of the world again. Fittingly, it is on a trip to Italy and in the city of Assisi, the home of Saint Francis, that Ortiz experiences God in nature: "The warmth, the fields, the light—nature itself was a healing source. For me the beauty was a sign that God had not died, that God was there."[18] In seeing God all around her, Ortiz is able to release the feeling of unworthiness, of shame bestowed upon her by her captors and those who denied the truth of her brutal torture for so many years.

To see the divine beauty of the world, in others, and in the earth necessitates seeing it in the self and allowing the self to become an agent of divine love, inspired by all the times that others showed divine love and mercy when they may have wielded force. This necessitates a life of social justice, of ethical care for others and the careful, thoughtful construction of a politics wherein the truth is always the most important thing to give to all people. As in Weil, this is not necessarily a dramatic or easy fix. It is a slow, thoughtful life of balance between grace and affliction that allows for the opening in oneself that can experience divine love and enact social justice. In Sister Dianna Ortiz's own words:

> I have forgiven God for not working some dramatic miracle. I've learned that God was working a quiet miracle all along, healing me through other people. I still have the horrible past with me—I carry it in my memory and in my skin and I always will—but laid over it, like new skin over a wound, is a newer past, a past of caring and love.[19]

Notes

1 I follow Roncalli's use of scene as an appearance in the political. For Weil, philosophy should involve ethical action that is closely related to Arendtian political action. Weil sets this ethical political action into actual scenes in her unfinished play, *Venice Saved* (VS).
2 I reference Sister Ortiz with warm thanks to Ron Collins, who brought my attention to her death in 2021 and noted the Weilian nature of Sister Ortiz's work.
3 According to Rowan Williams, Weil's philosophy suggests that "God is loved to the extent to which creation is destroyed." See Rowan Williams, "The Necessary Nonexistence of God," in *Simone Weil's Philosophy of Culture: Readings Toward a Divine Humanity*, ed. R. H. Bell (Cambridge: Cambridge University Press, 1993), 72. An emphasis on Weil's death and a misreading of her concept of decreation as a literal destruction rather than a spiritual transformation have caused further criticism that is often unfounded in both her work and the historical facts of her life. For example, see Francine du Plessix Gray, "At Large and at Small: Loving and Hating Simone Weil," *American Scholar* 70, no. 3 (2001): 8. www.jstor.org/stable/41213171. Also see Judith Gregory, "A Letter to Simone Weil," *Cross Currents* 40, no. 3 (1990): 368. www.jstor.org/stable/24459577. And see Claire Wolfteich, "Attention or Destruction: Simone Weil and the Paradox of the Eucharist," *Journal of Religion* 81, no. 3 (2001), 359. www.jstor.org/stable/1206400. The assertion that Weil debases the material world in favor of the divine is disputed by Eric Springsted, who argues that Weil does reconcile the

disjunction between body and spirit through the theory of mediation; her theology emphasizes Christ's role as mediator and ultimately seeks to overcome duality. The emphasis on interconnection with the earth offered by Springsted strikes me as the most productive and generous reading of Weil's life, but also the most accurate portrayal of her work. See Eric O. Springsted, *Christus Mediator: Platonic Mediation in the Thought of Simone Weil* (Chico, CA: Scholars Press, 1983), 8.
4 Roberto Esposito, *The Origin of the Political: Hannah Arendt or Simone Weil?* trans. Vincenzo Binetti and Gareth Williams (New York: Fordham University Press, 2017), 5.
5 Ibid.
6 See Simone Pétrement, *Simone Weil: A Life*, trans. Raymond Rosenthal (New York: Pantheon Books, 1976). For her visit to Germany, see p. 137. For the Spanish Civil War, see p. 268.
7 This is by no means unique to Weil, and the politics of agonism is a relevant branch of political philosophy, including Giorgio Agamben, *Homo Sacer* (Stanford: Stanford University Press, 1998); Hannah Arendt, *The Human Condition* (Chicago: University of Chicago Press, 1998); Bonnie Honig, *Political Theory and the Displacement of Politics* (Ithaca, NY: Cornell University Press, 1993); and Chantal Mouffe, *Agonistics: Thinking the World Politically* (New York: Verso, 2013).
8 This critique is taken up by Rowan Williams when he notes that Weil's ethical work on otherness suggests that "the necessarily frustrated subject, the limited point of view, is somehow the source of error, a corruption of some potentially divine subjectivity only thinkable for us in terms of negation, passivity, absence, death" (Williams, "The Necessary Nonexistence of God," 72). Williams herein articulates the frequent critique of Weil's decreation: her ethics of otherness seems to come at the expense of the existence of the I.
9 For more, see Friedrich Nietzsche, "European Nihilism," in *The Will to Power*, trans. Walter Kaufman and R. J. Hollingdale, ed. Walter Kaufmann (New York: Random House, 1967), 9–84.
10 Nietzsche, despite his notion of *amor fati*, does not choose love as his ultimate goal but the will to power, which leads to a dramatically different ethical imperative.
11 See note 3 for examples of these critiques.
12 Quoted in Sister Dianna Ortiz and Patricia Davis, *The Blindfold's Eyes: My Journey from Torture to Truth* (Maryknoll, NY: Orbis Books, 2002), 117.
13 Ibid., 15.
14 Ibid., 50.
15 Ibid., 127.
16 Ibid., 133.
17 Ibid., 39.
18 Ibid., 444.
19 Ibid., 475.

Bibliography

Esposito, Roberto. *The Origin of the Political: Hannah Arendt or Simone Weil?* Translated by Vincenzo Binetti and Gareth Williams. New York: Fordham University Press, 2017.
Gregory, Judith. "A Letter to Simone Weil." *Cross Currents* 40, no. 3 (1990). www.jstor.org/stable/24459577.

Nietzsche, Friedrich. "European Nihilism." In *The Will to Power*. Translated by Walter Kaufman and R. J. Hollingdale. Edited by Walter Kaufmann. New York: Random House, 1967, pp. 9–84.

Ortiz, Dianna, and Patricia Davis. *The Blindfold's Eyes: My Journey from Torture to Truth*. Maryknoll, NY: Orbis Books, 2002.

Pétrement, Simone. *Simone Weil: A Life*. Translated by Raymond Rosenthal. New York: Pantheon Books, 1976.

Plessix Gray, Francine du. "At Large and at Small: Loving and Hating Simone Weil." *American Scholar* 70, no. 3 (2001). www.jstor.org/stable/41213171.

Springsted, Eric O. *Christus Mediator: Platonic Mediation in the Thought of Simone Weil*. Chico, CA: Scholars Press, 1983.

Williams, Rowan. "The Necessary Nonexistence of God." In *Simone Weil's Philosophy of Culture: Readings Toward a Divine Humanity*. Edited by R. H. Bell. Cambridge: Cambridge University Press, 1993, pp. 52–76.

Wolfteich, Claire. "Attention or Destruction: Simone Weil and the Paradox of the Eucharist." *Journal of Religion* 81, no. 3 (2001). www.jstor.org/stable/1206400.

Chapter 7

REROOTING "WE REFUGEES": CONSIDERATIONS ON CONDITIONS OF DISPLACEMENT FROM HANNAH ARENDT AND SIMONE WEIL

Scott B. Ritner

Introduction

Both Hannah Arendt and Simone Weil lived as refugees, though their experiences as refugees were quite different. Arendt was forced to flee multiple times: from Germany to France (via Czechoslovakia and Switzerland) to the United States (via Portugal). She became a US citizen in 1950. Weil fled twice as well, but under different conditions. She fled from Paris to Marseilles during the 1940 German invasion and then to the United States (through Morocco) with her family. Unlike Arendt, Weil did not stay in New York. She traveled to London, where she worked with the Free French Forces for nine months until her death in England on August 24, 1943.

In 1943 both Weil and Arendt turned their attention to the conditions of their exile. Arendt's influential essay "We Refugees" appeared in the *Menorah Journal*, and Weil wrote her magnum opus, *The Need for Roots*, by request of the Free French about how to address the "trades union" question after liberation. Two figures from these asymmetrical texts, Arendt's short essay and Weil's monograph, form the foundation of this chapter. These figures are Arendt's refugee and Weil's déraciné. In this chapter, I will argue that the refugee and the déraciné are interrelated figures.

These subjectivities are relevant to the global migration crises in the twenty-first century.[1] There is no continent or region where there is not currently a migrant crisis complete with detention centers, border walls, refugee camps, destinations, through routes, natural barriers, rafts, border guards, human trafficking, kidnapping, humanitarian catastrophe, deportations, and so on. In this chapter, I mobilize Weil's and Arendt's interrelated subjectivities to challenge nationalist conceptions of belonging that rely on borders and documentation. It is an attempt—at a level of abstraction—to critique the state as the arbiter of identity by presenting the refugee as an intensification of the déraciné. I am compelled by the political question of what it means to cross a state border, especially a border that has been arbitrarily imposed by imperialist violence.[2] Such movements of people demand an examination of belonging.

The barriers to belonging that Arendt and Weil contest in 1943 are now bounded by post-1945 legal demarcations such as refugee and asylee, both of which stand apart from the term undocumented. In "We Refugees" and *The Need for Roots*, Arendt and Weil challenge the legitimacy claims of the state to make these demarcations. I will argue that Weil and Arendt's critiques serve as grounds upon which to challenge the policies of governments across the globe to hold migration at bay and punish those who cross or attempt to cross borders. In my parochial interest in critiquing US border regimes, it is important to note that these regimes are in effect at internal borders (of Native Reservations) and the northern border as well the border with Mexico that dominates public imagination[3] and lead to the abrogation of the declared republican values of the US state. The US state, as all states do, gives primacy to the restriction of claims to belonging thereby rejecting the liberal ideology to which it portends.

Bringing Weil and Arendt into conversation is important for thinking the imbrication of the refugee and the déraciné from the comfortable position of one born in a country that so many seek to arrive in and who is so unwilling to accept those who seek it.[4] No history of those fleeing religious persecution justifies the serial and systematic exclusion of those who seek refuge today. The shared history and founding mythologies of the United States and Israel as places to emigrate to for religious freedom is neither invalid nor politically accidental. These are the conditions from which US citizens cannot escape, but which citizens may be able to change. It is, then, imperative that there is a clear understanding of the subjective complexity of the refugee and the déraciné and a political basis for solidarity with refugees and the otherwise uprooted. Such solidarity[5] is necessary from a political standpoint, not only in the context of the current refugee crises but also in the context of the refugee crises to come as rising seas, climate catastrophes, neoimperialist economics, neoimperialist violence, internecine racism and terrorism, and extractive industry drive more and more people to migrate each year.

In relation to each other, Arendt's refugee was conceived as a specifically Jewish subjectivity, while Weil's déraciné is, at the very least, a modern European subjectivity, if not a universal category. Both Weil and Arendt's Jewishness and the Jewishness of their specific experiences as refugees from Nazi Germany and Nazi-Occupied France is germane to their experience and to their theorization, but it does not negate the universal possibilities of Arendt's refugee and the generality of Weil's déraciné. On the one hand, Arendt explicitly names the Jews of Europe as her archetypical refugee. On the other hand, Weil denotes deracination as something that touches everyone at different historical moments; diasporic Jews are only one example. As such, Weil suggests a virus-like spread of deracination through modernity and defines both oppression and resistance through the subjectivity of the déraciné.

My contribution is twofold: first, I introduce Weil's déraciné as a historically conditioned subject of modernity in *The Need for Roots*. Following that, I take up a systematic four-part analysis of Arendt's description of the refugee as a specific political subject in her essay "We Refugees," which I contextualize as an intensification of the déraciné. I then offer suggestions as to how deracinated solidarity with refugees may be practiced in the recent context of the Mexico-US border.

Weil's Déraciné

The déraciné is uprooted, but may not be geographically so, nor are they necessarily stateless. The déraciné is a subjectivity uprooted in oppression, one form of which is exclusion. Deracination is, at the very least, a European category universalizable for the purposes of understanding both a politics of uprootedness and a basis for political action. The déraciné is the living embodiment of the condition of modernity. In some way or another, humans are all uprooted; some more so than others, some as victims of violence or their inheritors, some as violators or their inheritors, still others ambiguously. What makes the déraciné universal in a time of migration is that it includes both domestic and international migration as well as those who are not uprooted geographically but are politically, culturally, linguistically, or otherwise displaced. Weil's déraciné inhabits a status as much as they do a place. They are the antihero of *The Need for Roots*.[6]

The Need for Roots is, among other things, a genealogical reconstruction of the French State from the centralization drive of Cardinal Richelieu through the Nazi conquest in 1940. Weil writes French history as a catalog of deracination within the "tradition of the oppressed."[7] Her diagnosis is that deracination has overcome France both by its own hand and through the Nazi occupation.

Deracination is the origin, in revolution and destination, via the imposition of national borders and resultant displacement, of the bourgeois state. For Weil, the state is not a steadying force that protects humanity from a condition of instability and war, as it is for Hobbes. Rather, the state realizes its potential only by bringing a great deal of instability to society through its destruction of free association among workers and peasants. Deracination in the wake of the creation of the modern state is a result of the twin forces of political and capital centralization, which include colonialist practice at home and abroad.[8] It was under Richelieu that the pacification of regional distinctions and the displacement of peasant populations took place. "His devotion to the State uprooted France. His policy was to kill systematically all spontaneous life in the country, so as to prevent anything whatsoever being able to oppose the State" (NR 115).[9] Weil's critique brings attention to the deracinating effects of the state—in this case personified in Richelieu—which acts as the conqueror of itself both in periods of expansion and consolidation, as Plato described in *The Laws*.[10]

The Need for Roots takes as its frame a monadic elision of centralization, assimilation, and imperialism inasmuch as they are the contributing factors to deracination. Weil argues that this is glossed over by the ideological guise of ersatz republicanism. She denotes the historical figures of Joan of Arc and the Cathar heretics of Oc as her models for the organized working classes of France both during the Nazi occupation and in her compromised utopian postwar France (NR 103–4). Force, as a central figure of history, is shown to be pernicious and ever present in the development of the modern nation and the modern state, as well as its radical extension in the fascism of both the Nazis and the French themselves.

The déraciné is a product of deracination, and so an understanding of the former as a historical process is necessary for a definition of the latter. Deracination can be understood as the historical product of the contradiction between Rousseau's narrative of fallenness in the *Discourse on the Origin of Inequality*—in which the advance of civilization is also the advance of unfreedom and human hardship—and Weil's diagnosis of the French State's idea of itself as the inheritor of Roman glory (NR 47, 140, 227). Both modernity and empire bring uprootedness. Weil writes of deracination: "The modern superstition of progress ... is bound up with the destruction of the spiritual treasures of those countries which were conquered by Rome, ... the idea of progress became laicized; it is now the bane of our times" (NR 227). According to Weil, the French State had always understood itself as the inheritors of the Romans (SE 102; NR 140).

This historical self-identification with Rome includes the identification as an imperial power, and Weil criticizes France without remorse for its "colonial greediness," which she includes among those "factors which have contributed to our defeat" (NR 86). In one of her more conservative claims, Weil argues that deracinated populations spread deracination. However, this mirrors her argument that the destructive centralization under Richelieu is the same as the destruction of overseas colonialism. She thus anticipates agreement with Frantz Fanon's claim that fascism is colonialism in the metropole (NR 81, 147).[11]

Whether at home or abroad, the oppressive implications of deracination in Weil's thought are heavily mediated by the state. The state both mediates the actual process of deracination, creating new collectivities of control and violence on the ruins of the old collectivities that provided roots, and in the process positions itself as the mediating agent that decides on the question of who does and does not belong. In other words, the narrative of deracination can be understood as a narrative of domestic colonization (or imperial colonization), or considering Weil's Platonism, it requires an understanding of the state as the conqueror of itself.[12]

Deracination can be understood as the confluence of historical social forces: centralization, colonialism, war, migration of all sorts, shifting borders, so-called primitive accumulation, capitalist accumulation, and the emergence of the modern state. Having explored the historical causes of deracination, it is of use to define rootedness and its absence. Weil defines rootedness explicitly, writing:

> To be rooted is perhaps the most important and least recognized need of the human soul. It is one of the hardest to define. A human being has roots by virtue of his real, active, and natural participation in the life of a community which preserves in living shape certain particular treasures of the past and certain particular expectations of the future. This participation is a natural one, in

the sense that it is automatically brought about by place, conditions of birth, profession and social surroundings. Every human being needs to have multiple roots. (NR 43)

Deracination is defined negatively as the absence of this real and active participation in multiple, pluralistic communities. The déraciné has been defined negatively, as a product of historical forces, to this point. Let us try to define them positively as well.

The organization of *The Need for Roots* delineates three interrelated forms of deracination: that of the workers, the peasants, and the nation. None of these three can be excluded from the other, as can be seen by the causes of deracination above. However, these three forms are distinct.

The deracination of the workers is related to their alienation from the means and ends of their labor, their coworkers, and themselves. Weil writes, "The French working-class movement which came out of the revolution was essentially a cry, less one of revolt than one of protest, in the face of the pitiless hardship of the lot reserved for all the oppressed" (NR 54). The revolutionary impulse of the deracinated, by her estimation, would only cause further deracination—as it did in the Soviet case—and thus protest without expectation of revolution must take its place to avoid the vicious circle. The urban déracinées are a revolutionary class without access to revolutionary politics.

Deracinated workers are cultureless in that they are robbed of their time by work itself. For Weil this makes the déraciné "a thinking being, for one hour or two, and a slave for the rest of the day," which "is such an agonizing spiritual quartering" that the weight of it cannot be overcome (NR 71). This forces the urban déracinées into a kind of idolatry, directing them into the throes of totalitarian cults of personality like those surrounding Hitler and Stalin.

In the early twenty-first century as in the mid-twentieth century, it is necessary to pay as much heed to rural deracination as urban deracination. A hesitant Marxist,[13] Weil cautions that "one should never bestow any public mark of attention on industrial workers, without bestowing another one of corresponding importance on the peasants" (NR 78). Rural deracination is more geographically based than that of the workers, and Weil's analysis is drawn from observations of both hinterland and empire. It is the peasant déraciné who is uprooted physically, as well as politically and morally. Forced off their lands by large-scale agriculture and absentee landlords, the peasant déraciné is uprooted and made into a migrant in their own right—if they are forced into the city or from the colonial or postcolonial state to a metropolitan one, this deracination is intensified.

Weil's déraciné is a tragic figure. On the one hand, they are an oppressed subject of modernity. On the other hand, they are an agent of further uprootedness. As individuals, déracinées have the potential to form collectives and to thereby reform society in their own image as a universal collectivity of the uprooted, an alliance of proletarians, peasants, and migrants of all sorts. As a collectivity in the throes of idolatry, deracinated nations experience uprootedness against the possibility of this universal character. Instead of being a baseline for a politics of hospitality toward Arendt's refugee, the deracinated nation pulls the ladder up behind themselves. The déracinées of the uprooted nation are drawn toward idolatry and perpetuate the violence that has been done on them. When the situation has reached such a point, the relative positions of the roots and the trunk of the trees have been swapped. Those collectivities that are meant to be roots are trunks, and the individuals meant to be trunks are roots. The universality of this position in modernity is the hyper-individualization of capitalist social organization and the subjugation of the individual by totalitarian ideologies and states. Because Weil leaves the déraciné as a revolutionary subject without access to revolutionary politics in *The Need for Roots*, she leaves this contradiction in *aporia*.

Weil's déraciné presents as the condition of modernity. By virtue of being in the state or being in relation to the state, the déraciné is exposed to differing degrees of violence or histories of violence. It does not flatten the difference between the lived experience of colonized subjects and the subjectivities of the colonizers because it offers these two subjectivities as relations vis-à-vis the histories of internal and imperial colonization. Furthermore, it offers a basis for the understanding of each legal person—that is, one who currently enjoys the right to have rights—as a potential refugee in the making. The refugee is the intensification to the level of the absolute of the déraciné. Both of which can in a Weilienne framework draw attention to both the new kind of human being (in its even newer formulation) that is encapsulated in Arendt's refugee subjectivity and, at the same time, the human being, as such.

Arendt's Refugee

The four elements of Arendt's conceptualization of the refugee are (1) the optimist, (2) the assimilationist (or the cosmopolitan patriot), (3) the politicized life, and (4) the Dachshund and the St. Bernard. Each of these elements provides a distinct moment in her 1943 essay "We Refugees." These four elements of the refugee are photographs of deracinated subjectivities imposed by the modern state on modern subjects. The refugee, as a hyper-déraciné, is a subjectivity and experience that Weil and Arendt shared in 1943.

The particular form of deracination that Arendt and Weil experienced in 1943 was based on a fundamental aporia—that they are both friends and enemies, prospective citizens and temporary residents, victims in need of aid and the representatives of an ongoing war all at the same time. Arendt's aporia, irresolvable as it is, is reducible to its identifying trait as a "new kind of human being—the kind that are put in concentration camps by their foes and in internment camps by their friends" (JW 265). The wartime crisis of deracination presented the world with a new kind of human being whose subjective qualities are constantly being renegotiated.

This new kind of human being is a subject in that they are subject to a state and a certain set of laws without their consent. In this sense they are *subjected* to the coercive forces that cause them to seek refuge and the coercive forces they encounter at the borders and in the interiors of the states that conditionally take them in. This new kind of human being is also a subject in the sense that they are constrained from the possibilities of living an autonomous life of their own choosing.[14] They are subjected to a particular set of social mores and expectations as the condition of their life as such because they must take refuge in order to live at all. This subject is, in part, defined by its "dangerous readiness for death" (JW 266). A readiness learned from the dire situations they needed refuge from.

What kind of person has the capacity, Arendt asks, to leave their home, even if the threat of violence and death is ever present?[15] It is the optimist who believes, despite evidence to the contrary, that they will have rights again (JW 264–7). They are convinced that they will become citizens and look forward to the day with hope. There is an interminable longing in the optimist that is dashed by their historical conditions. Their belief that they, personally, have done nothing wrong and therefore deserve no punishment is constantly tested, and their optimism relies very much on their ability to overcome what Arendt calls "mysterious shortcomings" in their own character (JW 268). This optimistic element of the subject we call the refugee must believe in themselves because the world has turned its back on them.

This optimistic refugee is a déraciné who does not want to be a refugee, preferring the terms newcomer or immigrant (JW 264). The optimistic déraciné goes from country to country being saved and expelled over and over, each time refashioning themselves as the most heartfelt patriots and trying to repair their uprootedness with new attachments. Both now and then, Arendt's refugees are seeking to rebuild their lives after they have lost their homes. But rebuilding in each place requires an entirely new identity. This is the second moment of Arendt's new refugee subject: the optimist is a Jew who does not want to be a Jew because, in that historical moment, the refugees of the world were the Jews (JW 271). They want to be something else entirely; they seek to be subject to something, tied to something in an endless state of hopefulness and anticipation, never tiring of being disappointed, no longer a perpetual other. And being an optimist, they desire to anesthetize their Jewishness because that is the only way to anesthetize their refugee status and become the kind of subject that has the right to have rights—the kind of subject who is limited by some sort of national persuasion pursuant to their belonging to a state.

So a German Jew becomes a Czech patriot, becomes an Austrian patriot, becomes a French patriot (even when the French government considers them an enemy alien), becomes an American patriot (even when the US government considers them a temporary refugee) all in an attempt to become a subject who has the right to have rights, a settled identity, and a reliable future—in other words to no longer be a déraciné (JW 271). The optimist desires to be rooted in those identities they once had as a Jew and a German coincidentally. Every subject who has achieved what the optimist desires, even if only nominally and fleetingly, reinforces their optimism that it will last, if only they are loyal enough. It is this cosmopolitan patriotism that Arendt identifies as being particularly Jewish in her times.

However, this assimilationist tendency is, most certainly, complicated by the historical formation of migrant and diasporic cultural frames and, thus, has a universal capacity rather than a specifically Jewish one. Whereas it was one thing to become an American as a German Jew, and quite another to become a Jewish American, the same can be said about the migrant communities of contemporary times. It is certainly one thing to be a Honduran refugee; it is quite another to be a Honduran American in both the legal and the subjective senses. My purpose here is not to reify the arbitrary boundaries of citizenship and nationality but instead to point out that the social relationship between the human being and what we call them is mediated, at least in the eyes of the state, by this distinction. While, on the one hand, migrant communities offer the sounds, tastes, and concerns of the motherland, there is, at the same time, a double assimilation that takes place, wherein cultural realities are flattened or smoothed in order to create a coherent national community.[16]

Arendt describes the desperate trading of each patriotism for the next as based on the material reality of *needing to be saved*, some multiple times. She writes: "The more optimistic among us would even add that their whole former life had been passed in a kind of unconscious exile and only their new country now taught them what a home really looks like" (JW 265). But even for this assimilationist subject, the cosmopolitan patriot, leaping from patriotism to patriotism, is not an autonomous choice. Because in 1943 these refugees, rather than being political exiles (for bad behavior), are a new kind of refugee and the definition of the refugee was changing along with them to mean "those of us who have been so unfortunate as to arrive in a new country without means and have to be helped by refugee committees" (JW 264). The need to curry favor and prove oneself to one's new country and new hosts at every turn becomes increasingly important. One's social standing and one's status are inextricably linked.

The assimilation of each new patriotism is an act of fulfilled optimism and an act of desperation at the same time. And so, Arendt's refugee subject gets a little bit clearer: the optimist who seeks to have rights again is simultaneously the cosmopolitan patriot who fleetingly trades loyalty for the partial fulfillment of the rights the optimist desires. Each concurrent act of optimism and desperation—for Arendt—builds tension in the *aporia* between who one has been, who one is, and who one wishes to become, namely a subject with rights.

Here, Hagar Kotef's problematization of how to act when one's material conditions are based in the deracination of a people or peoples is brought into relief.[17] Two further questions must be asked: (1) what is identity when the state is the primary actor in defining hospitality and hostility? And (2) is this identity an intensification of the condition of modernity that is deracination?

As such, this requires the introduction of the third element of Arendt's new refugee subjectivity. One could say that this element is a necessary condition of the new subjectivity that is at stake in this essay, perhaps it is even *the* sufficient condition. This is the subject who does not have the right to have rights. In other words, this subject had rights and is without rights in their new home. Because this subject once had rights, the refugee, the immigrant, the newcomer has left family and friends behind in dangerous conditions. But they left because the conditions from which they fled were not within their control, or because something about those conditions changed, became dangerous, and made fleeing from those conditions into uncertainty and internment by their potential saviors more attractive than staying at home.

But this new home still regarded them differently. The more optimistic they were, the more likely their otherness was to be noticed. Their lives became completely politicized. Whether it is their existence within the exceptional conditions of the internment camp or the simple act of shopping for groceries with accented English (JW 269). Their rightlessness is total not only because they wish for their rights to return but also because they once had what they now so desperately want.

And with each turn, the diasporic statelessness of the Jewish people intensified, if only because it had been ever so fleetingly overcome in the late nineteenth and early twentieth centuries with the origin of the modern European state and emancipation of the Jews. Perpetually excluded from the right to have rights, there is a necessity to "disguise an imaginary stigma" (JW 273). Each act becomes political. For example, the former self-construction of difference for the purpose of community and solidarity becomes the basis for exclusion and persecution not only by the native people (native in the lowercase sense of one born into citizenship of a certain state, thereby overlapping but not synonymous with the Indigenous) but also by the very same community they wish to be a part of, or could be seen to be a part of by the native community. Arendt gives the example of the Jews arriving in France and being called "Polaks" by the French and "*Jaekes*" by the assimilated French Jews. But the children of the assimilated Jews also call these newcomers "Polaks." The bonds of solidarity among Jews (even though they are Jews from Germany and Poland rather than from Hungary and Russia, or France itself) are broken down, and even in Jewish society, the individual must prove and reprove themselves again and again (JW 270–1). This collective origin is overinterpreted and therefore misinterpreted.

This third element of refugee subjectivity is the deracinated politicized life. It is both Jewish and universal. It is also the most extreme position of the déraciné that is the refugee; the *aporia* of politicization—of being categorized but not belonging, of being officially unofficial—is perhaps the most complicated reality in Arendt's essay. Beyond the general assimilation in each concurrence of cosmopolitan patriotism, there is a second reconstruction of each individual narrative that also becomes necessary. This third element of refugee subjectivity opens the aporia between the human being and the great man (JW 270). Which makes up the content of what I see as the fourth element of Arendt's refugee subject.

Arendt presents this subjectivity to her reader in the parable of the Dachshund who was once a Saint Bernard. When the bonds of solidarity in the past and the prospects for it in the future are broken and clouded, respectively. It is in these moments that the refugee reconstructs their narrative based not on where they have been but on what they have done.

Arendt's parable gives us a look at the affective experience of feeling small and disconnected when formerly living a life in which one's status was not constantly in question. The refugee was once somebody to their neighbors, to their friends, and to society. In reconstructing their own narrative of how they came to be stateless and how they desire to be a subject with rights again, there is a desire to make what was once a human into a "great man" because, it is in fact easier to become that than it is to simply be a human being. To have a past that is spectacular gives the promise of a future that is equally bright when one has been stripped down to bare life.

Because of their prior deracination, this great individual did not realize that their greatness was only in relation to that context in which they lived until their hyper-deracination upon being made a refugee. And so, the great individual's problem is a way of keeping themselves as well as their saviors and potential future friends distracted from their original identities, namely their identity as a universalized déraciné, a Jew, and a refugee.

To recap the four elements of the refugee in Arendt's essay: the first is the optimist, the subject who wishes to have rights. The second is the uprooted patriot, the one who assimilates in order to have at least the proximity to rights but remains essentially rightless. The third is the rightless figure *in quod*, the politicized human being who has nothing but their own life. And the fourth is the subject who has lost their rights and wishes to return in some way from their current position as a human being (which is difficult) to their previous socially rooted life as a great individual. Each of these intensifies the deracination that is the condition of modernity, making its potential threats to life and limb very, very real.

This yearning for greatness drives the refugees into despair, and the stable déraciné into idolatry and totalitarianism. This yearning is a hallmark of Weil's déraciné and Arendt's refugee—it is indicative of a mutual lack of rootedness. So why such drastically different results from the universal condition and the intensified status of being officially unofficial? Is the refugee fated to be detained or repatriated by the déraciné? The current policies of the governments of the United States, Australia, and European Union suggest that this is likely. And it is not for nothing that these three, among others, are deeply implicated in settler colonial histories of uprooting.

Suggestions in Lieu of Conclusions

What I am suggesting here is that the refugee and the déraciné can be understood as asymmetrical reflections of each other in a sort of carnival mirror in which one sees themselves recognizably and settled but simultaneously foreign and unrecognizable. I further suggest that this reflection may be the basis for a profound political hospitality by the déraciné toward the refugee.

The possibilities for hospitality are opened by the asymmetrical uprootedness of those who have the capacity to give sanctuary and those who need it. The déraciné who is not a refugee may have the right to have rights but only contingently—déracinées are always only one legal decision away from being rightless themselves. Thus, there is also an asymmetrical reflection of material vulnerability between the déraciné and the hyper-deracinated refugee. At the border, the refugee is devoid of protections, whereas in the déraciné's homeland or adopted home, they (the déraciné and the refugee) are instead under threat of losing protections they have. The significance of this distinction is massive and, as Weil and Arendt's studies in subjectivity unmask, dangerously contingent.

These reflections negatively define the relationship between the merely deracinated déraciné and the hyper-deracinated refugee. In the positive, as a source of potential hospitality, the narrative structure of Weil's déraciné serves as a corrective to the lines of distinction drawn between the person born in a certain place or the citizen and the refugee or the migrant. Conceiving of ourselves in our historical condition (especially in settler colonies and the postcolony, but also in the internally colonized European states), there is the promise of a radical openness to hospitality rather than from a more amorphous and prefigurative ethical demand to simply not oppose the arrival of newcomers.

In addition to her critique of the state and the explication of deracination, Weil does put forward a positive conception of political action that can be taken by uprooted collectivities, though it does not result in rerooting. The upshot of her pessimistic attitude toward the revolutionary act of rerooting is that acts of hospitality toward and solidarity with those who are more violently uprooted make one "acquire a taste for helping those in misfortune, it is clearly a good thing" (NR 210). It is reasonable to wonder if Weil's déraciné, like Arendt's refugee, can locate hospitality within the context of the state itself. In *The Need for Roots*, hospitality is consistently found outside of the state, and hospitality is therefore an abolitionist act against the state and borders. Transitively, this makes hospitality an abolitionist act against the refugee as a formal legal category, but not as a politically lived experience (NR 120, 127).

This hospitality is based on a reflection in which the distinction between the universal déraciné and the specific form of déraciné that is the refugee is observable. By understanding the refugee as the intensification of the déraciné, political linkages demand more than mere sympathy. Remembering that the déraciné, like the refugee, is a historically conditioned subject rather than an ontological subject, it is then a position from which action can be taken. Indeed, those who are uprooted, in the minimal sense, may act in ways that refuse to allow the state to determine who is and is not someone deserving of a future. If enacted, this solidarity can be a sort of siege laid upon the state at its points of entry and regulation of refugees.

The proliferation of No Borders camps and activism, especially in Europe, which aim to aid refugees and migrants in both attaining material needs and making political demands on the states they wish to cross into, is an example of this. In March of 2019, as a migrant camp was being built on the Tijuana–San Diego border of Mexico and the United States, there were calls by the Border Angels for antiborder activists to gather there and provide material and political aid to migrants. In February 2022, the migrant camp in Tijuana was cleared by the Mexican government with bulldozers. Border Angels, as an activist organization, strategically places provisions of water and food in the deserts of the southwestern

United States for migrants who are risking everything to cross the US–Mexican border. As deracinated citizens of imperial and postimperial powers, these activists mobilize to aid refugees and other migrants. In doing so, they take up the challenge of deracinated solidarity I argue for in this chapter.

Notes

1 These articles and subjectivities have significance for the politics of the SARS-CoV-2 vaccination drives in the United States and elsewhere. Republican Senator Ted Cruz attempted to add an amendment to the Covid-19 relief bill excluding undocumented migrants from vaccination eligibility. The Democratic party also only supported vaccine availability for legal residents and had written the bill that way. The idea that a respiratory disease could not spread from an undocumented resident to a documented one is preposterous.
2 Ariella Aïsha Azoulay, *Potential History: Unlearning Imperialism* (New York: Verso, 2019), 33.
3 This is documented with exquisite precision by the Kanien'kehá: ka anthropologist Audra Simpson in her book *Mohawk Interruptus*. See Audra Simpson, *Mohawk Interruptus: Political Life across the Borders of Settler States* (Durham, NC: Duke University Press, 2014). Other Native scholars, including Nick W. Estes and Roxanne Dunbar-Ortiz, have taken up this point in their work as well. I am grateful to two undergraduate students at SUNY Potsdam—John George (who, like Simpson, is Kanien'kehá: ka) and Corina Tulevich—for codesigning and reading through an independent study on Native American politics with me in spring 2022.
4 See Hagar Kotef, "Fragments," *Critical Inquiry* 44, no. 2 (2018), 343–9.
5 I use this term in the way it has been generally used in the socialist/communist/anarchist tradition to which, I argue elsewhere, Weil certainly belongs. It is worth noting that Weil's relationship to this conception is not without some hesitancy: in a conversation hosted by Incite Seminars, Kenny Novis brought to my attention that Weil offers a critique of solidarity as a formulation of "la première personne du pluriel [the first-person plural]" in her essay on "The Pythagorean Doctrine." See Simone Weil, *Intuitions Pré-chrétiennes* (Paris: Gallimard, 1951), 140. See also Scott B. Ritner, "Simone Weil's Heterodox Marxism: Revolutionary Pessimism and the Politics of Resistance," in *Simone Weil, Beyond Ideology?*, ed. Sophie Bourgault and Julie Daigle (New York: Palgrave, 2020), 185–206 .
6 For considerations on heroism and greatness in *The Need for Roots*, see Scott B. Ritner, "Against Greatness," *Theory & Event* 26, no. 2 (April 2023). As Arendt describes in *The Human Condition*, a hero is no one more than someone about whom a story is told. See Hannah Arendt, *The Human Condition* (Chicago: University of Chicago Press, 1998), 184.
7 Walter Benjamin, "On the Concept of History" and "Paralimpomena to 'On the Concept of History,'" in *Selected Writings, Vol. 4: 1938–40* (Cambridge, MA: Belknapp Press, 2006), 392, 394, 403.
8 Frantz Fanon described fascism as domestic colonialism in *The Wretched of the Earth*, trans. Richard Philcox (New York: Grove, 2004), 48.
9 My emphasis.
10 Plato, *The Laws*, trans. Trevor J. Saunders (New York: Penguin, 2004), 627a.

11 Fanon, *The Wretched of the Earth*, 48.
12 Plato, *The Laws*, 627a.
13 Ritner, "Simone Weil's Heterodox Marxism."
14 Kwame Anthony Appiah, "Stereotype and the Shaping of Identity," *California Law Review* 88, no. 1 (January 2000), 41–53.
15 Arendt was quite familiar with Hobbes's *Leviathan*. In *Leviathan* the implications of the "rational passion" that is the fear of violent death is both an existential imperative and also the constitution of the Leviathan itself. This framework is the basis for many subsequent state theories in which the fear of violent death even goes so far as to justify the creation of the subject via conquest, or rather through the sovereign allowing the subject. Thomas Hobbes, *Leviathan with Variants from the Latin Edition of 1668*, ed. Edwin Curley (Indianapolis, IN: Hackett, 1994), book II, chapter XX.
16 Jewish American communities are particularly intriguing in this regard, dominated as they are by Ashkenazi cultural practices and those who present as white to the point of outward exclusion of Sephardic communities and Jews who do not have European ancestry.
17 Hagar Kotef, "Fragments," *Critical Inquiry* 44 (Winter 2018), 343.

Bibliography

Appiah, Kwame Anthony. "Stereotype and the Shaping of Identity." *California Law Review* 88, no. 1 (January 2000): 41–53.

Arendt, Hannah. *Jewish Writings*. Edited by Jerome Kohn and Ron H. Feldman. New York: Schocken, 2008.

Azoulay, Ariella Aïsha. *Potential History: Unlearning Imperialism*. New York: Verso, 2019.

Benjamin, Walter. "On the Concept of History" and "Paralimpomena to 'On the Concept of History.'" In *Selected Writings, Vol. 4: 1938–40*. Cambridge, MA: Belknapp Press, 2006, pp. 389–411.

Fanon, Frantz. *The Wretched of the Earth*. Translated by Richard Philcox. New York: Grove, 2004.

Hobbes, Thomas. *Leviathan with Variants from the Latin Edition of 1668*. Edited by Edwin Curley. Indianapolis, IN: Hackett, 1994.

Kotef, Hagar. "Fragments." *Critical Inquiry* 44, no. 2 (2018): 343–9.

Plato. *The Laws*. Translated by Trevor J. Saunders. New York: Penguin, 2004.

Ritner, Scott B. "Simone Weil's Heterodox Marxism: Revolutionary Pessimism and the Politics of Resistance." In *Simone Weil, Beyond Ideology?* Edited by Sophie Bourgault and Julie Daigle. New York: Palgrave, 2020, pp. 185–206.

Ritner, Scott B. "Against Greatness." *Theory & Event* 26, no. 2 (April 2023).

Simpson, Audra. *Mohawk Interruptus: Political Life across the Borders of Settler States*. Durham, NC: Duke University Press, 2014.

Weil, Simone. *Intuitions Pre-Chretienne*. Paris: Gallimard, 1951.

Chapter 8

ATTENTION AS A CONTESTED ETHICAL AND POLITICAL RESOURCE: SIMONE WEIL AND HANNAH ARENDT ON THE INNER ORIGINS OF FREEDOM

Paolo Monti

Digital Public Sphere and Attention Economy

In the past decade, the impact of social media on the public sphere of democratic societies has fostered a debate on new forms of manipulation of public opinion. In a digital "regime of visibility,"[1] access to the flow of information and communication is ubiquitous and pervasive. What matters the most, in this context, is not the now widespread ability to fabricate and disseminate claims, images, and symbols but rather the capacity to orient the public's attention toward some of them. Social media is, in this sense, a grand technology of attention that establishes a powerful form of communicative intermediation by training the gaze of an immense public worldwide and then reselling it for commercial and political purposes.[2]

In some ways, the new digital public sphere carries impressive democratic potential. Any individual with basic technological means can now reach a global audience, thus generating massive phenomena of political mobilization. From the perspective of deliberative and participatory democracy, this appears as an extraordinary chance to pursue higher standards of political transparency and widespread direct involvement, consistently with the ideal of the public use of reason cherished by the tradition of the Enlightenment. However, as recent political trends have shown, populist movements, authoritarian leaders, and conspiracy theorists have been, in fact, the most effective at exploiting these new systems worldwide. Their communication is well paired with the inner workings of social media, as the populist style of simplification, emotionalization, and negativity operates in tune with the dopamine-driven feedback mechanisms upon which these platforms are designed. Consequently, their political message performs very efficiently in this new kind of "attention economy," whereas experts and traditional information providers are regarded with suspicion.[3]

This trend has led many observers to speak of a crisis of democracy, as the traditional institutions of political representation struggle to adapt and populist movements rise to power in several countries around the globe.[4] The conundrum at the heart of this crisis is that this more accessible individual participation of citizens in global spaces of publicity seems to bring about new forms of authoritarian rule more than it creates innovative forms of democracy. This threat poses systemic problems concerning the structures and regulations of the digital public sphere, but also points to matters of the ethics of citizenship concerning the conditions of free and responsible individual agency in this transformed political sphere.

To pursue these ethical questions, we need an appropriate philosophical framework to connect individual attention, moral conduct, and the risk of collective political unfreedom. In these pages, we seek such a framework in Simone Weil's and Hannah Arendt's explorations of the concept of attention. During the most troubled years of the twentieth century, both authors experienced how the joint effect of the unprecedented political participation of the masses and the advent of new forms of communication and propaganda could lead to the rise of nationalist sentiments and authoritarian leaders. And both authors, through different paths, came to reflect on how deeply attention is related to the precarious conditions of individual moral judgment and the risk of collapse of the democratic polity.

Simone Weil: Attention as Nonacting Action

Simone Weil's writings highlight the importance of attention as a renunciation to the superficial illusions of will and choice to pursue a selfless and receptive disposition toward truth, beauty, and goodness, "the authentic and pure values in the activity of a human being" (NB 449). By shaping our ability to establish an undivided relationship with those values, attention produces a moral disposition to avoid evildoing:

> That action is good which we are able to accomplish while keeping our attention and intention totally directed towards pure and impossible goodness, without veiling from ourselves by any falsehood either the attraction or the impossibility of pure goodness. …
>
> The attention turned with love towards God (or in a lesser degree, towards anything which is truly beautiful) makes certain things impossible for us. Such is the non-acting action of prayer in the soul. There are ways of behaviour which would veil such attention should they be indulged in and which, reciprocally, this attention puts out of the question. (NB 416)

Attention, therefore, is an elevated kind of individual agency that detaches the agent from the threat of social idolatry and reshapes their commitments and behaviors accordingly. This has important political implications, since not all forms of political engagement are equally compatible with it. In her critique of political parties, Weil illustrates how the claims on the party activist's attention raised by collective mechanisms of identification and belonging end up being incompatible with a proper dedication to public interest:

> The goal of a political party is something vague and unreal. If it were real, it would demand a great effort of attention, for the mind does not easily encompass the concept of the public interest. Conversely, the existence of the party is something concrete and obvious; it is perceived without any effort. Therefore, unavoidably, the party becomes in fact its own end. This then amounts to idolatry, for God alone is legitimately his own end … . It is impossible to examine the frightfully complex problems of public life while attending to, on the one hand, truth, justice and the public interest, and, on the other, maintaining the attitude that is expected of members of a political movement. The human attention span is limited—it does not allow for simultaneous consideration of these two concerns. In fact, whoever would care for the one is bound to neglect the other … . Even for those who do not compromise their inner integrity, the existence of such penalties unavoidably distorts their judgment. (APP 10)

Weil here characterizes attention both as a quantitative resource, a limited supply that needs to be spent appropriately, and as a qualitative property of one's judgment, an attitude that needs to be cultivated and protected, especially against the dominating mechanisms of political propaganda.[5] The origins of any political action that is genuinely free from the pressure of collective movements lie in solitary contemplation and meticulous studies, whose higher purpose is not to accumulate knowledge but rather to train our disposition to be fully attentive. Ultimately, the fruit of attention is the ability to act lovingly, a creative act that stems from a focus on what is absent from our immediate engagements with reality:

> Love for our neighbor, being made of creative attention, is analogous to genius.
> Creative attention means really giving our attention to what does not exist. Humanity does not exist in the anonymous flesh lying inert by the roadside. The Samaritan who stops and looks gives his attention all the same to this absent humanity, and the actions which follow prove that it is a question of real attention. (WG 149)

In times dominated by collective dehumanizing tendencies, it takes a considerable effort of attention to see the dignity of humanity in the suffering of others and to direct personal and collective action toward the realization of that humanity.[6] This effort, however, is not about exerting one's will but rather about cultivating a pure desire for that which is absent, and it calls for our action, especially when its realization appears beyond our reasonable reach: "All true good carries with it conditions which are contradictory and as a consequence is impossible. He who keeps his attention really fixed on this impossibility and acts will do what is good" (NB 410).

Hannah Arendt: Thinking Attention as Precondition for Judgment

The concept of attention appears in Hannah Arendt's late writings, especially *The Life of the Mind*. In her reading of Augustine's *Confessions*, she highlights the role of attention as a specific form of interaction between will and intellect through which the self comes to properly connect sensations and reality and to jointly understand past, present, and future, thus transcending the incessant flow of fleeting impressions and desires:

> We can see without perceiving, and hear without listening, as frequently happens when we are absent-minded. The "attention of the mind" is needed to transform sensation into perception; the Will that "fixes the sense on that thing which we see and binds both together" is essentially different from the seeing eye and the visible object ... In other words, the Will, by virtue of attention, first unites our sense organs with the real world in a meaningful way, and then drags, as it were, this outside world into ourselves and prepares it for further mental operations: to be remembered, to be understood, to be asserted or denied. For the inner images are by no means mere illusions. (LM 100)

Attention establishes a meaningful relationship between the "inner human" and the object of their consideration; on this premise, it is then possible to take a stance when facing the world, to assert or deny it. It is in this sense that the exercise of attention establishes the conditions of individual agency:

> This Will could indeed be understood as "the spring of action"; by directing the senses' attention, presiding over the images impressed on memory, and providing the intellect with material for understanding, the Will prepares the ground on which action can take place. (LM 101)

Arendt appreciates how this Augustinian perspective illuminates the origins of our ability to formulate judgments. She could not complete the section of *The Life of the Mind* specifically devoted to *Judgment*, but we nonetheless have some clues about her ideas on the matter. In her introduction to the section on *Thinking*, she illustrates her intentions with an almost word-by-word reprise of a passage from the essay "Thinking and Moral Considerations," published in *Responsibility and Judgment* in 1971. Here she reconsiders the phenomenon of the banality of evil and comes to characterize Eichmann's thoughtlessness specifically as a lack of "thinking attention":

> Inconsistencies and flagrant contradictions in examination and cross-examinations during the trial had not bothered him. Cliches, stock phrases, adherence to conventional, standardized codes of expression and conduct have the socially recognized function of protecting us against reality, that is, against the claim on our thinking attention which all events and facts arouse by virtue of their existence. If we were responsive to this claim all the time, we would soon be exhausted; the difference in Eichmann was only that he clearly knew of no such claim at all. This total absence of thinking attracted my interest. Is evil-doing, not just the sins of omission but the sins of commission, possible in the absence of not merely "base motives" (as the law calls it) but of any motives

at all, any particular prompting of interest or volition? ... Is our ability to judge, to tell right from wrong, beautiful from ugly, dependent upon our faculty of thought? (RJ 160)

Arendt is interested in thinking through attention because of its role in our ability to form proper moral judgments, regardless of the particular subject at stake:

Could the activity of thinking as such, the habit of examining whatever happens to come to pass or to attract attention, regardless of results and specific content, could this activity be among the conditions that make men abstain from evil-doing or even actually "condition" them against it? (LM 5)

In this context, attention displays, again, distinct quantitative and qualitative properties. It is quantitative, as it is characterized as a resource that can be exhausted by overstimulation from the constant claims of the world, but also left untapped. And it is qualitative, as it is a thinking kind of attention, best cultivated in solitude that allows one to differentiate between right and wrong (LM 75).

Attention and Totalitarian Mechanisms: Derealization and Uprooting

Weil's and Arendt's characterizations of attention differ in some relevant ways. For Weil, attention is not an active effort of the will but a selfless desire, a hollowing of human faculties by renouncing their constant engagement with immediate purposes and social attachments and opening up to the highest values. This operates an ethical and political deliverance of the agent, which is outright impossible to achieve as a voluntary effort. The roots of political agency are spiritual, Weil argues, contrary to the assumptions of the revolutionary projects of the Enlightenment: "Freedom without supernatural love—that of 1789—is entirely empty, a simple abstraction, with no possibility of ever becoming real" (NB 466).

Arendt's dealings with the concept draw directly from Augustinian sources; therefore, they construe attention as an active expression of the human faculties.[7] Attention is here a mode of the will, a unifying effort of the self that actively gathers its faculties around its object, thus preparing the conditions for a thoughtful judgment and, subsequently, a just action. At a political level, the ability to resist the call of totalitarian rule is grounded upon this capacity to freely formulate thoughtful moral judgments: "Those few who were still able to tell right from wrong went really only by their own judgments, and they did so freely ... They had to decide each instance as it arose, because no rules existed for the unprecedented" (EJ 295).

Despite these differences, Weil's and Arendt's perspectives also hold striking similarities. Both appreciate the quantitative, resource-like properties of attention and its qualitative aspects as well. Both identify attention as an inner prerequisite for the formulation of value-based moral judgments that exceed the mere application of general rules to specific situations. Both, finally, frame a meaningful connection between the exercise of attention and the ability to resist sociopolitical mechanisms of idolatry and conformity.

Their convergent understandings of attention are useful to also make sense of their compatible views about the inner workings of the totalitarian machine, as highlighted by Roberto Esposito:

> For both authors, this machine tends toward the annihilation of human presence via the double yet combined procedure of the derealization of that which exists, in conjunction with the ideological construction of a world that is so false that the real appears to be unbelievable. Once deprived of any notion of reality, men are ready for the experience of uprooting and subsequent deportation that consequently allows totalitarianism to reach its ultimate goal; that is, to treat them like things in order to render them "superfluous."
>
> Both authors explain that this is made possible through the arrest of thought—Weil expresses it more specifically in terms of the faculty of attention—which brings about a collapse in the boundary between good and evil that is specifically designed to render each category the mirror image of the other.[8]

As shown above, the "arrest of thought" is actually characterized in terms of attention by Arendt as well, at least in some of her late writings. In this sense, not only both authors point toward the phenomena of derealization and uprootedness as fundamental gears of the ideological and totalitarian machines, but they also both come to the conclusion that attention is a focal point where these machines interact with the individual mind and push it toward the collapse of its ability to formulate moral judgments.

The notion of derealization highlights how social mechanisms create a buffer between the individual mind and reality, to the point of gradually substituting tangible communal experiences with a shared unreality whose dwellers are more easily distracted and misdirected. According to Weil, this trait is present in most modern ideologies: utilitarianism, economic liberalism, Marxism, and Nazism. Each of these "rests upon the supposed existence of a wonderful little piece of mechanism thanks to which force, on entering into the sphere of human relations, becomes an automatic producer of justice" (NR 236). But this is a fundamental lie for Weil. All these mechanisms are just blind manifestations of force that cannot automatically create justice, since justice can only be the outcome of conscious human agency:

> Where force is absolutely sovereign, justice is absolutely unreal. Yet justice cannot be that. We know it experimentally. It is real enough in the hearts of men. The structure of a human heart is just as much of a reality as any other in this universe, neither more nor less of a reality than the trajectory of a planet. (NR 237)

It is in this sense that, according to Weil, the goals of political parties are "unreal": they exhaust the attention of their followers through constant demands of engagement with collective mechanisms, in exchange for an ideological unreality that will never come to pass. Arendt's portrait of Eichmann shows a person deeply integrated into such a mechanism: his "cliches, stock phrases, adherence to conventional, standardized codes of expression and conduct" fulfill their function of shielding him "against reality" and neutralizing his "thinking attention," as he is entirely committed to operating efficiently within the bureaucratic machine in the pursuit of inhumane goals he seems unable to morally question (RJ 160).

Derealization is the antechamber of uprootedness. Weil observes that, detached from the claim of genuine human values and immersed in the mechanisms of social idolatry, the citizens have their roots severed from the "real, active and natural participation in the life of a community which preserves in living shape certain particular treasures of the past and certain particular expectations for the future" (NR 40). The role of attention is, again, crucial in this process that shrinks the width and depth of one's thinking and binds the individual to the here and now of the inner workings of the social machine.[9] Arendt echoes the image of uprootedness in her observations over the "nonradical" nature of the greatest evils. The kind of evil enacted by those who actively cooperated with the Nazis lies on the surface of history; it has no conscious connection with a deeper understanding of one's past or one's future; it is favored by isolation, superficiality, and indifference:

> The greatest evildoers are those who don't remember because they have never given thought to the matter, and, without remembrance, nothing can hold them back. For human beings, thinking of past matters means moving in the dimension of depth, striking roots and thus stabilizing themselves, so as not to be swept away by whatever may occur—the Zeitgeist or History or simple temptation. The greatest evil is not radical, it has no roots, and because it has no roots it has no limitations, it can go to unthinkable extremes and sweep over the whole world. (RJ 95)

In the face of derealization and uprootedness, what is morally required is thus an exercise of attention that goes in the exact opposite direction from the abandonment to the social mechanisms of force: the creative miracle of fixating on the reality of those human values that can only be brought into existence through our free agency,[10] the task of continually reconnecting our human interactions with the moral resources that are available to our conscious judgment.

Digital Platforms and Democratic Crisis: An Interpretive Framework

Based on the analysis conducted so far, let us reconsider our initial intent: to draw from Weil's and Arendt's work to articulate a philosophical frame that connects attention, individual conduct, and the risk of collective political unfreedom in a way that is useful to address the undemocratic tendencies of the contemporary digital public sphere. The articulation of this framework has both an interpretive and a normative side. There is an interpretive side, because Weil's and Arendt's notions of derealization and uprootedness offer valuable insights to clarify some of the salient political phenomena determined by the impact of media technologies. And there is a normative side, because their characterization of attention is useful for defining some ethical demands of citizenship in this context.

The promise of a surge of democratic participation and transparency on the wings of the global disintermediation operated by the internet appears now appropriately framed by the Weilian warning against "the supposed existence of a wonderful little piece of mechanism thanks to which force, on entering into the sphere of human relations, becomes an automatic producer of justice" (NR 236). The subtle reintermediation of the public sphere operated by social media platforms has been consistently connected to phenomena that disrupt the democratic process through the viral circulation of fake news, the proliferation of conspiracy theories, and the increasing polarization of the citizenry.[11] In all these phenomena, the new media are often found to be operating as social mechanisms that create a buffer between the individual mind and its dealings with reality, to the point of gradually building a shared unreality where people are more easily distracted and misdirected by actors that have the influence and expertise to exploit the inner workings of the digital environments. The circulation of false and fabricated information has an obvious misdirecting impact on the attention of citizens, whose focus is shifted toward inexistent threats and alternative versions of the events. But, in turn, the citizens' lack of attention is also actively enacting this misdirection: in a series of studies on social media behaviors, Pennycook and others have observed that users' inattention is one of the main factors that accelerate the diffusion of fake news and that, conversely, the activation of people's attention on the accuracy of their beliefs reduces their individual contribution to the circulation of misleading information.[12] On the digital platforms, the citizens are both recipients and emitters: they are subject to competition for their attention, but they also actively enhance or corrupt the epistemic properties of the communicative environment based on the quality of attention with which they partake in it.

These forms of derealization via distraction and misdirection support corresponding phenomena of uprooting via belief polarization. As social media algorithms push interaction among like-minded users to maximize their engagement, the circulation of fake news and conspiracy theories among them gradually generates social circles that function as echo chambers and prioritize affiliation over information and deliberation.[13] Robert Talisse has highlighted how civic polarization is built upon belief corroboration: citizens interacting within the same group tend to hold the same beliefs more and more intensely and to adhere to an increasingly extreme version of those beliefs, not as a response to a change in the justificatory resources available to them but as a consequence to the constant corroboration of those beliefs they receive from other group members.[14] As Weil observed in political parties, the mechanisms of belonging inside echo chambers have a claim on the individual attention that trumps any focus on the substance of what is actually in the public interest.[15] Social media are fertile ground for collective corroboration, and the affiliations that emerge in that environment end up overpowering other connections entertained by the citizens: family ties, bonds of civic friendship and solidarity, communities of practice, local communities all get internally segmented along the lines of polarized political boundaries.[16] In this sense, increasing levels of civic polarization signal a contemporary form of uprooting: the rise of collective forms of belonging with no deep roots in the history of a community but rather grounded upon Arendtian phenomena of "thoughtless" adherence to collective symbols, slogans, and conventions that shield from the complexity of society.

Disguised Domination and Citizens' Freedom: An Ethics of Attention

If we consider this interpretive framework through the lens of nondomination theory, it appears that the joint influence of derealization and uprooting exposes the citizens to the arbitrary influence of political leaders, identity groups, and authoritarian institutions that exert their mastery through the strategic use of mechanisms of distraction, misdirection, and corroboration enabled by this new form of media. Similar to the historical moment contemplated by Weil and Arendt, our times see the rise of unprecedented forms of political participation but also reveal the fragility of the citizens' attention, which becomes arguably the most contested ethical and political resource. Once this resource is dispersed and appropriated, the citizens remain apparently immersed in a public space of communication and exchange but are effectively deprived of their freedom. This form of domination is, indeed, particularly insidious as it disguises the manipulation of the citizens' capacity of judgment under an illusion of discursive control. According to Philip Pettit's influential characterization of the concept, to be in discursive control one must meet two requirements: "the ratiocinative capacity to take part in discourse" and "the relational capacity that goes with enjoying relationships that are discourse-friendly."[17] The first requirement is threatened by the contemporary forms of derealization, like the circulation of fake news and conspiracy theories, which introduce important cognitive distortions in the ethical and political thinking of citizens. The second requirement is endangered by the contemporary forms of uprootedness, with echo chambers and phenomena of civic polarization fragmenting the political community as a unified community of conversation.

In the light of the role of attention within these phenomena of derealization and uprooting, we can specify two conditions for the exercise of the citizens' discursive control to be defended from this form of disguised domination: first, a condition of detachment from mechanisms of attention manipulation; second, a condition of civic friendship grounded in the awareness of one's coimplication with the humanity of others. The fulfillment of these conditions depends not only on systemic arrangements but also, crucially, on the individual disposition and conduct of the citizens. The detachment condition needs to be supported by regulating the mechanism of digital intermediation through which social media platforms exploit the public attention for commercial and political purposes, but it can be fully realized only when the citizens preserve and nurture their capacity for reflexiveness, understanding, and judgment. The civic friendship condition needs to be supported by public education, civil society activism, and political participation, but it can be fully realized only when the citizens remain open to consciously engaging with interlocutors across their polarized political boundaries.[18] In this sense, Weil and Arendt's lesson suggests that the conditions of enduring freedom and solidarity in a political community encompass a commitment of its members to an ethics of citizenship that is, in relevant ways, an ethics of attention. In their account, attention has both quantitative and qualitative properties, and both dimensions are indeed morally relevant.

From a quantitative perspective, attention is a scarce but vital resource of citizenship whose protection is increasingly essential in order to preserve the conditions of democratic rule. Exceeding or falling short of what is right in the use of this resource can be construed, in Aristotelian terms,[19] as a pair of opposite epistemic vices that expose the citizen to an increased risk of domination. More specifically, we can speak of a civic virtue of attentiveness as a means between an Arendtian vice of lack of attention, which she stigmatizes in Eichmann's insensibility toward the claims of humanity and his lack of any motive, and a Weilian vice of excessive attention, which she sees embodied in the political party activist whose attention is entirely absorbed by the commitment to group affiliation. As we have noted, both these tendencies find relevant contemporary correspondences in experiences of distraction and inattention on one side, and phenomena of corroboration and polarization on the other.

The virtuous measure of attention for the citizen, however, is not a purely quantitative middle ground between untapped or exhausted individual resources. For both Weil and Arendt, the quality of attention is revealed in the ability to give weight to the singular reality of values in our human interactions despite their conspicuous absence from the mechanisms of human sociality. Thinking attention destroys any automatism, and "this destruction has a liberating effect" on our "faculty to judge particulars without subsuming them under those general rules," without reiterating unexamined habits or enacting thoughtless group mentalities (RJ 188–9). The virtuous exercise of attention enables a counterprocess of realization and rooting: attentiveness shields the citizens' judgment from what is pushed on them through demands of constant engagement to rather focus on values that are missing from those concrete circumstances as well as respond to the call for their realization.[20] In Arendt's words, "When everybody is swept away unthinkingly by what everybody else does and believes in, those who think are drawn out of hiding because their refusal to join is conspicuous and thereby becomes a kind of action" (RJ 188). The political significance of the civic virtue of attentiveness is, therefore, mainly negative: it establishes attention as a site of resistance against domination and thus creates the conditions for the formulation of moral judgments that, ethically, make "certain things impossible for us" (NB 504) and, politically, "may prevent catastrophes ... in the rare moments when the chips are down" (RJ 189). The citizens' political freedom as discursive control is dependent, now perhaps more than ever, on the inner origins of this individual capacity to resist.

Notes

1 See Marie-José Mondzain, *Le Commerce des Regards* (Paris: Éditions du Seuil, 2003).
2 The recent literature on the systemic importance of attention management for the global economy and politics is multifaceted. Among others, see Christopher Mole, Declan Smithies, and Wayne Wu (eds.), *Attention. Philosophical and Psychological Essays* (Oxford: Oxford University Press, 2011); Wayne Wu, *Attention* (London: Routledge, 2014); Tim Wu, *The Attention Merchants* (New York: Alfred Knopf, 2016); Claudio Celis Bueno, *The Attention Economy. Labour, Time, and Power in Cognitive Capitalism* (Lanham, MD: Rowman and Littlefield, 2017); Peter Doran, *A Political Economy of Attention, Mindfulness and Consumerism* (London: Routledge, 2017); Paul Atchley and Sean M. Lane (eds.), *Human Capacity in the Attention Economy* (Washington, DC: American Psychological Association, 2020).
3 See Yochai Benkler, Rob Faris, and Harold Roberts, *Network Propaganda: Manipulation, Disinformation, and Radicalization in American Politics* (Oxford: Oxford University Press, 2018); Jan A. G. M. van Dijk and Kenneth L. Hacker, *Internet and Democracy in the Network Society* (London: Routledge, 2018).
4 See Nadia Urbinati, *Me the People. How Populism Transforms Democracy* (Cambridge, MA: Harvard University Press, 2019).
5 Weil was an acute observer of how new forms of media and new styles of political communication were used to suppress freedom: "Collective pressure is exerted upon a wide public by the means of propaganda. The avowed purpose of propaganda is not to impart light, but to persuade. Hitler saw very clearly that the aim of propaganda must always be to enslave minds. All political parties make propaganda. A party that would not do so would disappear, since all its competitors practice it" (APP 16).
6 This connection between attention and solidarity in the thought of Simone Weil is widely explored in Robert Chevanier, *Simone Weil. L'attention au réel* (Paris: Michalon, 2009).
7 For a thorough investigation of the influence of Augustine in Hannah Arendt's action theory and moral philosophy, see Stephan Kampowski, *Arendt, Augustine, and the New Beginning* (Grand Rapids, MI: Wm. B. Eerdmans, 2008).
8 Roberto Esposito, *The Origin of the Political. Hannah Arendt or Simone Weil?* (New York: Fordham University Press, 2017), 3.
9 It is the case of the exploited members of the working class: "There are social conditions in which an absolute and continuous dependence on money prevails—those of the wage-earning class, especially now that piece-work obliges each workman to have his attention continually taken up with the subject of his pay. It is in these social conditions that the disease of uprootedness is most acute" (NR 41).
10 This understanding of free agency as bringing into existence what is of value against any apparent necessity is also consistent with the Arendtian concept of natality: "The miracle that saves the world, the realm of human affairs, from its normal, 'natural' ruin is ultimately the fact of natality, in which the faculty of action is ontologically rooted. It is, in other words, the birth of new men and the new beginning, the action they are capable of by virtue of being born" (HC 247).

11 See Cass R. Sunstein, *#Republic: Divided Democracy in the Age of Social Media* (Princeton: Princeton University Press, 2017).
12 See Gordon Pennycook and David G. Rand, "The Psychology of Fake News," *Trends in Cognitive Sciences* 25, no. 5 (2021), 388–402; Gordon Pennycook et al., "Shifting Attention to Accuracy Can Reduce Misinformation Online," *Nature* 592 (2021), 590–5.
13 See Emanuele Brugnoli et al., "Recursive Patterns in Online Echo Chambers," *Scientific Reports* 9, art. 20118 (2019); Matteo Cinelli et al., "The Echo Chamber Effect on Social Media," *PNAS* 118, no. 9 (2021), 1–8.
14 See Robert Talisse, *Overdoing Democracy: Why We Must Put Politic in Its Place* (Oxford: Oxford University Press, 2019), 95–127.
15 The Weilian concept of attention entails, instead, a pluralization of public and political discourse; see Shari Stone-Mediatore, "Attending to Others: Simone Weil and Epistemic Pluralism," *Philosophical Topics* 41, no. 2 (Fall 2013), 79–95.
16 A significant literature about the effects of political polarization on families and local communities is developing. See Shanto Iyengar, Tobias Konitzer, and Kent Tedin, "The Home as a Political Fortress: Family Agreement in an Era of Polarization," *Journal of Politics* 80, no. 4 (2018), 1326–38; Benjamin R. Warner, Colleen Warner Colaner, and Jihye Park, "Political Difference and Polarization in the Family: The Role of (Non)accommodating Communication for Navigating Identity Differences," *Journal of Social and Personal Relationships* 38, no. 2 (2021), 564–85.
17 Philip Pettit, *A Theory of Freedom: From the Psychology to the Politics of Agency* (Oxford: Oxford University Press, 2001), 70.
18 For an interesting analysis of the relationship between attention and polarization that articulates Weilian concepts in support of deliberative democracy, see Pascale Devette and Jonathan Durand Folco, "Retrouver la réceptivité: écoute, attention et résonance pour débattre dans un monde polarisé," *Éthique publique* 22, no. 1 (2020).
19 See *Nicomachean Ethics*, 1108b11: "There are three kinds of disposition, then, two of them vices, involving excess and deficiency respectively, and one a virtue, namely, the mean": Aristotle, *Nicomachean Ethics* (Oxford: Oxford University Press, 2009), 34.
20 Arendt frames this as a structural connection between thinking and judging, consciousness and conscience: "Judging, the by-product of the liberating effect of thinking, realizes thinking, makes it manifest in the world of appearances, where I am never alone and always much too busy to be able to think" (RJ 189).

Bibliography

Aristotle. *Nicomachean Ethics*. Translated by David Ross. Edited by Lesley Brown. Oxford: Oxford University Press, 2009.

Atchley, Paul, and Sean M. Lane, eds. *Human Capacity in the Attention Economy*. Washington, DC: American Psychological Association, 2020.

Benkler, Yochai, Rob Faris, and Harold Roberts. *Network Propaganda: Manipulation, Disinformation, and Radicalization in American Politics*. Oxford: Oxford University Press, 2018.

Brugnoli, Emanuele et al. "Recursive Patterns in Online Echo Chambers." *Scientific Reports* 9, art. 20118 (2019).

Bueno, Claudio Celis. *The Attention Economy: Labour, Time, and Power in Cognitive Capitalism*. Lanham, MD: Rowman and Littlefield, 2017.
Chevanier, Robert. *Simone Weil. L'attention au reel*. Paris: Michalon, 2009.
Cinelli, Matteo et al. "The Echo Chamber Effect on Social Media." *PNAS* 118, no. 9 (2021): 1–8.
Devette, Pascale, and Jonathan Durand Folco. "Retrouver la réceptivité: écoute, attention et résonance pour débattre dans un monde polarisé." *Éthique publique* 22, no. 1 (2020).
Doran, Peter. *A Political Economy of Attention, Mindfulness and Consumerism*. New York: Routledge, 2017.
Esposito, Roberto. *The Origin of the Political: Hannah Arendt or Simone Weil?* New York: Fordham University Press, 2017.
Iyengar, Shanto, Tobias Konitzer, and Kent Tedin. "The Home as a Political Fortress: Family Agreement in an Era of Polarization." *Journal of Politics* 80, no. 4 (2018): 1326–38.
Kampowski, Stephan. *Arendt, Augustine, and the New Beginning*. Grand Rapids, MI: Wm. B. Eerdmans, 2008.
Mole, Christopher, Declan Smithies, and Wayne Wu, eds. *Attention: Philosophical and Psychological Essays*. Oxford: Oxford University Press, 2011.
Mondzain, Marie-José. *Le Commerce des Regards*. Paris: Éditions du Seuil, 2003.
Pennycook, Gordon, and David G. Rand. "The Psychology of Fake News." *Trends in Cognitive Sciences* 25, no. 5 (2021): 388–402.
Pennycook, Gordon et al. "Shifting Attention to Accuracy Can Reduce Misinformation Online." *Nature* 592 (2021): 590–5.
Pettit, Philip. *A Theory of Freedom. From the Psychology to the Politics of Agency*. Oxford: Oxford University Press, 2001.
Stone-Mediatore, Shari. "Attending to Others: Simone Weil and Epistemic Pluralism." *Philosophical Topics* 41, no. 2 (Fall 2013): 79–95.
Sunstein, Cass R. *#Republic: Divided Democracy in the Age of Social Media*. Princeton: Princeton University Press, 2017.
Talisse, Robert. *Overdoing Democracy: Why We Must Put Politic in Its Place*. Oxford: Oxford University Press, 2019.
Urbinati, Nadia. *Me the People. How Populism Transforms Democracy*. Cambridge, MA: Harvard University Press, 2019.
van Dijk, Jan A. G. M., and Kenneth L. Hacker. *Internet and Democracy in the Network Society*. London: Routledge, 2018.
Warner, Benjamin R., Colleen Warner Colaner, and Jihye Park. "Political Difference and Polarization in the Family: The Role of (Non)accommodating Communication for Navigating Identity Differences." *Journal of Social and Personal Relationships* 38, no. 2 (2021): 564–85.
Wu, Tim. *The Attention Merchants*. New York: Alfred Knopf, 2016.
Wu, Wayne. *Attention*. New York: Routledge, 2014.

Part III

ART, AESTHETICS, AND THE VULNERABILITIES OF POLITICAL APPEARANCES

Chapter 9

PAYING ATTENTION TO AFFLICTION: HANNAH ARENDT AND SIMONE WEIL ON TRAGIC STORYTELLING

Pascale Devette

Introduction

The banning of the graphic novel *Maus* by Art Spiegelman from the school curriculum in Tennessee is but one example of a larger pattern of the silencing of stories featuring otherness.[1] In the context of the contemporary resurgence of extremist neo-Nazi organizations and other racist groups, this phenomenon of censorship is becoming increasingly dangerous.[2] Now more than ever, stories dealing with the notion of plurality and offering an experience of alterity are needed to contrast with the current atmosphere of ethnonationalism and the fear of the unknown, otherness, and the foreign.

As early as 1950, Hannah Arendt wrote that Auschwitz and the "death factories" represented radical changes to the basic conditions of human existence.[3] In response, *The Human Condition* offers a radical anthropology of freedom, one grounded in action, that attempts to confront and adjust to the new dangers of totalitarianism. There she addresses, at length, a number of pressing social and political quandaries that the existence of the camps imposes on political thought. This essay, however, focuses less on Arendt's account of action and more on the impact that the tragic experience of the concentration camps has had on Arendt's approach to storytelling.

My aim is first to show that, for Arendt, storytelling has the power to expose the suffering inherent in action and identify the realities of affliction and mourning in the world around us. In particular, I hope to make clear that the more our stories relate to notions of affliction and mourning, the greater our need to reconfigure not just our actions but also our ways of telling and receiving stories. On the one hand, I argue that there is an evident need to imbue our narratives with a strong idea of social justice, while, on the other hand, I argue that there is also a need to reconfigure our sense of receptivity. Being open to listening to stories of affliction is more demanding than other forms of story; it requires the extrication of the listeners from themselves in order to welcome otherness.

To better identify the challenges that prevent us from giving this kind of attention to storytelling, and to better understand the relationship between truth, silence, and affliction, I then turn to the work of Simone Weil. According to Weil,

> When affliction is seen vaguely from a distance, either physical or mental, so that it can be confused with simple suffering, it inspires in generous souls a tender feeling of pity. But if by chance it is suddenly revealed to them in all its nakedness as a corrosive force, a mutilation or leprosy of the soul, then people shiver and recoil. The afflicted themselves feel the same shock of horror at their own condition. (HP 332)

As Weil explains, we rarely pay attention to affliction, which is often hidden by good intentions, indifference, disgust, or even disguised by ideological justifications. As a result, affliction is hidden behind complex relations of power when it should be at the center of our political concerns.

Finally, I will study the accounts of some of the survivors of the concentration camps, in particular Primo Levi and Jean Améry, in order to illustrate how this "testimonial" literature invokes a unique form of exchange with the readers. It is extremely difficult to tell a story to try to give an account of what took place in the camps. Storytelling, thus, attempts to restore an experience deployed under the sign of absence where something is irremediably left out in the telling.[4] This loss calls for the listener to be attentive not only to what is said but also to what cannot be written and to consider the silent meanings behind the word, fundamental to the story. To get the whole story, listeners must be enabled to grasp the meaning of silences and fractures within the story. The words must let us perceive the perforating silence; they must be able to make us feel, in the present, what remains unfinished and untold in the story. The testimonial accounts of the Shoah illustrate, in a radical way, the importance of this transmission of silence.[5]

More than a simple "reactivation" of memory, this understanding of storytelling constitutes an attempt to bequeath a shared responsibility for future generations, as heirs not only of Auschwitz but also of Armenia, Hiroshima and Nagasaki, the Gulags, Rwanda, Bosnia and Herzegovina, Burma and, unfortunately, so many others. "Tragic stories," a term that can encompass the testimonial literature of genocides of all stripes, are haunted by the imperative to transmit experiences of unspeakable cruelty in the name of those who did not return. By bringing to the present experiences of silence and absence, these stories offer ethical and political reference points by which to ground ourselves as we move into the future. Tragic stories give an account of the disarray of the absurd death, just as they fight against the indifference toward anonymity that threatens the memory as soon as it becomes a comfort.[6]

Today, the comfortable space of anonymity threatens the potency of memory. One may wonder if the memory transmitted by the tragic stories of survival in the camps has been effectively received by subsequent generations. The last witnesses of the Nazi concentration camps are about to disappear, and there soon will be no one left alive to communicate those particular tragic stories. Eventually, the memory of the camps will become a subject of distant history, and all that will remain are the tragic stories, whose imperative of reception remains at issue. My hope is that, by engaging with the works of Hannah Arendt and Simone Weil and their respective accounts of storytelling, attention, and affliction, we can effectively reconfigure our approach to storytelling and the transmission of the tragically intransmissible. Methodologically, I will not seek to compare the thoughts of Arendt and Weil but rather try to complement one with the other in order to deepen our appreciation of the art of "tragic storytelling."[7]

Arendtian Storytelling: Revealing Action through Suffering

Discussing *The Human Condition*, Paul Ricœur writes that "the connection between action and story is one of the most striking themes of the whole treatise on *The Human Condition*."[8] Despite its importance to her larger vision, Arendt's account of the relationship between action and storytelling is somewhat convoluted, and it can be difficult to navigate the distinctions between action, speech, and storytelling. Moreover, Arendt is not always clear about the place of storytelling within her own conceptual constellations: is it a form of action, or is it a work of art? Is it primarily related to the public realm or to the private realm? Are there different kinds of stories? If so, what are they?

Much work has been done examining the link between storytelling and action in Arendtian scholarship.[9] Among those exploring this topic, Julia Kristeva proposes a concept of narrative that is directly rooted in the public space. As she understands it, storytelling is irresistibly drawn to the place of action, to the same public space, in order to complete the action by revealing its meaning.[10] Against the idea that the work of art ought to be confined strictly to the private sphere, Kristeva writes that "only action as narration, and narration as action, can fulfill life in terms of what is 'specifically human' about it."[11] Storytelling, thus, appears to be a form of *praxis* similar to acting, what we might call an "active telling." For Kristeva, action and narrative are consubstantial; they belong to the same essence.[12] For action to convey meaning, it needs to be narrated, and it can do so only as long as it continues to be depicted in the stories we tell. In this way, she complexifies Arendt's public sphere. By showing that action, although it cannot be reduced to any causality, is not wholly independent, Kristeva responds critically to classical interpretations of Arendt, such as those put forward by George Kateb and Hannah Pitkin, which pay little attention to the crucial element of storytelling in politics.[13]

From this vision of narrative as the other side of action, Kristeva reiterates that, for Arendt, "the art of narrative resides in the ability to condense the action into an exemplary moment, to extract it from the continuous flow of time, and reveal a *who* ... that is what a good story tells."[14] The main role of storytelling is to bring to light the agent, the *who* of an action, and to represent them in a relatable framework whose temporality will have more duration than the process of the action itself. Storytelling is a revelation of the agent that allows us to infinitely interpret and reinterpret what took place. And indeed, so many of our stories come back, again and again, to the feats of heroes whose greatness makes their lives ever tellable and significant.

The question Kristeva leaves open, however, is: what are we to make of testimonial stories that reveal neither an agent nor a heroic action but, on the contrary, attempt to give an account of a process of near-total destruction? How can we appreciate the testimonial narratives of those who were dispossessed of their agency, survivors whose stories represent the attempt to name an abyss even though the genocide has mutilated their language?[15] How is it possible to give an account of the *meaning* of the lives of people whose deaths were devoid of any *sense*? This is the difficulty of writing after the Shoah. As Giorgio Agamben reminds us, in the extermination camps "people did not die; rather, corpses were produced."[16] Death itself was deprived of its own meaning. How, then, can storytelling leave a mark of what took place when the operation of the concentration camps ensured the suppression of evidence?

While the question of how to write poetry after Auschwitz has been discussed at length by figures like Theodore Adorno, I would like to reflect more specifically on the storytelling aspect of narrative testimony.[17] In so doing, I want to show that testimony, at least a certain tragic form of it, betrays a crucially private dimension that redeploys the role of storytelling in politics. Rather than revealing a *who*, whose exploits are open to continuous reinterpretation, it is rather the impossibility of accounting for the *who* that is at stake in these stories. Instead of telling the meaning of a life by identifying its history in a relatable framework, tragic testimonials project a permanent gap between the unimaginable barbarism and the impossibility of attaching meaning to it. They neither reveal the greatness of a hero, nor do they give expression to an accomplished life. They instead try to transmit what remains intransmissible. Such stories, therefore, have a very different kind of political and individual effect than heroic stories.

If tragic stories are to play an essential role in the public sphere, their work must actually begin in the private sphere where they might challenge us to disengage from ourselves in order to encounter something different and, in so doing, develop within ourselves the capabilities of listening, care, and attention to otherness. Such stories encourage us to work on ourselves in private rather than expose ourselves in public. And the more they reveal the fragility of the world, the more they attempt to make the invisible visible and the inaudible audible, the more that they ultimately demand from us.

With this in mind, while I share Kristeva's emphasis on storytelling (or narrative), I am less interested in complexifying Arendt's notion of the public realm than in showing how Arendt's ideas about storytelling and narration allow us to reflect on the dignity of the private as a prepolitical space. Although this dignity may only be implied in Arendt's work, it nonetheless remains fundamental to her vision of human life and politics. Indeed, the Arendtian distinction between the private and the public realms (the "futility" of the former and the "dignity" of the latter) might not be as strict as many commentators have suggested.[18] Sharing this perspective, Patchen Markell proposes that we think about the art of Arendtian storytelling as a unique form of world-shaping work. For Markell, narrative, together with action, institutes "a relation of provocation and response between things in their meaningful appearances—not just walls or laws but artifacts of all sorts—and what we say about and do to them and the world they constitute."[19] It is in terms of this provocative relation that I want to interrogate the kinds of provocative relations that tragic narratives are able to instigate as they work to reveal experiences of grief.

Storytelling in general reminds us that art not only is intended for individual human beings or generations of human beings but also has a wider purpose. Stories belong, first and foremost, to "the world which is meant to outlast the life-span of mortals, the coming and going of the generations" (PF 207). They embody and sustain the *heart* of human life, not by producing any final lasting sense of meaning but by challenging readers to continuously engage with and reimagine the significance of a story that is not their own. Such stories contribute to the active search for the meaning of life rather than completion of it.[20]

Unlike action, art survives obscurity: it does not need to be seen or read to persist. Artworks can sometimes disappear from attention for centuries only to return with renewed meaning and impact. Similarly, many works of art have gone virtually unnoticed in their time of creation only to be discovered long after the death of its creator. It is this persistence that enables art to secure a lasting memory and a place for action long after its initial enactment. In fact, one of the dangers of placing narrative art on the side of the action is that it exposes it to the same kinds of vulnerabilities as action when its purpose is actually to redeem action from those vulnerabilities.[21]

Storytelling is intertwined with inner relationships and outer relationships that weave together the history of the world from a particular perspective. This interweaving is noticeable in *Men in Dark Times*, where Arendt examines at length the lives of different writers through political, literary, and biographical lenses.[22] Indeed, in addressing William Faulkner, Arendt reminds us that literature does not heal but rather highlights again and again what has not been looked at (or looked at too little, or badly). Arendt recalls that for Hermann Broch, "writer in spite of himself," art had the vocation and "the task to coin the world we live by" (MD 249). The story told in writing takes time that the word spoken in action does not require, but it is this slowness that enables it to have such an intense impact on us.[23] Arendt observes, for example, that it took "nearly thirty years" before Faulkner's *A Fable* displayed "the inner truth of the event," namely the First World War (MD 20). As she writes:

> The tragic hero becomes knowledgeable by re-experiencing what has been done in the way of suffering, and in this pathos, in resuffering the past, the network of individual acts is transformed into an event, a significant whole. The dramatic climax of the tragedy occurs when the actor turns into a sufferer; therein lies its peripeteia, the disclosure of the dénouement. But even non-tragic plots become genuine events only when they are experienced a second time in the form of

suffering by memory operating retrospectively and perceptively. Such memory can speak only when indignation and just anger, which impel us to action, have been silenced—and that needs time. (MD 20-1)

Only with time is action revealed in its full impact so that everything it has touched, everything it has modified, weakened, or even destroyed also comes to appearance. Because it narrates what happened, and because it shows the multiple entanglements, intricacies, and networks that make up the entire framework of a story, storytelling does not and cannot simply repeat an isolated action. It is only when time has passed that one can grasp the extent of what was played out. Even the actor, learning what she has done by listening to her own story, must relive her action in the mode of a suffering that she must endure. Paradoxically, it becomes visible in its totality only once the action itself has long since disappeared. Storytelling, thus, distances itself from life, always appearing after the fact, only when everything has already played out.

Arendt emphasizes this distinction between narrative and life in her analysis of Isak Dinesen (also known as Karen Blixen; MD 106).[24] Recalling the story of Dinesen's relationship with her first cousin, Hans Blixen, Arendt identifies a point of continuity (and as a kind of strange repetition) between her story and that of her father's, who was also deeply in love with his own cousin. Arendt suggests that the death of Dineson's father, which was a source of great suffering for the young woman, drove her to conceive of her own life in the image of the broken history between her father and his cousin. Dinesen's relationship with Blixen is said to be motivated by her ambition to restore a lost possibility, to connect with her father's wider family, and to make her life conform to the life of another, namely her father. Unsurprisingly, the relationship fails and the marriage does not last, and this part of Dinesen's life story appears as an utterly sterile moment in a wider narrative. What this strange episode reveals, however, is that stories are meant only to observe what has occurred, what has come and passed, and must not be treated as a model for life. To do so is to risk reducing freedom to a preconceived formula. Art, for Arendt, is not life and life is not art.[25] To confuse the two is to make a youthful error, one that, Arendt observes, appears again and again in Dinesen's writings. Indeed, Dinesen's tendency to conceive of life as "following a preconceived pattern" is repeated in other ways and transmitted in and through many of her short stories (MD 106).

In the end, Arendt takes two lessons from Dinesen's life and approach to storytelling:

While you can tell stories or write poems about life, you cannot make life poetic, live it as though it were a work of art (as Goethe had done) or use it for the realization of an "idea." Life may contain the "essence" (what else could?); recollection, the repetition in imagination, may decipher the sense and deliver to you the "elixir"; and eventually you may even be privileged to "make" something out of it, "to compound the story." But life itself is neither essence nor elixir, and if you treat it as such it will only play tricks on you. (MD 109)[26]

It was only as Dinesen approached fifty that she began to write. Under the effect of mourning lost love and the vanishing of her African freedom, writing seems to be a way for her to live her past over again. As Arendt explains, it was "the bitter experience of life's tricks" that prepared her "for being seized by the *grande passion* (great passion) which indeed is no less rare than a chef-d'oeuvre" (MD 109). The task of storytelling is not to repeat life but to transform it into something meaningful. By making memory tangible in writing, the meaning of our lives begins to emerge in a way previously unimagined. In Arendt's thought, without narrative, there would be no way of securing for posterity, a life, a history, or a world; memory would wither away as quickly as the individuals to whom they belong.

Of course, some stories, in particular those that speak of mourning and grief, create a real "tragic impact" on the establishment of meaning in our lives (MD 21). Arendt admits that she deliberately "mention[s] tragedy because it more than the other literary forms represents a process of recognition" (MD 20). For her, tragedy is a question of trying to recognize the meaning of life (not life itself), and the price of that story is that life. As she explains:

> [Story] is always the "dead letter" in which the "living spirit" must survive, a deadness from which it can be rescued only when the dead letter comes again into contact with a life willing to resurrect it, although this resurrection of the dead shares with all living things that it, too, will die again. (HC 169)

In tragic storytelling, it becomes possible to see the past from a position of otherness, to look at it as something external to oneself. This does not mean, however, that the past becomes an object of indifference. On the contrary, it touches us in an even more profound manner because it can no longer be easily and readily assimilated into the self. Of course, it takes time to be able to put the "spirit" of this loss into the "dead letter." One must first tame the anger, humiliation, pain, regret, and sorrow, all of which accompanies mournful memory. In Arendt's words, such storytelling is something that "needs time" (MD 21).

Arendt and Weil Paying Attention to Afflicting Storytelling

Arendt begins her chapter on the concept of action in *The Human Condition* with the quote of Dinesen: "All sorrows can be borne if you put them into a story or tell a story about them" (HC 175). Indeed, the afflicting nature of grief shown in literature is precisely what, through the beauty of the writing, is made visible. This revelation allows for the experience of grieving that "represents a process of recognition" (MD 20). However, Arendt sometimes seems to confuse recognition with reconciliation. Stories, through their tragic effect, allow for the recognition of affliction, but this does not mean that there is reconciliation with what has taken place. On the contrary, I would like to highlight that tragic storytelling brings contradiction to the forefront for the reader. This kind of narrative does not bring resolution, but it does show the effects of "force" on people, on the one hand, and what sometimes escapes force while remaining perishable and exposed, on the other.[27] This is something that Arendt seems to admit at times, notably when she writes that the narrative "solves no problem and assuages no suffering" (MD 21). Therefore, not all sorrows are bearable if we tell them, and tragic storytelling is not what makes one able to accept affliction. It is rather with tragic stories that we can see, and sometimes feel, affliction fully and in its reality.

I want to put forward the idea that tragic stories convey the impossibility of solace. In other words, tragic stories present affliction in such a way that we are able to feel what remains unspeakable or, at least, incommunicable in its totality. They allow us to experience the absence of meaning and the feeling of emptiness. The reception of tragic stories is less pleasant and easier for the reader than the ones that teach moral lessons or that are happy or that give certainties. But the tragic, nonetheless, cultivates in the reader a capacity for deep and free attention. And so, tragic stories could potentially have political meaning in new ways for two specific reasons. First, it is extremely demanding and rare to pay attention to real affliction without looking for solace. Second, tragic stories make visible situations that are usually little considered, disdained, or, again, whose affliction is neutralized by ideological justifications. Arendt is keenly aware that the afflicted are usually consciously ignored by others. She mentions it, for example, in *On Revolution* while quoting John Adams at length:

> The poor man's conscience is clear; yet he is ashamed … . He feels himself out of the sight of others, groping in the dark. Mankind takes no notice of him. He rambles and wanders unheeded … . He is not disapproved, censured, or reproached; *he is only not seen* … . To be overlooked, and to know it, are intolerable. (OR 59)

For Arendt, even more than its material destitution, the absence of visibility makes the heaviness of the anonymity present in misery difficult to grasp. And yet, despite its invisibility, the need for someone to receive the cry of the miserable remains. More complex than physical hunger, misery is a hunger to exist in humanity, to come out of the shadows, to break the silence, and to be seen as well as heard.

Here, the thought of Simone Weil pairs well with Arendt's account of storytelling.[28] For Weil, paying attention to affliction is extremely demanding and rare. Affliction is not a purely subjective feeling; it refers, rather, to a social, political, and individual condition in which a person counts for almost nothing. To be afflicted is to lose the sense of one's own reality; it is to always be on the verge of falling out of existence entirely. As Weil puts it:

> Affliction is not a psychological state; it is a pulverization of the soul by the mechanical brutality of circumstances … Affliction is something which imposes itself upon a man quite against his will. Its essence, the thing it is defined by the horror, the revulsion of the whole being, which it inspires in its victim. (SWR 462)

Affliction reveals the artificial nature of individual sovereignty. It is not only the painful experience of individual vulnerability and limitation but also the radical dispossession of the self and the loss of a well-grounded relationship with the world. In addition to physical pain and inner suffering, true affliction is accompanied by what might be called social decay. In this sense, affliction is also a humiliation. The afflicted person is marked by a sense of shame and self-loathing, which can contribute to the acceptance of mistreatment by the afflicted since they begin to see themselves as coming from an inferior layer of humanity.

Affliction, in this sense, is an existential phenomenon, an awareness of counting for nothing, but it is also an epistemic phenomenon. It marks the limit of the intellect's capacity to understand and find meaning in a given situation. From a spiritual point of view, affliction entails total abandonment. Far from generating a sense of compassion in the other, the afflicted generates a sense of repulsion in others. Bystander's pity, Weil argues, camouflages the reality of affliction with good feelings. In this way, affliction creates spaces of silence and unintelligibility. Thoughts flee affliction because it is an ultimately absurd and meaningless condition that stands outside the realm of discursive meaning. Words, as human creations, can never adequately give an account of this inhuman ordeal. Based on this Weilian insight, we can begin to see how tragic narratives seek to articulate—to testify, paradoxically—what in the experience of the affliction remains necessarily inarticulable.

Only stories that manage to leave room for silence can become artworks capable of communicating affliction without consolation and without justification. As Weil remarks about *The Iliad*: "This poem is a miracle. Its bitterness is the only justifiable bitterness, for it springs from the subjections of the human spirit to force, that is, in the last analysis, to matter" (IF 211). It is in this context that Weil mentions how precious *The Iliad* is, because, for her, this story does not overshadow the suffering caused by the Trojan War. It tells the life of people, those who participate in the war, allies, and enemies, just as it tells the life of those who wait, far from Troy, for the end of combat. Absent consolation and justification, *The Iliad* tries only to tell of the horror of war with pure lucidity.

The question we might ask, then, is to what extent tragic stories have historical "truth" value. As already mentioned, the art of storytelling does not necessitate the perfect reconstruction of what happened. Indeed, stories more often than not fail to give a descriptively sufficient account of what was destroyed. As Adriana Cavarero explains:

> When history is produced through extreme horror, narrating is not merely "reconstructing" the thread of a life story; it is above all opposing the work of destruction that has devoured life itself. It is ultimately a making against destroying, a creating against demolishing, a doing against undoing.[29]

To some extent, tragic storytelling creates unhappy feelings that are difficult to handle for the reader, in the sense that the work manages, at times, to make affliction fully real in its harshness and to convey it to others. This act of creation is perhaps the most difficult one, considering, with Weil, that affliction always tends to be concealed. The creation here fights the derealization.

As a reader of Weil, Imre Kertész finds a tragic element in the "spirit of storytelling" that attempts to communicate affliction, insofar as the representation of it awaits an active reception from the reader.[30] As a teenage survivor of concentration camps, Kertész was a journalist ostracized by the Hungarian communist regime. He was haunted by the call to write about Auschwitz while knowing that only a few would have an interest in it. It is undeniable to him that the collective realization of what took place during the Holocaust created a tragic culture, one calling for a catharsis. And yet, as Kertész notes, "the mechanical repetition of commemorations is more at the service of institutional oblivion than of cathartic remembrance."[31] The Holocaust, understood as a culture, produces endless tragic stories, while the call for reparations remains rarely heard. In order for the properly critical charge of these stories to be properly received, listeners must undergo a subjective process that extends beyond the museumization of memory.[32] We ought not seek to appease or resolve the affliction present in such tragic stories. Instead, we ought only to recognize it, to give it space to come into existence. From a Weilian perspective, this means receiving the account of affliction without trying to "derealize" it or diminish its harshness. It also means being able to receive within ourselves the contradiction and the nonreconciliation proper to these accounts.

Tragic Storytelling and the Experience of the Irreconcilable and Unspeakable

Good storytelling, Arendt argues, comes from the "human capacity to think" (HC 264). The process of writing, as the testimony of the "one who has returned," is a form of exchange with the reader. The question is, what do stories told by survivors of genocide make us think about? Here the storyteller shares an experience with their audience, the totality of which escapes even the teller of the tale. Genocide emerges from the desire to erase a people from the face of the world. To recount stories of genocide is to try to find the words that convey this process of erasure. This is a process challenged by the fact that what is destroyed in this manner is destroyed forever. What is told through tragic storytelling, thus, reveals more than mere history. It contains the subjective mark of a noncoincidence to oneself, of a radical exit from humanity, and the diminution of plurality in the world.

History is marked by the disappearance of victims, both politically, through the various massacres, and epistemologically, being erased from the collective memory. Several first-hand accounts of the Nazi camps, for example, deal with this situation of erasure, with an emphasis on mourning.[33] This is the case in the works of Primo Levi (*If This Is a Man*), Charlotte Delbo (*Auschwitz and After*), David Rousset (*Les Jours de notre mort*), Imre Kertész (*Galley Diary*), Elie Wiesel (*Night*), Robert Antelme (*L'Espèce humaine*), or Jean Améry (*At the Mind's Limits: Contemplations by a Survivor of Auschwitz and Its Realities*). Each of these authors tells a particular story that deploys their own experience in a particular way.

Jean Améry, for instance, gives an intellectual account of life in the camps, of the torture endured and the difficulty of having survived. He attempts to transport the reader into the place of the survivor. Primo Levi, on the other hand, writes more simply, and his style is less philosophical than Améry's. Levi tries, through the recollection of precise daily details, to give an account of the lost lives by speaking as little as possible about his own. He describes primarily his relationships with others and takes the reader along with him as a counterpart to those relationships. Charlotte Delbo, finally, addresses the question of memory in a space without past or future. Her testimony attempts to convey the impossibility of imagining a world based on the loss of memory and death.

Although each of these authors starts from shared experiences, their stories are fully unique.[34] The horror and suffering they experienced do not make these survivors "siblings"; their voices do not merge to become one.[35] All of them, however, mention that the tragic experience of the camps was marked with the visceral need to survive to tell their stories, and they were comforted by the idea of being listened to by their loved ones.[36]

Without ignoring the differences between them, we nevertheless find in these testimonies the same difficulty: how is it possible to give an account of the process of destruction of the Nazis while giving a voice to the victims? It is immensely challenging to find words that describe the barbarity in its daily nonsense while also giving voices to victims, to become the bearer of their memory, even though the extreme conditions have made it impossible to have any kind of conventional relationship with them. The survivors are bound by an oath made to their fellow prisoners, the missing and the dead, to communicate what had happened.

For Charlotte Delbo, who pays tribute at length to the women she knew, fulfilling this oath was difficult but still much easier than it was for Primo Levi who struggled to write the testimonial stories of persons unknown to him, many of whom had already been reduced to complete anonymity before they died.[37] Levi relates that:

> All the *mussulmans* who finished in the gas chambers have the same story, or more exactly, have no story; they followed the slope down to the bottom, like streams that run down to the sea. On their entry into the camp, through basic incapacity, or by misfortune, or through some banal incident, they are overcome before they can adapt themselves; they are beaten by time, they do not begin to learn German, to disentangle the infernal knot of laws and prohibitions until their body is already in decay, and nothing can save them from selections or from death by exhaustion. Their life is short, but their number is endless; they, the *Muselmanner*, the drowned, form the backbone of the camp, an anonymous mass, continually renewed and always identical, of non-men who march and labour in silence, the divine spark dead within them, already too empty to really suffer ... They crowd my memory with their faceless presences, and if I could enclose all the evil of our time in one image, I would choose this image which is familiar to me: an emaciated man, with head dropped and shoulders curved, on whose face and in whose eyes not a trace of a thought is to be seen.[38]

Levi, who only began to write after the Shoah, argues that his testimony is inhibited by the impossibility of giving a full account of the Nazi's destruction, since the aim of the camps was to make a part of humanity disappear, collectively and in every individual. Jews selected by the SS were systematically isolated from other prisoners and regularly exterminated.

In particular, Levi recalls the systematic destruction of witnesses by the *Sonderkommandos* (special Mazi unit).[39] Constantly renewing the concentration camp's "workforce" (prisoners) guaranteed the impossibility of testimonies; the dead witnesses became completely anonymous.[40] It is in this sense that the testimony of the survivors is haunted by those who disappeared before even appearing as humans. This subtle aspect of the testimony is as significant as the part that can be properly spoken. Testifying must leave a part of silence in what is rendered. First, because the horror experienced never belongs to anyone (although it implants itself deep inside each person and modifies their subjectivity). Second, because the lack of witness testimony means that the greatest suffering is muzzled (although it must still be accounted for). As Levi explains:

> We survivors are not only an exiguous but also an anomalous minority: we are those who by their prevarications or abilities or good luck did not touch bottom. Those who did so, those who saw the Gorgon, have not returned to tell about it or have returned mute, but they are the "Muslims," the submerged, the complete witnesses, the ones whose deposition would have a general significance.[41]

Again, the testimony is doubly silent because the words to account for the dead are out of place and out of proportion as if they were being emptied by the very act of being spoken. Indeed, "one hesitates to call their death death."[42] The event of the Shoah is incommensurable to language. It is an abyss, Arendt argues, opened by "the fabrication of corpses ... Something has happened there to which we cannot reconcile ourselves. None of us can" (EU 14).

In the extreme intimacy with the most radical tragedy, there remains the unattainable. Indeed, how can you transmit this improbable (and yet real) space where there is a merger of the human and the inhuman, the subject and the object, the living person and the corpse? This nonplace, which should have never existed, is where "living corpses" are made to speak.[43] Moreover, the *Muselmanner* themselves, the "drowned," says Levi, "even if they had paper and pen, the drowned would not have testified, because their death had begun before that of their body."[44] It is in this sense that the partly silent testimonies of the survivors are as significant as the part that can be properly spoken.

It is in fact a double challenge, because of the terrible difficulty (becoming even more terrible because of its necessity) of giving dignity to the dead when they have already been transformed into anonymous masses. The process of being heard, if it succeeds, is itself inhibited by the danger of seeing one's own testimony encompass the diverse silent realities of those who died. Additionally, one's own testimony as a survivor reified into that of a "professional concentration camper," per Améry's ironic formula. Indeed, reception can become problematic when it tries to take possession of meaning. When this happens, it is enough to only repeat and crystallize a narrative to claim to grasp its history and close the process of defining its meaning. This is perhaps what Améry was trying to say in his second preface to *At the Mind's Limits: Contemplations by a Survivor of Auschwitz and Its Realities*. In the winter of 1976, shortly before committing suicide, he wrote:

> I had no clarity when I was writing this little book, I do not have it today, and I hope that I never will. Clarification would also amount to disposal, settlement of the case, which can then be placed in the files of history My book meant to aid in preventing precisely this. For nothing is resolved, no conflict is settled, no remembering has become mere memory.[45]

The memory carried by the stories of the Shoah does not repair its horrors; it attempts to bring into appearance lives that were shattered, knowing that this appearance can never be completed or satisfied. The "deposition" of the survivors is therefore partial and painful because the survivors carry with them the fear of taking over the places and the voices of those who did not return. It is precisely because tragic storytelling is partial and situated that the (non)meaning is never completed, inviting us to return again and again to renew and repeat our efforts.

The stories of the Shoah passed on by the survivors represent the limit of what Arendt mentions when she referred to Dinesen that not all sorrows are bearable even if they are told and even if they are made into a story. Without omitting the "therapeutic" character of the writings, these stories are attempts to overcome what is in fact insurmountable. They do not testify to a feeling of sorrow, to a counterbalance of public humanity, nor to chance and necessity. They give an account of an abyss in the history of the world. One must turn away from oneself to fully perceive the silence embedded within these stories and to properly receive the otherness they carry.

Conclusion

Arendt's critical project is to "tell us things no one has yet had ears to hear" (PF 94). Weil's project is to protect the infinitely fragile. The challenge, when it comes to tragic storytelling, therefore, is to understand the conditions that enable us to do the work of reception. For proper transmission to take place, such stories must not only be carefully crafted and conveyed in a way that is understandable, but, more importantly, the audience must also learn how to pay attention to those stories, which are so often camouflaged by social noise, power relations, and the hypervisibility of certain groups to the detriment of others.[46]

For Arendt, culture is the least utilitarian of all man-made things. It is a kind of relationship of the individual with the world, a way of arranging its universe and taking care of it. The arts, like literature, give a certain permanence to the world and address the question of meaning beyond the present time. For Arendt, "in order to become aware of appearances," we first must be free to establish a certain distance between ourselves and the object, and the more important the sheer appearance of a thing is, the more distance it requires for its proper appreciation. This distance cannot arise unless we are in a position to forget ourselves, the cares and interests and urges of our lives, so that we will not seize what we admire but let it be as it is, in its appearance. (PF 207)

To accept an artwork requires that we be capable of a kind of disengagement in which we give attention to others without regard for oneself, at least momentarily. In this way, the space of action must be separated from the space of contemplation in order for us to stand back and observe the action *before* being able to speak about it. The same is true of the person receiving the story: one must be receptive to the otherness of the work, paying attention to it without regard to oneself. In this sense, I hope to echo the work of Schoonheim who states:

> The transition from the private to the public sphere involves a transfiguration of subjective feeling into public assertion; in the case of the loss of a loved one, in Arendt's words, "the transfiguration of grief into lamentation." Even if Arendt did not yet use the terms public and private in 1951, her task of redeeming the lost lives transforms the night time thoughts of her friends and family members into a public outcry over their death.[47]

By conceptualizing the notion of tragic storytelling, I wanted to show that Arendt's insight into the role of storytelling could be fully reconciled with a concern for the private, understood as a place to cultivate one's individual capacities of reception, attention, and openness to others. If Arendt says little about how to create distance from oneself, Weil makes up for this with her concept of attention. Pure attention, according to Weil, is always decentered. It is necessary to persist in the effort of attention without preconceiving its object, to let it happen as it is, so that our perception will be momentarily free from self-perception. Paying attention, being able to rise above oneself and receive affliction are in a way consubstantial and appear with practice, over time.

To really direct someone's attention to affliction implies consent. To be pure, attention requires the release of a part of "oneself" in order to let oneself be touched by affliction. To pay attention to affliction "is to experience non-being. It is the state of extreme and total humiliation which is also the condition for passing over into truth. It is the death of the soul … It is more difficult than suicide would be for a happy child. Therefore, the afflicted are not listened to" (HP 331–2). It is perhaps in this sense that Weil considers true attention a miracle.

Tragic storytelling, as embodied in the testimony of concentration camp survivors, reminds us of the importance of the gap (between reality and the words spoken) and the noncoincidence of the self so that we might become capable of receiving the experience of affliction. Moreover, as Primo Levi shows, the survivors make an extraordinary effort to tell the stories of people more engulfed than themselves in affliction. This is indeed an extraordinary effort because, in addition to returning to the site of their own trauma, the survivors, through their stories, attempt also to pay attention to those more afflicted than themselves. To do this, Weil believes it is necessary that the soul passes "through its own annihilation to the place where alone it can get the sort of attention which can attend to truth and to affliction."[48] To survive and tell the story of the annihilation of others, one must therefore pass through the moments of self-annihilation, when the survivor's attention is focused on the nameless *Muselmanner* without a face of his own. They must find the words to transmit the intransmissible.

It is only insofar as an artwork manages to make the silence of affliction audible, without providing any justification, that it can be qualified as tragic and direct people toward a "decentering of the self." The content of certain artworks has the power to make affliction visible beyond the limits of language. Tragic artwork offers both the rough bitterness of affliction and the fragile sensitivity that sometimes escapes that affliction in small ways. The more these stories are embedded in the relationality of the world (in the sense that they reveal the tragic tension that inhabits and constitutes this world), the more imperative it is that we learn to properly receive them. It is in this light that Arendt conceives of tragedy as what happens when the tragic character of the world fades. On the one hand, tragedy occurs when the world no longer allows for action and the plurality associated with it. On the other hand, tragedy occurs when there is no awareness of the tragic in the narrative or, again, when the narratives are simply not received or even perceived. As she explains:

> The tragedy began … when it turned out that there was no mind to inherit and to question, to think about and to remember. The point of the matter is that the "completion," which indeed every enacted event must have in the minds of those who then are to tell the story and to convey its meaning, eluded them; and without this thinking completion after the act, without the articulation accomplished by remembrance, there simply was no story left that could be told. (PF 6)

The history reconfigured in tragic storytelling is always and still disfigured. Its irresolution invites the reader to *amor mundi*, to a renewed concern for the world and the perishable things that constitute it. It is also a call for awareness for the tragedies that are currently unfolding in the shadows of flashes, tweets, and Realpolitik. If this sort of receptivity could one day, probably too late, change the course of things, it will be transmitted through storytelling.

Notes

1   *Maus*, the first and only graphic novel to ever win a Pulitzer Prize, is based on the interviews of the author with his father, a Holocaust survivor. On January 10, 2022, the McMinn County School Board in Tennessee voted unanimously to ban the book due to rough language and nudity. See Art Spiegelman, *The Complete Maus: A Survivor's Tale* (New York: Pantheon Graphic Library, 1996). At the beginning of January 2022,

a school board in McMinn County (Tennessee) voted unanimously to ban *Maus* from the school curriculum.
2 See Cas Mudde, *The Far Right Today* (Cambridge, MA: Polity Press, 2019) and Barbara Perry and Ryan Scrivens, *Right-Wing Extremism in Canada* (Cham: Palgrave Macmillan, 2019), among others.
3 Hannah Arendt, "Social Science Techniques and the Study of Concentration Camps," *Jewish Social Studies* 12, no. 1 (1950): 49–64.
4 This difficulty can be found in many other situations of oppression. Without wishing to hierarchize or standardize misfortunes, it is generally hard for survivors to give an account of their misfortunes (and to be heard). In Canada, the accounts of First Nations survivors of the residential schools—a system of forced assimilation aimed at "killing the Indian in the child" that lasted from 1883 to 1996—reveal a breakdown in the transmission of the culture. The children who survived the residential schools were dispossessed of their mother tongue. They could no longer turn to their own people to recount the horrors they had suffered. The other children, those who are still found in unmarked graves near the schools, could not say anything at all. The reality of their deaths is just beginning to emerge in the political arena with the discovery of the bodies of at least 751 children in 2021. See An Antane Kapesh, *I Am a Damn Savage: What Have You Done to My Country?* (*Eukuan nin matshi-manitu innushkueu; Tanite nene etutamin nitassi?*) (Waterloo: Wilfrid Laurier University Press, 2020).
5 The term "Holocaust" will be used to describe a non-Jewish experience of the Nazi camp, and "Shoa" will be used to describe the Holocaust according to a Jewish person.
6 Here absurdity is meant in the strong Camusian sense as the opposite of reconciliation. This implies that the subject learns to inhabit the tear present in oneself and with the world at the same time. See Albert Camus, *Le Mythe de Sysiphe* (Paris: Gallimard, 1942), 85.
7 There are obviously several studies comparing Weil and Arendt; see, in particular, the important collective directed by Michel Narcy and Étienne Tassin, *Les catégories de l'universel, Simone Weil et Hannah Arendt* (Paris: L'Harmattan, 2002), as well as the book by Sylvie Courtine-Denamy, *Three Women in Dark Times: Edith Stein, Hannah Arendt, Simone Weil* (Ithaca, NY: Cornell University Press, 2001), or Roberto Esposito's *The Origin of the Political: Hannah Arendt or Simone Weil?* (New York: Fordham University Press, 2017). See also the excellent article by Sara MacDonald, "Simone Weil and Hannah Arendt on the Beautiful and the Just," *European Legacy* 24, nos. 7&8 (2019), 805–18.
8 Paul Ricoeur, "Action, Story and History: On Re-reading The Human Condition," *Salmagundi* 60 (1983), 67.
9 As already noted, Ricoeur finds the notion of storytelling in Arendt to be complex. It entangles both these categories of action and work, on the one hand, just as it involves distinctions between the public and private realms, on the other. On this difficult point in Arendt's thought, see, among others, Lisa J. Disch, "More Truth Than Fact: Storytelling as Critical Understanding in the Writings of Hannah Arendt," *Political Theory* 21, no. 4 (November 1993), 665–94; Patchen Markell, "Arendt's Work: On the Architecture of *The Human Condition*," *College Literature* 38, no. 1 (2011), 15–44; and Liesbeth Schoonheim, "The 'Rightful Place in Man's Enduring Chronicle': Arendt's Benjaminian Historiography," *History of European Ideas* 46, no. 6 (2020): 844–61. Without denying the importance of action, the notion of work and, in particular, storytelling constitutes a fundamental category for Arendtian thought, especially as a response to the loss of the world.

10 Julia Kristeva, *Hannah Arendt: Life Is a Narrative* (Toronto: University of Toronto Press, 2001).
11 Ibid., 8.
12 This conception of storytelling resonates with the one put forward by Leslie Paul Thiele, who argues that the very nature of action is to be narrated: the event, being by nature unpredictable, transforms experience in such a way that one cannot directly grasp the action, and thus experience it, without going through the narrative. Thiele proposes to conceive of narrative by emphasizing the idea that it must be understood in Arendt's thought in light of the fact that Arendt is "a theorist of action who understood its intrinsically narrative nature." For Thiele, action as freedom "appears after its execution exhibit freedom by way of the original narratives that their actions foment. Freedom is expressed in the co-development of an ever-unfolding, and inherently unpredictable plot that solicits novel responses and judgments." Leslie Paul Thiele, "The Ontology of Action: Arendt and the Role of Narrative," *Theory & Event* 12, no. 4 (2009).
13 For Kateb and Pitkin, storytelling is linked with a stylistic and aesthetic conception of Arendt's politics. See George Kateb, "Democratic Individuality and the Claims of Politics," *Political Theory* 12, no. 3 (August 1984), 331–60; and Hannah Pitkin, *The Attack of the Blob: Hannah Arendt's Concept of the Social* (Chicago: University of Chicago Press, 1998). For Pitkin, Arendt holds a virilized vision of politics, as actors appear as children, as "little boys clamoring for attention ('look at me! I'm the greatest!' 'No, look at me!') and waiting to be reassured that they are brave, valuable, even real … Though Arendt was female, there is a lot of *machismo* in her vision." Hannah Pitkin, 'Justice: On Relating Private and Public,' in *Hannah Arendt, Critical Essays*, ed. Lewis P. Hinchman and Sandra K. Hinchman (Albany: State University of New York Press, 1994), 281.
14 Kristeva, *Hannah Arendt*, 17–18.
15 On the issue of language in concentration camps, see Michaela Wolf, *Interpreting in Nazi Concentration Camp* (New York: Bloomsbury Academic, 2016).
16 Giorgio Agamben, *Remnants of Auschwitz: The Witness and the Archive* (New York: Zone Books, 1999), 72.
17 For Adorno, poetry after Auschwitz contains the shame related to the impossible transfiguration of suffering, concluding that "to write lyric poetry after Auschwitz is barbaric." Theodor Adorno, "Commitment," *New Left Review* 1, nos. 87&88 (1974), 84. In response, Primo Levi considered that "after Auschwitz it is barbaric to write poetry except about Auschwitz": Anthony Rudolf, "Primo Levi in London (1986)," in *The Voice of Memory: Interviews 1961–87*, ed. Marco Belpoliti and Robert Gordon (Cambridge, MA: Polity Press, 2001), 23–33.
18 See Bonnie Honig, *Feminist Interpretations of Hannah Arendt* (University Park: Pennsylvania State University Press, 1995).
19 Patchen Markell, "Arendt's Work: On the Architecture of *The Human Condition*," *College Literature* 38, no. 1 (2011), 36.
20 If Arendt sees in *Oedipus Rex* the importance of the city insofar as it allows us to sustain the weight and suffering of human life, there is no need to mention how many other interpretations of *Oedipus Rex* are possible. Storytelling can bring meaning to life, and if the meaning is inspired and directed in a certain direction, it is neither fixed nor unitary.
21 Let us recall that action is always embedded in a network of human relationships and that, in this sense, it is impossible to foresee the type of relationships it generates in the world, as well as the effects it implies, just as its character remains anonymous

and cannot be associated with a sovereign vision of the actor who would exhaust it by leading it to its end. See Étienne Tassin, *Le trésor perdu: Hannah Arendt, L'intelligence de l'action politique* (Paris: Payot & Rivages, 1999); and Seyla Benhabib, "Time, Action and Narrative in Nietzsche and Arendt," *Raisons politiques* 70, no. 2 (2018), 15–28.

22 Arendt's approach, however, is not that of a biographer but a "hybrid approach" of merging theory and storytelling.

23 "No philosophy, no analysis, no aphorism, be it ever so profound, can compare in intensity and richness of meaning with a properly narrated story" (MD 22).

24 See Hedwig Marzolf, "Écrire sa vie. L'équivoque de la 'philosophie du conter' de Hannah Arendt," *Raison publique* 19, no. 2 (2014): 139–64.

25 The dangers of this construction are multiple. It implies considering life as an object to be managed according to a foreseen finality, which inevitably hinders the capacity to perceive and think the world outside this finality, just as it conforms action to a teleology. Life modeled on a narrative loses its unpredictability and becomes clichéd and uniform; action becomes behavior. Also, as storytelling becomes self-referential, it no longer acts as a mediation allowing both to apprehend other stories than one's own and, thus, to experience various forms of otherness. The field of experience and reception narrows—just as the "enlarged thought," a concept dear to Arendt—withers away. There is no longer an "in-between" to welcome what is expressed differently, what lives differently, in short to open up to what one does not expect.

26 This process of distancing herself from the romantic tradition is important in Arendt's intellectual journey and is notably present in her book on Rahel Varnhagen, where she shows how Rahel sought to shape her personality and live her life "as if it were a work of art" (RV).

27 I use the term "force" in the sense that Simone Weil does in *Iliade ou le poème de la force* (*The Iliad, or the Poem of Force*). Also see Jane E. Doering, *Simone Weil and the Specter of Self-perpetuating Force* (Notre Dame, IN: University of Notre Dame Press, 2010).

28 For a study of affliction, attention, and compassion in the work of Simone Weil, see the very rich and interesting contribution of Evans, "The Nature of Narrative in Simone Weil's Vision of History: The Need for New Historical Roots," and Jane E. Doering and Ruthann Knechel Johansen's *When Fiction and Philosophy Meet: A Conversation with Flannery O'Connor and Simone Weil* (Macon, GA: Mercer University Press, 2019); and Christopher Thomas's "Simone Weil: The Ethics of Affliction and the Aesthetics of Attention," *International Journal of Philosophical Studies* 28, no. 2 (2020), 145–67.

29 Adriana Cavarero and Elvira Roncalli, "Narrative against Destruction," *New Literary History* 46, no. 1 (2015), 14.

30 According to Kertész, Weil would have understood in a few months of work in factories what two totalitarian experiences had made him understand. See Imre Kertész, *Eurêka. L'Holocauste comme culture* (Arles: Actes Sud, 2010).

31 Kertész, *Eurêka*, 33 (my translation).

32 Catherine Coquio, "Envoyer les fantômes au musée? La critique du kitsch concentrationnaire chez Imre Kertész et Ruth Klüger," *Gradhiva, Revue d'anthropologie et d'histoire des arts* 5 (2007).

33 This chapter only discusses stories from Nazi camps, but several parallels are possible with the literature on the Soviet gulag.

34 All three were Auschwitz survivors. Charlotte Delbo was a political prisoner, while Jean Améry and Primo Levi were both Jewish resistance fighters.

35 One can think, for example, of the dispute between Améry and Levi concerning "forgiveness" and "resentment." As Irène Heidelberger-Leonard discusses, quoting Améry: "Unlike Levi, I am not a forgiving person and I have no understanding for gentlemen who were part of the 'directing staff' of IG-Auschwitz": Irène Heidelberger-Leonard, "Deux frères ennemis: Jean Améry et Primo Levi," in *Primo Levi à l'œuvre. La réception de l'œuvre de Primo Levi dans le monde*, ed. Philippe Mesnard and Yannis Thanassekos (Paris: Éditions Kimé, 2008), 437.
36 Primo Levi, *If This Is a Man* (New York: Orion Press, 1959).
37 Charlotte Delbo, *Aucun de nous ne reviendra* (Paris: Les Éditions de Minuit, 1970).
38 Levi, *If This Is a Man*, 103.
39 The *Sonderkommandos* assisted the Jews when they undressed. They collected their belongings and then ushered them into the gas chambers. The *Sonderkommandos* were also responsible for removing the bodies from the chambers and extracting teeth or hair from the prisoners.
40 It is important to mention that, although the concentration camp system ensured the destruction of the witnesses, some survived and reported on the experience of the *Sonderkommandos*. It is the case, for example, of the drawings and paintings of David Olère. Even more anonymous than the concentration camps were the death camps, such as Sobibor and Treblinka, that carried out immediate and systematic killings.
41 Primo Levi, *The Drowned and the Saved* (New York: Simon and Schuster, 2017), 70. The use of the term *muslim* here is synonymous with the term *Muselmanner*, both of which refer to the starvation, exhaustion, and impending death of concentration camp prisoners.
42 Levi, *If This Is a Man*, 103.
43 Weil associates this image with the slaves from *The Iliad*. For her,

> a person's being a thing is a logical contradiction. Yet what is impossible in logic becomes true in life, and the contradiction lodged within the soul tears it to shreds. This thing is constantly aspiring to be a man or a woman, and never achieving it—here, surely is death but death strung out over a whole lifetime; here, surely is life, but life that death congeals before abolishing. (IF 211)

44 Levi, *The Drowned and the Saved*, 70.
45 Jean Améry, *At the Mind's Limits: Contemplations by a Survivor on Auschwitz and Its Realities* (Bloomington: Indiana University Press, 1980), xi.
46 For Simone Weil: "Relations between the collectivity and the person should be arranged with the sole purpose of removing whatever is detrimental to the growth and mysterious germination of the impersonal element of the soul ... What man needs is silence and warmth; what he is given is an icy pandemonium" (HP 331–2). The impersonal extends beyond the person and allows, among other things, to hear the truth of affliction.
47 Schoonheim, "The 'Rightful Place in ...,'" 851–2.
48 Ibid., 333.

Bibliography

Adorno, Theodor. "Commitment." *New Left Review* 1, nos. 87&88 (1974): 84.
Agamben, Giorgio. *Remnants of Auschwitz: The Witness and the Archive*. New York: Zone Books, 1999.

Améry, Jean. *At the Mind's Limits: Contemplations by a Survivor on Auschwitz and Its Realities*. Bloomington: Indiana University Press, 1980.

Benhabib, Seyla. "Time, Action and Narrative in Nietzsche and Arendt." *Raisons politiques* 70, no. 2 (2018): 15–28.

Brossat, Alain. "La place du survivant. Une approche Arendtienne." *Revue d'Histoire de la Shoah* 3, no. 164 (1998): 79–90.

Camus, Albert. *Le Mythe de Sysiphe*. Paris: Gallimard, 1942.

Cavarero, Adriana, and Elvira Roncalli. " Narrative against Destruction." *New Literary History* 46, no. 1 (2015): 1–16.

Coquio, Catherine. "Envoyer les fantômes au musée? La critique du kitsch concentrationnaire chez Imre Kertész et Ruth Klüger." *Gradhiva, Revue d'anthropologie et d'histoire des arts* 5 (2007): 38–51.

Courtine-Denamy, Sylvie. *Three Women in Dark Times: Edith Stein, Hannah Arendt, Simone Weil*. Ithaca, NY: Cornell University Press, 2001.

Delbo, Charlotte. *Aucun de nous ne reviendra*. Paris: Les Éditions de Minuit, 1970.

Disch, Lisa J. "More Truth than Fact: Storytelling as Critical Understanding in the Writings of Hannah Arendt." *Political Theory* 21, no. 4 (November 1993): 665–94.

Doering, E. Jane. *Simone Weil and the Specter of Self-perpetuating Force*. Notre Dame, IN: University of Notre Dame Press, 2010.

Doering, E. Jane, and Ruthann Knechel Johansen. *When Fiction and Philosophy Meet: A Conversation with Flannery O'Connor and Simone Weil*. Macon, GA: Mercer University Press, 2019.

Esposito, Roberto. *The Origin of the Political: Hannah Arendt or Simone Weil?* New York: Fordham University Press, 2017.

Evans, Christine Ann. "The Nature of Narrative in Simone Weil's Vision of History: The Need for New Historical Roots." In *The Beauty That Saves: Essays on Aesthetics and Language in Simone Weil*. Edited by John M. Springsted Dunaway. Macon, GA: Mercer University Press, 1996, pp. 55–68.

Fricker, Miranda. *Epistemic Injustice: Power and the Ethics of Knowing*. Oxford: Oxford University Press, 2011.

Heidelberger-Leonard, Irène. " Deux frères ennemis: Jean Améry et Primo Levi." In *Primo Levi à l'œuvre. La réception de l'œuvre de Primo Levi dans le monde*. Edited by Philippe Mesnard and Yannis Thanassekos. Paris: Éditions Kimé, 2008, pp. 433–42.

Honig, Bonnie. *Feminist Interpretations of Hannah Arendt*. University Park: Pennsylvania State University Press, 1995.

Kapesh, An Antane. *I Am a Damn Savage: What Have You Done to My Country?* (*Eukuan nin matshi-manitu innushkueu: Tanite nene etutamin nitassi?*). Waterloo: Wilfrid Laurier University Press, 2020.

Kateb, George. "Democratic Individuality and the Claims of Politics." *Political Theory* 12, no. 3 (August 1984): 331–60.

Kertész, Imre. *Eurêka. L'Holocauste comme culture*. Arles: Actes Sud, 2010.

Kristeva, Julia. *Hannah Arendt: Life Is a Narrative*. Toronto: University of Toronto Press, 2001.

Levi, Primo. *If This Is a Man*. New York: Orion Press, 1959.

Levi, Primo. *The Drowned and the Saved*. New York: Simon and Schuster, 2017.

MacDonald, Sara. "Simone Weil and Hannah Arendt on the Beautiful and the Just." *European Legacy* 24, nos. 7&8 (2019): 805–18.

Markell, Patchen. "Arendt's Work: On the Architecture of *The Human Condition*." *College Literature* 38, no. 1 (2011): 15–44.

Marzolf, Hedwig. "Écrire sa vie. L'équivoque de la 'philosophie du conter' de Hannah Arendt." *Raison publique* 19, no. 2 (2014): 139–64.
Mudde, Cas. *The Far Right Today*. Cambridge, MA: Polity Press, 2019.
Nancy, Michel, and Étienne Tassin. *Les catégories de l'universel, Simone Weil et Hannah Arendt*. Paris: L'Harmattan, 2002.
Perry, Barbara, and Ryan Scrivens. *Right-Wing Extremism in Canada*. Cham: Palgrave Macmillan, 2019.
Pirro, C. Robert. *Hannah Arendt and the Politics of Tragedy*. DeKalb: Northern Illinois University Press, 2000.
Pitkin, Hannah. "Justice: On Relating Private and Public." In *Hannah Arendt, Critical Essays*. Edited by Lewis P. Hinchman and Sandra K. Hinchman. Albany: State University of New York Press, 1994, pp. 261–88.
Pitkin, Hannah. *The Attack of the Blob: Hannah Arendt's Concept of the Social*. Chicago: University of Chicago Press, 1998.
Ricoeur, Paul. "Action, Story and History: On Re-reading The Human Condition." *Salmagundi* 60 (1983): 60–72.
Rudolf, Anthony. "Primo Levi in London (1986)." In *Primo Levi, The Voice of Memory: Interviews 1961–87*. Edited by Marco Belpoliti and Robert Gordon. Cambridge, MA: Polity Press, 2001, 23–33.
Schoonheim, Liesbeth. "The 'Rightful Place in Man's Enduring Chronicle': Arendt's Benjaminian Historiography." *History of European Ideas* 46, no. 6 (2020): 844–61.
Spiegelman, Art. *The Complete Maus: A Survivor's Tale*. New York: Pantheon Graphic Library, 1996.
Tassin, Étienne. *Le trésor perdu: Hannah Arendt, L'intelligence de l'action politique*. Paris: Payot & Rivages, 1999.
Thiele, Leslie Paul. "The Ontology of Action: Arendt and the Role of Narrative." *Theory & Event* 12, no. 4 (2009).
Thomas, Christopher. "Simone Weil: The Ethics of Affliction and the Aesthetics of Attention." *International Journal of Philosophical Studies* 28, no. 2 (2020): 145–67.
Wolf, Michaela. *Interpreting in Nazi Concentration Camps*. New York: Bloomsbury Academic, 2016.

Chapter 10

EMBODYING THE IN-BETWEEN: AN ARENDTIAN
REFLECTION ON SIMONE WEIL'S *VENICE SAVED*

Thomas Sojer

This chapter imagines a possible past in which Hannah Arendt might have visited a theater that was playing Simone Weil's *Venice Saved*. In light of this fabulation, let us reconsider Weil's play as a metaphor for "the political" as coined by Hannah Arendt. By drawing on selected passages from Arendt's writings we will elaborate on various concepts and terms taken from the realm of theater. My objective in this chapter is twofold: First, I want to offer insights how applying an Arendtian sense of theater to *Venice Saved* helps to analyze and explain some key differences in both thinkers. Second, I hope to show how these careful distinctions enrich a reading of *Venice Saved* as a metaphor for ultimately rejecting "the political" in favor of a passivity beyond passivity that lends itself to the higher good which is impersonal and unrelated to any political form. In addition, resonating voices of Homi K. Bhabha, Judith Butler, and Adriana Cavarero support a broader reflection on *Venice Saved*.

Venice in France

Imagine a small theater in Marseille at the end of September in 1940. Walter Benjamin, Heinrich Blücher, and Hannah Arendt are in town. They decide to visit an amateur production hosted by the local premier literary magazine *Les Cahiers du Sud*. The play, *Venice Saved*, is a three-act tragedy written by a French refugee high school teacher. We are speaking of Simone Weil. Like her three imagined German visitors, she is fleeing the persecution of dissidents and Jewish people. Backstage, Ms. Weil, probably also acting as director this night, moves hastily giving final instructions. She has carefully chosen each word and gesture, every note in the melody and every beat in the rhyme, that the sixteen actors will perform. Tragically, those who know Weil's biography well are all too aware that no such event ever happened since the play was never finished. Simone Weil was forced to flee once again, to Casablanca, and then

New York, and eventually to London where she died tragically in 1943. Her play, *Venice Saved*, was her only attempt at drama and it is an attempt that will remain forever "in the making."

The importance of Weil's decision to write a play in face of the catastrophe of World War Two, rather than an essay or a story, for example, should not be overlooked. As J. P. Little has pointed out, the questions that inspired Weil's "most mature social theory" were mainly the same ones that she explored in the dramatic and concentrated poetical form of *Venice Saved*.[1] Correspondingly, we can in read in Arendt that she understood theater as "the political sphere of life [is] transposed into art" (HC 188). Applying this Arendtian sense of theater, the chapter identifies the actual stage of *Venice Saved* as the Arendtian space of appearance that is actualized through the performance of acting and speaking with fellow citizens in the public sphere. Thus, the stage is read as being continually recreated by action, classifying the who-ness of individual bodies on stage and in front of it.

In theater, as in politics, acting bodies gather, not only as coactors but also as actors in front of an audience, to reconfigure and transform the pre-existing conditions of the material and institutionalized constellation that prefigures performances. This is not a purely passive relation, as theatrical assemblages can break through "the fourth wall" into the audience, thus revealing an immersive affective power. Witnessing this power firsthand, the iconic chancellor of Western Germany Willy Brandt famously spoke about "the political significance of theatre."[2] With this political significance comes the danger of propagandist theater that was instrumentalized to give birth to affect-driven collectives.[3] History attests to this danger, for example, in the *agitprop theater* in Soviet Russia or the large-scale industry of Nazi propaganda theater.[4] Rejecting the vulgarities of totalitarian propaganda, *Venice Saved* can be read as lucid outlier in the world of exploitative theater, offering a uniquely dissenting and subversive voice.[5] On this basis, the objective of an Arendtian reading of *Venice Saved* is to hint at the play's underlying performative account of the precarious and highly fragile state in which bodies (dis-)appear on stage.

Certainly, the content and themes of *Venice Saved* are of first importance, but I would like to add the importance of the performative perspective to a literary thematic focus as the latter has already been analyzed by numerous Weil scholars.[6] The way that certain human bodies appear and become visible on and in front of the stage, while at the same time, withdrawing from appearance as more-than-human bodies performing an assigned role, is too central to the play's metaphorical account of politics to be ignored. Thus, my exploration aims to amplify and exceed strategies of simple representation on stage.

When watching *Venice Saved* one is confronted with the uncanny consequences of the existential void, of necessity, both inner and outer, beauty, ignorance, fallenness, muteness, nakedness, radical transformation, and the unlimited circles of violence. Against this backdrop, masking oneself and each other provides at least ephemeral possibilities to speak and act politically. However, all those whose masks are ripped off become exposed objects that can no longer speak for themselves. These lives no longer have a protective *persona*, that is, the theatrical mask, in between them and the others. They experience their incapability of action and speech and thus they necessarily lose their freedom.

According to my reading of selected passages from Arendt's writings, passages in which she refers to the world of theater, the very act of dramaturgical imitation can provide a specific innovative form to reflect metaphorically on the conditions of *who-ness* in the "finding of oneself to others" instead of "the finding oneself to itself."[7] Put more concisely, for Arendt, the art of *acting* (in the sense of play acting) becomes an insightful metaphor for the idea of *acting* in the political sense, as it is always already finding and revealing oneself to others.[8] In this regard, Arendt describes an affinity between theater and politics using the metaphor of the play to argue that there is but one way action in general becomes "fully manifest" and that is "only in the performing act itself" (EJ 151).

Every now and then, Hannah Arendt refers to ancient Greek theater within the horizon of Hellenistic society and Aristotelian political theory to promote her concept of theater as a metaphor for the political. J. Peter Euben epitomizes the significance of ancient Greek theater in Arendt's political theory with the formula: "Theater provided a place and moment when citizen spectators could judge refracted versions of themselves on stage."[9] Such mirroring and hence critically reflective quality of theater, both as a cultural institution and as a metaphor for an Arendtian sense of "the political," can be read in light of Arendt's (Kantian) notion of "proper distance, the remoteness or uninvolvedness or disinterestedness, that is requisite for approbation and disapprobation, for evaluating something at its proper worth."[10] For Arendt, in order to recognize other people in the community as equal, unique, and vulnerable, one must distance oneself from the other to allow an in-between space of reflection. From this demand for distance, however, arises a series of paradoxes. For one, we must be able to maintain this distance while also being responsible toward and caring for others in both public and private spheres. Indeed, the permanent risk here is that we might lose the foundational solidarity and social cohesion that we intended to reinforce by distancing ourselves from the other in the first place. Here, theater can serve as a balance.

Based on Euben's interpretation of Arendt's creative metaphorizing of theater, that is, that theater may function as refracted mirror that allows proper distance and critical reflection, I want to highlight selected cultural practices and techniques of acting and spatially arranging bodies within *Venice Saved* as a social event, allowing for experimentation with distancing oneself from the other as well as converging oneself with the other.[11] In my opinion Paul A. Kottman sums this up brilliantly when he writes about ancient Greek tragedy in the thought of Arendt: "What makes the theatre political, in Arendt's view, is not the imitative or mimetic quality of the work as such; rather it is the fact that tragedy "imitates" "man in his relation to others." Put simply, it is the relationality of the scene that lends the theater its political sense."[12] This notion of relationality provides salient resources for a nuanced understanding of the stage in *Venice Saved* as an Arendtian space of appearance on which different strategies of embodying and classifying the who-ness of individual bodies become possible or impossible.

When we retrieve an authentic understanding of the stage as a disruptive confrontation of bodies, theaters exhibit a metaphorical and actual space to experience "the political" in a way that perforates the accustomed private-public and social-political domains.[13] While scholars generally agree that Arendt was reluctant to engage with "the question of the body,"[14] I want to evoke a possibly deviant, or at least new position on this issue by Charles des Portes who has proposed a strong body-positive reading of Arendt. Des Portes suggests that, for Arendt, "corporeality is the *first* condition of politics as it makes possible the uniqueness of the 'who'"[15] and that, in relation to other bodies, the body "is the condition of plurality because of its requirement to distinctness."[16] In this regard, I read Arendt's attempt to metaphorize theater in such a way that *only* the distinct bodies surrounding each other in action and speech can "create a space between the participants which can find its proper location almost anywhere and anytime. It is the space of appearance in the widest sense of the word, namely, the space where I appear to others as others appear to me, where men exist not merely like other living or inanimate things but make their appearance explicitly" (HC 198–9).

Against this backdrop, a speculative Arendtian reflection on *Venice Saved* can be particularly illuminating. As Katherine T. Brueck points out, Simone Weil conceived her play on the model of Greek tragedy.[17] Accordingly, Weil deliberately chose the classical Aristotelian unities of time, space, and action which demand that dramatic tragedies not exceed a period of 24 hours, that they take place in a single location, and that they have only one principal line of action (VS 58). Likewise, the stage instructions for act one underline that "all the characters are assumed to be there for the whole act, moving around in the room" (VS 59). With this in mind, I suggest reading the material and temporal unities as viable strategies that Weil applies to direct the audience in constructing and inhabiting one single organic theatrical realm including both actors and spectators.

In the next segment, we focus on the metaphor of masking and thereby arrive at a juncture where Weil's dramaturgical staging meets Arendt's sense of theater as a metaphor for "the political," that is, a liberating vision of togetherness in speech and action.

Masking: How Classifying the Who-ness of the Individual Body Becomes Possible

The abundance of existing lines, versions, and stage directions of *Venice Saved* has prompted several artists around the world to complete parts of the missing text in order to stage the play. While appreciating the newer versions and creative appropriations of Weil's *Venice Saved*, I want to stress that we do not know how the finished play would have ultimately looked. The unfinished state of the material of Weil's play may give the impression that the barefaced rawness of the work-in-progress fragments attests to a greater originality of thought than the polished publications of other writers conceal. And yet, no reading of *Venice Saved* can claim to provide a closer interpretation of Weil's play none but all efforts to read it will

10. Embodying the In-Between

always remain a speculative exercise. Each speculation about the final outcome, thus, will always be a kind of fabulation, akin to my story of Blücher, Benjamin, and Arendt visiting the production. Rather than see the unfinished nature of the play as a limitation, I argue that it provides us with the opportunity to be creative when reading Weil's fragments. It enables us to carry Arendtian insights into our reading of *Venice Saved* despite Weil's and Arendt's differing approaches and intentions. In so doing, we can formulate new perspectives that help to accentuate the broad lines of the fragmentary play.

On stage, six characters (Jaffier, Pierre, Renaud, and three officers) enter and function as the head of a conspiracy to conquer Venice for the purpose of annexing it to the Habsburg empire in the 17th century. Surprisingly, only five of the six revolutionary men speak during the first act. Jaffier, the tragic hero and beloved of all, does not speak. The muteness of Jaffier allows us to explore a first speculative Arendtian reflection on *Venice Saved* by drawing on Arendt's thoughts about the masks worn by ancient actors, or the *dramatis personae*. As Arendt puts it in *On Revolution*, "The mask as such had to hide, or rather to replace, the actor's own face and countenance, but in a way that would make it possible for the voice to sound through" (OR 106).[18] For Arendt, this twofold function of hiding as well as actualizing a body's speakability qualified the metaphor of the *persona* to enter into legal terminology.

In case of Jaffier, as will be shown below, his uncanny muteness is turned into the opposite when his body is "masked" under social and military leadership. Accordingly, to exemplify this insight Arendt looks to Roman society, where the possibility of speech and action among the plurality of others opens the public space of the city:

> The distinction between a private individual in Rome and a Roman citizen was that the latter had a persona, a legal personality, as we would say; it was as though the law had affixed to him the part he was expected to play on the public scene, with the provision, however, that his own voice would be able to sound through. The point was that "it was not the natural Ego which enters the court of law. It is a right-and-duty-bearing person, created by the law, which appears before the law." Without his persona, there would be an individual without rights and duties, perhaps a "natural man"—that is, a human being or homo in the original meaning of the word, indicating someone outside the range of the law and the body politic of the citizens, as for instance a slave—but certainly a politically irrelevant being. (OR 106–7)

In light of this passage, I will call the "part one is expected to play on the public scene," with the provision, however, that "one's own voice is able to sound through," that is, the precondition for action, speech, and freedom: *masking*. To put it in another way, it is my objective to explain Arendt's account on political agency in terms of metaphorical practices of *masking*.

Venice Saved provides us with a good example of masking, metaphorizing the conditions for speech, action, and freedom. In the second scene, Renaud, a

Spanish lord, gives a speech about the impending doom of Venice. Weil writes that Renaud's speech, "should have the same effect on the spectator as it has on Jaffier" (VS 50). However, in this scene we do not get any information about the effect it has on Jaffier. It is only in hindsight, in scene three, that Weil reveals Jaffier's reaction. There, Renaud tells Pierre that he saw "Jaffier's face go pale and lose its composure as Jaffier listened" (VS 50). Concerned for their plan above all else, Renaud who "loves Jaffier too" advises Pierre, the leader of the conspiracy and Jaffier's best friend, to kill Jaffier (VS 62). Jaffier's failure in masking puts his very life at risk. At this juncture it is worthy to focus on what has been exposed that ultimately calls for Jaffier's death. Renauld refers to Jaffier's face as betraying "such weakness" (VS 62). On that account, we might ask what showing weakness actually reveals? Is it the personal failure of Jaffier or, perhaps, the unavowable vulnerability of the conspiracy itself? In *Venice Saved* this remains unresolved. Weil does not give us more information about what motivated the change in Jaffier's face. She tells us simply in the stage directions that it was a change "in his soul and this change remains mysterious" (VS 52).

Pierre eventually saves Jaffier's life and creates "something between" the natural weak man and the social man by *masking* him—without Jaffier ever speaking for himself. The first masking of Jaffier is Pierre's public declaration of his intimate friendship with Jaffier. Pierre tells Renaud that he "would sacrifice the whole world and every man alive for" Jaffier (VS 64). Jaffier receives a second masking as Pierre asks for additional testimonies and the officers describe Jaffier as a "natural leader" who officers and soldiers want to obey (VS 63). I want to read this scene in the following way: Pierre's posterior masking of Jaffier hides the natural "weak" private face of Jaffier. Concurrently, the further masking by other's testimonials reestablishes Jaffier's capacity for political speech and action. Attributed with the masking of familial relationship (by Pierre) and institutional leadership (by his soldiers) Jaffier not only stays alive but also takes command of the conspiracy when the Venetian military drafts Pierre in his duty as a Venetian officer. In response to his new position, Jaffier, now fully "masked," raises his voice for the first time.

Hence, we can observe that humans are deaf to "naked face speech," that is, without a mask, and only become capable of dialogue when masked. With the concept of the *dramatis personae*, Arendt provides a corresponding image to show how such a "dialogue between the deaf" can, nonetheless, take the shape of actual communication. This seems to indicate how both Arendt in her political theory and Weil in her stage directions stress the ambivalent dynamics of speakability. Both try to recover the inextricably *relational* and primordially *dysfunctional* nature of communication, in other words, how the pursuit of recognition involves the (mis-)recognition of "one's own fundamental situation and circumstances"[19] when being at the mercy of the other. Arendt observes that from this perspective the precarity of the space of appearance is one major aspect why theater can serve as a metaphor for politics:

> The performing arts, on the contrary, have indeed a strong affinity with politics. Performing artists—dancers, play-actors, musicians, and the like—need an audience

to show their virtuosity, just as acting men need the presence of others before whom they can appear; both need a publicly organized space for their "work," and both depend upon others for the performance itself. Such a space of appearance is not to be taken for granted wherever men live together in a community. (BPF 154)

Or, as Julia Kristeva puts it in her reading of Arendt's metaphorical use of theater, the actor becomes someone who is "at once an agent and a recipient."[20] Additionally, in *The Human Condition* Arendt outlines some of the key principles behind her reading of ancient Greek theater culture, stressing the metaphorical strength of theater for an understanding of the political regarding the human condition in his relationship to others:

The specific revelatory quality of action and speech, the implicit manifestation of the agent and speaker, is so indissolubly tied to the living flux of acting and speaking that it can be represented and "reified" only through a kind of repetition, the imitation or mimesis, which according to Aristotle prevails in all arts but is actually appropriate only to the drama, whose very name (from the Greek verb *dran*, "to act") indicates that playacting actually is an imitation of acting. The imitative element lies not only in the art of the actor, but, as Aristotle rightly claims, in the making or writing of the play, at least to the extent that the drama comes fully to life only when it is enacted in the theater. Only the actors and speakers who re-enact the story's plot can convey the full meaning, not so much of the story itself, but of the heroes who reveal themselves in it. In terms of Greek tragedy, this would mean that the story's direct as well as its universal meaning is revealed by the chorus, which does not imitate and whose comments are pure poetry, whereas the intangible identities of the agents in the story, since they escape all generalization and therefore all reification, can be conveyed only through an imitation of their acting. This is also why the theater is the political art par excellence; only there is the political sphere of life transposed into art. By the same token, it is the only art whose sole subject is man in his relationship to others. (HC 187–8)

This passage demonstrates the distinctive way of dramaturgical acting in which unique who-ness is tied to action and speech and both are approached as relational, that is, one is always already at the mercy of others in order to reveal oneself as a *who*. Arendt reedited this passage for the German translation of *The Human Condition*. In so doing, she highlighted the "So-und-nicht-anders-Sein der handelnden Personen, die der Schauspieler unmittelbar in ihrem eigensten Medium darstellt."[21] To put it differently, *in the making* or writing of the play the absent *who* of the character can only appear when another, nonfictional body offers itself to the absent body to perform its speech and action for it. For example, the actor portraying Hamlet reveals oneself as a particular *who* before the audience in the theater on any given performance, but also before the enormous sociocultural *who* that is Hamlet, Prince of Denmark.

With this in mind, I read Arendt in such a way that there is no primordial "original" that is going to be revealed but a "coming-to-presence"[22] in the face of others. In this respect, Arendt adds another paradigmatic sentence to the German translation of *The Human Condition* that is absent in the English original. This sentence relativizes her previous argument of the precarious space of appearance: "Der politische Bereich im Sinne der Griechen gleicht einer solchen immerwährenden Bühne, auf der es gewissermaßen nur ein Auftreten, aber kein Abtreten gibt, und dieser Bereich entsteht direkt aus einem Miteinander, dem 'mitteilenden Teilnehmen an Worten und Taten.'"[23] The real-life stage of the political and the actions decided there—in contrast to its metaphorical meaning in theater—provided their agents, once publicly present, with a *permanent* space of appearance. Accordingly, for Arendt's free agent, who is among the other free agents in the public sphere, any withdrawing from appearance by disappearing is no real option or possibility. In comparison, Homi K. Bhabha writes critically about such unreserved affirmation of a liberating vision of togetherness that he reads in Arendt:

> This repetition of the agent, reified in the liberal vision of togetherness, is quite different from my sense of the contingent agency for our postcolonial age. The reasons for this are not difficult to find. Arendt's belief in the revelatory qualities of Aristotelian *mimesis* are grounded in a notion of community, or the public sphere, that is largely consensual ... [by contrast] social violence is, for Arendt, the denial of the disclosure of agency, the point at which "speech becomes mere talk, simply one more means towards the end."[24]

Against this backdrop, I share Bhabha's sense of the contingent and precarious agency. Here, I think it is particularly interesting to highlight the concept and architecture of the stage as a material limit, obstacle, and instrument of symbolizing a metaphorically distancing "in-between" that troubles bodies also in nonconsensual ways. In this perspective, the material stage can be read as addressing the performative acts on it in a new light, that is, the precarity in the finding of oneself to others that manifests particularly along the storyline and stage directions of *Venice Saved*. This becomes most evident when in the third act Jaffier experiences himself as a speechless animal and only utters a lonely monologue into the audience. I will go into this in detail in the next but one segment.

First, however, the following segment focuses on the breaking point between Weil's stage directions and Arendt's metaphorical reflections on masking. While Arendt's metaphorical use of theater holds on to the optimistic promise of agency, speech, and freedom in the public sphere, Weil uses the second act of *Venice Saved* to exemplify how the metaphorical mask, while enabling political action and speakability, may lead to a dangerous disembodiment and a lack of distance because of their inherent social fabrication.

The Disembodiment of Masking

In the stage directions of the first act, Weil writes that the six characters should become present in "joy, pride, [and] intoxication in action and in power without any shadow of concern" and, as Weil notes in view of the audience, "the spectator is to desire the success of the enterprise" (VS 62, 50) and "to give form to the sentiment that it is the good that is abnormal" (VS 51). Inlaid onto the dialogues and bodily gestures of *Venice Saved*, Weil presents evil as the lack of distance, which in turn results from giving in to force, that is, paradoxically believing that one is a free agent in executing force. Yet, as Weil's play develops, we learn from Weil's stage directions that the true subject of the conspiracy is not Jaffier (or Pierre or the Habsburg empire) but force itself. It violently carries away all who touch it and think to control it. Expressed in the language of dreaming, delusion, and unreality, force renders everyone and everything immediately graspable, it turns everything, particularly persons into mere things at hand. Raptured by the intoxication of force, evil appears as the most natural thing ever, and thus, in *Venice Saved* "evil should be shown to be vulgar, monotonous, dismal and boring" (VS 51).[25] Weil ties this effect of (lost) affect in evil to a kind of contagious disembodiment or collective embodiment without limitations, notably in the metaphor of dreaming. Gazing together at Venice, Renaud and Jaffier share in a vision of disembodied dreaming. Weil emphasizes through Renaud's mouth that "men of action and enterprise are dreamers":

> [Jaffier:] We, a few unknown men, will become its [Venice's] masters. And I think I must be dreaming. [Renaud:] Yes, we are dreaming. Men of action and enterprise are dreamers; they use arms to make others dream their dreams. The victor lives his dream; the vanquished lives another's dream. All the men of Venice who live through the next night and day will spend the rest of their lives wondering if they wake or dream … To see today these men of Venice, so proud, who think that they exist. They each believe they have a family, a house, goods, books, rare paintings. They take themselves seriously. And as of now they no longer exist … . Every object on every day will remind somebody … that he is alive only as long as you want him alive. And their life as well as will model itself on your thought. Their life and their death will only be your dream. (VS 72)

Drawing on Arendt's metaphor of masking as the condition to appear in public space and to speak and act, we might ask if in *Venice Saved* the necessary masking turns out to be social illusion, that is, *dreaming*. When the newly socially masked Jaffier starts speaking for the first time in the passage above he proclaims himself to be the future master of Venice and reexplains the previous change of his face, that is, the moment of his social *unmaskedness*, saying that he was "feeling pity at the idea of the city being sacked" (VS 69). In contrast to the "men of action and enterprise," pity appears as a deficiency, a kind of paralysis or inability to act while dreaming is considered action par excellence.

Jaffier then looks at sunset: "The dying sun still covers her [Venice] with its final rays. If it only knew, then it would stop out of pity. But the sun has no pity for her, nor, alas do I" (VS 87). Notably, the course of the sun takes on a highly ambivalent position. On the one hand, it sets the condition of possibility for the destruction of Venice. On the other hand, in the eyes of the Venetians who enjoy their city anew this fateful morning, it represents the guarantee for the carefree continuation of the city as a space of appearance. Here, however, a political question arises, namely, how, in the midst of the omnipresence of force, could one withdraw from force without becoming passively complicit in it. The sun rises onto annihilation but does it not also usher in new beginnings? Significantly, Jaffier's unreflective use of the term "pity" as paralysis resonates with a common argument, notably also made by Arendt, which contrasts pity with *dispassionate* solidarity:

> Pity may be the perversion of compassion, but its alternative is solidarity. It is out of pity that men are "attracted toward *les hommes faibles*," but it is out of solidarity that they establish deliberately and, as it were, dispassionately a community of interest with the oppressed and exploited. (OR 88)

Akin to the dispassionate nature of solidarity, Weil puts Jaffier's excuse into perspective emphasizing that the condition of "true pity" is found only in the place of "infinite distance." Weil writes accordingly, "pity is an attribute that is truly divine. There is no human pity. Pity implies an infinite distance. There is no compassion for what is near Jaffier" (VS 54). Consequently, I propose a reading of *Venice Saved* that addresses a certain loss in the entanglement of masking and the primacy of action. This is the loss of, as Weil says, "true pity," and thus of nothing less than reality itself. From this perspective, the coming into view of a unique *who* due to the space of appearance in speech and action risks a kind of blindness, in the words of Weil, a blindness to one's own enmeshment with force.

Retrospectively, Jaffier's sudden gift of voice, speech, and freedom by the power of masking suggests another reading of his uncanny muteness which has lasted to this moment in the storyline. The plot twist is congruent with Weil's notion of *reading* which she explicates in the *Notebooks* as follows: "One reads, but also one is read by others. Interpositions of such readings. To force somebody to read himself as you read him (slavery). To force others to read you as you read yourself (conquest). Mechanism? More often than not, dialogue between the deaf" (NB 43). Force, which is implicit to reading (and masking), in *Venice Saved*, makes its agents believe that power was fatefully given to or taken from them while, in reality, everything is at the immediate and indiscriminate disposal of force. Beyond a mere literary embellishment or metaphor, the idea of "infinite distance" poses a cognitive conundrum irritating the illusory "promises of force" to gain limitless power. This conundrum is based on the fact that distances constitute a span between two distinct situated things. However, calling a distance infinite spotlights the impossibility of perceiving this distance in the sphere of matter and its "corporeality."

Weil, in a manner reminiscent of Plato[26], argues, however, that beauty is an exception to the rule in which limited matter shows the quality of infinite distance. Plato writes in the *Symposium* that the contemplation of beautiful bodies leads to the contemplation of the inconceivable beauty in itself. Yet, beauty in Plato's and Weil's thought does not simply mark an aesthetic pleasure, but precisely the impossible possibility of infinite distance. Accordingly, we can read in Weil's

Notebooks: "Beauty is a sensual attraction that maintains one at a certain distance and implies a renunciation including the most intimate form of renunciation, that of the imagination. One wants to devour all other desirable objects. Beauty is something that one desires without wanting to devour it. We simply desire that it should be" (NB 335).[27] For Jaffier, whose body dwells in the very center of the city he is going to sack, Violetta the daughter of a leading Venetian politician, is suddenly *embodying* such beauty that establishes an infinite distance in relation to his *persona*. The encounter with the young woman is ripe for his dramatic subjectivation process. In contrast to his earlier disembodied dreaming, when Jaffier is now facing Violetta, he finds himself thrown into a space of "infinite distance." Weil explains this change by writing in the instructions that Jaffier "gives expression to love for Venice made incarnate for him by Violetta … . The moment of Jaffier's meditation at the end of the second act is the moment when reality enters into him, because he has paid attention" (VS 52–3). Additionally, it may shed some light on what happens between Jaffier and Violetta when we consider how Weil describes beauty in the following way:

> Beauty: a fruit which we look at without trying to seize it … To love purely is to consent to distance, it is to adore the distance between ourselves and that which we love … distance is the soul of beauty. (NB 615)

The bodily encounter with the beauty of Violetta reveals to Jaffier that it is impossible for someone who recognizes reality, that is, who *loves*, to destroy and that he has no choice but to save it. Thus, the "Platonist" Violetta is right when she makes the claim that Venice's "beauty is a better defence than that of soldiers, better than the concerns of statesmen" (VS 82). While the men on stage ridicule Violetta for this statement, it presents a central thought that J. P. Little identifies as central to Weil's "most mature social theory" at work in *Venice Saved*.[28]

From this perspective, Violetta's claim that beauty is a better defense than either arms or diplomacy is far more than a simple leap between the aesthetic and the ethical. Athanasios Moulakis's notion of "Weil's politics of self-denial" sheds light on what is so central to Weil's "most mature social theory." For Weil, it is only the disposition of public life *relating* to the higher good that can protect human civilization from its (self-)annihilation. Moulakis writes:

> Democracy, as well as the law and the person, cannot be absolute goods for Weil because they are part of a middle region, a region that comes very close to the Platonic metaxy … For her metaxy is the bridge that allows the uniting of man with his true self, the "eternal part" of the soul with God. She included in the concept art, methodical science, and of course, the prototype of all the others, work … there is no guarantee for democracy, or for the protection of the person against the collectivity, without a disposition of public life relating to the higher good which is impersonal and unrelated to any political form. The *modi* by which the good is crystallized in society, the legitimizing ties to justice, must be invented, since, according to Weil, there are no models.[29]

Disapproving of the existing literary and theatrical solutions to the double betrayal of Jaffier, Weil decided to restage anew the novelistic material authored by the Abbé de Saint-Réal. Weil's Platonist revision was the third version after the English version *Venice Preserv'd* (1682) by Thomas Otway and its German adaptation *Das gerettete Venedig* (1904) by Hugo von Hofmannsthal. The two already existing theatrical performances offended Weil due to their lack of understanding that the doomed city had not been saved by inner-worldly mechanisms. Weil fiercely argued against the interpretation that Venice was saved by Jaffier simply falling in love with Violetta; in other words, Jaffier saved Venice *for* Violetta. Weil's interpretation why in the end Venice was saved is of a distinctive "supernaturalist" and "redemptive nature."[30] In her perspective, hidden behind this love episode between Jaffier and Violetta, something happened that has a decisive political significance: reality enters into human consciousness due to an event of infinite distance in the experience of beauty. At the same time, the concept of infinite distance marks a clear departure from the Aristotelian optimism of political agency that guides Arendt's anti-Platonist theorization of the public realm. In the following segment, we look at an aspect where, in my reading, Weil entirely departs from Arendt's thinking, rejecting the primacy of action in favor of an openness for the event of the supernatural.

Unmasking: When Classifying the Who-ness of the Individual Body Becomes Impossible

Jaffier has fallen prey to the beauty of Violetta and, through Violetta, the beauty of Venice. He finally reveals the conspiracy to the Venetian officials. It is important to emphasize that Jaffier can only save Venice at the very last moment because of his top social and military position, his action, speech, and freedom, that is, his mask. Yet, at a single blow he becomes a traitor as Venice suddenly starts killing all conspirators despite the fact that the Venetian officials just moments before had solemnly promised to Jaffier to spare those Jaffier had listed. Venice allows Jaffier alone, of all conspirators, to stay alive and even to enter their Venetian army at a top rank, though, if he declines, he will be expelled from Venice forever. Reminiscent of the biblical Books of Job and Isaiah, the entire third act involves Jaffier standing mostly mute as a *body without a mask*. The Venetians insult him, and Jaffier speaks but no one on stage can hear his voice any longer, but only the audience can. Correspondingly, emphasis of the third act falls on Jaffier's bodily immobility as he stands motionless facing the audience. For Weil, what is immobile lends itself to the attentiveness of necessity in the same way as beauty does, however mostly in ways of suffering. Jaffier then enters into an *intimate soliloquy* that turns into a monologue with the silent audience traversing the fourth wall:

> And now I'm like an animal. And in my greatest need my voice can no longer be heard ... my pain is mute and my crime only wearies me in vain. No sign of emotion on the hard faces around me. When I hear their words, I hear only a

noise that hurts me, for nothing replies to me ... Is this a dream where I am? Have I ceased to be a man? ... If only I could exist and never see the sun ... The sun makes me afraid; death tears away the last veil, makes me still more afraid; for death will strip my soul naked. God my soul has need of flesh, in order to hide its shame. (VS 102–3)

In light of this passage, I want to refer back to the actual stage as a material limit, obstacle, and instrument of symbolizing a metaphorically distancing "in-between" that troubles bodies in nonconsensual ways: the stage becomes at the same time a relational threshold between Jaffier and the audience and marks the unbridgeable divide between their two worlds. Weil highlights in the stage directions the idea of "Jaffier's supplication and despair" in order to "insist perhaps even more on the *silence* that answers him" (VS 54). Such a theatrical repetition and imitation performs, to put it in the vocabulary of Weil, *decreation*, which is the repetition and imitation of the decentering of God in the act of creation or, to name an important biblical model for Weil in the Hebrew bible, in the suffering of Job.[31] In this regard, Weil writes in the stage instructions:

> Thus perfect detachment alone allows us to see the nakedness of things, without the fog of lying values. This is why it was necessary for Job to suffer boils and the dung heap: so the beauty of the world could be revealed to him. For there is no detachment without pain. And there is no pain that can be borne without hatred and lies unless there is detachment. (*Venice Saved* should reproduce this movement). (VS 52)

Significantly, in the very moment of Jaffier's total detachment, the sun rises and everyone including Jaffier suddenly moves and leaves the stage, also leaving the fate of Jaffier unknown to the audience; then Violetta enters the stage and stands alone singing a hymn about the glorious day. At this moment, she can be read as impersonating Venice, living the life of the newborn city: fully unaware of what happened, she does not know that she and the entire city were "only" secured by her beauty, "infinitely precious ... a precarious happiness, fragile—a happiness of chance" (VS 54).

Simone Weil's theatrical adaptation of *Venice Saved* may come across as tacky (to say the least) and highly irritating in its clichédness and flat character figurations, not to mention the infuriating gender stereotypes and meager narrative developments. To dwell on this, however, is to miss the point of this play. Composing *Venice Saved* while facing persecution, Weil is convinced that within the material of the Abbé de Saint-Réal, something extraordinarily decisive manifests itself, namely that, in times of utmost need, redemption is not accomplished through action alone, but rather that every action must *open* itself to the possibility of "relating to the higher good which is impersonal and unrelated to any political form."[32] In the concluding segment, I briefly want to refer to the reflections on Arendt by Judith Butler and Adriana Cavarero, which, in my reading, allow exploring some further bodily aspects of *Venice Saved* even after our departure from Arendt insomuch as, for Weil, every opening to the supernatural always takes place in bodily terms.

Embodying the In-Between Relation That Both Binds and Differentiates

The exposed vulnerability of Violetta's female body, embodying the entire city, beautiful in the eyes of Jaffier, should not be read too easily as a result of the male gaze. As Weil contends, beauty awakens us from the dream inflicted by force and is thus a matter of attention to necessity, and this is why, for Weil, "theatre must manifest both interior and exterior necessity" (VS 57) to reveal the illusionary promise of force to control it in action. For her, the decisive junction of inner and outer necessity exists foremost in the force-driven interaction between bodies situated within these inner and outer necessities. I want to support a reading that in *Venice Saved* a primary *in-between* is constituted by means of the performance of the concrete bodies on stage.[33] This becomes evident in the following scene in *Venice Saved*, for example: while Jaffier's officers fantasize about raping Violetta (VS 84), Jaffier interrupts them asking if they will also have the courage to kill all of the friends they have in Venice. One of the officers replies with a memory of another sacking: "They saw me and threw themselves at me, clutching my cloak; I pushed them away, not even recognizing them" (VS 85). In the officer's words, we encounter an association of the inability to recognize a *who* present in front of us and our physical attitude of rectitude that refuses to turn to the supplicant. The association of the inability to recognize a *who* present in front of us and our physical attitude of rectitude reminds me of Adriana Cavarero's adaption of Arendt: to recognize the relation of "oneself to others," for Cavarero, requires one to actually *incline* toward the other with one's body, paying attention to the other with one's body in a way that allows the other to act and speak. In this regard, Cavarero invokes Arendt's idea of relational subjectivity and calls upon the bodily gesture of the mother figure:

> Embodying the other in relation to the newborn over whom she leans, the mother not only confirms that scene's relational and antivertical character, but also, by predisposing it to an altruistic ethics, requires that it be understood in terms of dependence.[34]

For Cavarero, it is inclining oneself *to others*, affirming the dependence of the other, that the other can appear as an irremediably unique being.

Interestingly, we can see inclination in Jaffier metaphorically expressed in the event of beauty when he is mute and is paying attention. Against this background, *Venice Saved* may present an alternative form of *who-ness* in the event of beauty differing from masking, speech, action, and freedom. To put it differently, we can ask what the condition for an event of beauty in the eyes of Simone Weil might look like? One could answer this question with these stage instructions by Weil: "[It] is not what is social; it is a human milieu of which we are no more conscious than the air we breathe. A contact with nature, the past, tradition, a μεταξύ [metaxy]" (VS 52).

To shed further light on the nature of such *in-between* events (metaxy events), I want to consider Judith Butler's critical reading of Arendt on the question of how bodies appear. Butler notes that the notion of *appearing* in Arendt must be amplified:

> I am, as a body, not only for myself, not even primarily for myself, but I find myself, if I find myself at all, constituted and dispossessed by the perspective of others. So, for political action, I must appear to others in ways I cannot know, and in this way, my body is established by perspectives that I cannot inhabit but that, surely, inhabit me. This is an important point because it is not the case that the body only establishes my own perspective; it is also what displaces that perspective and makes that displacement into a necessity. This happens most clearly, when we think about bodies that act together. No one body establishes the space of appearance, but this action, this performative exercise, happens only "between" bodies, in a space that constitutes the gap between my own body and another's. In this way, my body does not act alone when it acts politically. Indeed, the action emerges from the "between," a spatial figure for a relation that both binds and differentiates.³⁵

I read Butler's passage on the in-between relation that both binds and differentiates in the following way: bodies are acting on stage in such a way that bodies depend on each other in disclosing who-ness precisely in the way they physically act together: one in front of the other, as subjects and objects likewise, distinct and unique persons. Together the bodies share and create a common space. Their who-ness does not depend on any existing particular political entity but "is made precisely when bodies appear together, or rather, when through their action, they bring the space of appearance into being." It is an embodied set of social relations that both binds and differentiates, the in-between, that bodies are constituted as well as dispossessed by the perspective of others. In Butler, the bodies no longer appear because of a simply given public space, but instead, allying with other bodies, they mutually expose their who-ness ideally *in-between* fragile networks of dependency and care, love, and attention that have become emblematic as the physical gestures of their bodies, or as Weil puts it, "a human milieu of which we are no more conscious than the air we breathe."

In a similar manner, *Venice Saved* can be a metaphor ultimately rejecting the idea of any existing "political" as it discloses dependent persons in an event of beauty that is *relational* and relies on receptivity provided by a human milieu rather than individual action. In the play, the physical gestures of infinite distance and immobility refer to an event of beauty that leads to recognizing the who-ness of the one who is beautiful only "between" bodies. Thus, Venice *is not* beautiful for Jaffier in terms of an object, but the event of beauty takes place when he encounters Violetta, and this relationality in-between, unclosing for the event of beauty, prevents him from destroying Venice. The story of how this vision can fail by turning into unlimited circles of violence and yet still function as scene of salvation is the story taking place on the stage of *Venice Saved*. It is a story that ultimately leads to the resignation of action in favor of a passivity beyond passivity that lends itself to the higher good which is impersonal and unrelated to any political form.

Conclusion

So, what is the result of this encounter between Arendtian metaphorizing of theater and Weil's play? In summary, *Venice Saved* ultimately rejects the idea that politics is about action for its own sake and instead presents a view of action as a means of orienting oneself toward or away from an opening for the emergence of a higher, supernatural good. From this perspective, it would be too simplistic to reduce the differences between Simone Weil and Hannah Arendt to their philosophical figureheads, Plato and Aristotle, a move that has become all too obvious. Instead, I want to argue that the decisive difference lies in the situatedness of both writers: while Arendt was witness to the end of Second World War and the ensuing struggle for justice, Weil's outlook stalls in a moment of extreme despair. This difference, which cannot only be called Platonic and Aristotelian, is revealed in the way *Venice Saved* gives up on Arendt's imperative that one must act. This is despite the fact that Weil and Arendt follow the common path of thought that action is inevitable up to the point of resignation.

Notes

1 Janet Patricia Little, "Society as Mediator in Simone Weil's 'Venise Sauvée,'" *Modern Language Review* 65, no. 2 (1970): 298. In their English translation of the play (VS), Silvia Panizza and Philip Wilson provide a summary of the main themes of *Venice Saved*. They are as follows: (1) history as the place of philosophical perception, (2) the 'social' as the Great Beast in contrast to the 'city', (3) roots and rootlessness, (4) remaining truthful to supernatural law, (5) decreation, (6) beauty, and (7) the Christian cross and affliction (VS 13–38).
2 Willy Brandt, "The Political Significance of the Theatre," *Comparative Drama* 7 (1973): 222.
3 See Weil OL for the issues of the "collective" or the "great beast" of society in Weilian thought.
4 See Erika Fischer-Lichte, *Theatre Sacrifice Ritual: Exploring Forms of Political Theatre* (Oxford: Routledge, 2005), 96.
5 For the relation of Simone Weil's *Venice Saved* to the contemporary propaganda theater, see Thomas Sojer, "Theatre as Creative Failure: Simone Weil's Venise sauvée Revisited," *Platform: Journal of Theatre and Performing Arts* 1 (2019): 17–30.
6 For an overview of research on *Venice Saved*, see introduction to the play in VS.
7 Charles des Portes, "Hannah Arendt's Hidden Phenomenology of the Body," *Human Studies* 45 (2022): 154.

8   Here the others refer to both the absent body that is reenacted (the role played) and to the other present bodies (the actor, the other actors, and the audience) who become aware of the who's reenacted presence. For example, the actor portraying Hamlet reveals oneself as a particular who before the audience in the theater on any given performance, but also before the enormous sociocultural who that is Hamlet, prince of Denmark.
9   Peter J. Euben, "Arendt's Hellenism," in *The Cambridge Companion to Hannah Arendt*, ed. Dana Villa (Cambridge: Cambridge University Press 2000), 159.
10 Hannah Arendt, *Lectures on Kant's Political Philosophy* (Chicago: University of Chicago Press, 1992), 67.
11 Often these strategies are coined by the term *somatechnics*, that is, "how embodiment is always already technological, and how technology is always already embodied and embedded" (176). See Iris van der Tuin and Nanna Verhoeff, "The Notion of 'Somatechnics,'" in *Critical Concepts for the Creative Humanities* (London: Rowman & Littlefield, 2022), 176. Additionally, *somatechnics* alludes to Ann Pirruccello's term of somatic practice in reference to Weil's performative philosophy. See Ann Pirruccello, "Making the World My Body: Simone Weil and Somatic Practice," *Philosophy East and West* 52, no. 4 (2002): 483.
12 See Paul A. Kottman, "Memory, Mimesis, Tragedy: The Scene before Philosophy," *Theatre Journal Baltimore* 55, no. 1 (2003): 82.
13 See Rieke Trimcev, *Politik als Spiel. Zur Geschichte einer Kontingenzmetapher im politischen Denken des 20. Jahrhunderts* (Nomos: Baden Baden, 2018), 208–70.
14 des Portes, "Hannah Arendt's Hidden Phenomenology," 139.
15 Ibid., 153.
16 Ibid., 154.
17 Katherine T. Brueck, *Redemption of Tragedy: The Literary Vision of Simone Weil* (New York: State University of New York Press, 1995), 68.
18 In her essay "The Social Question," the second chapter of OR, Arendt tells us that while Marx favored the metaphor "birth-pangs of revolutions," those who actually enacted the French Revolution "draw their images from the language of theatre" (OR 106).
19 Patchen Markell, *Bound by Recognition* (Princeton: Princeton University Press, 2009), 5.
20 Julia Kristeva, *Hannah Arendt: Life Is a Narrative*, vol. 1 (New York: Columbia University Press, 2001), 78.
21 Translation by the author: "Being-so-and-not-other of the acting persons, whom the actor portrays imminently in their own most unique being-a-medium": Hannah Arendt, Vita activa oder Vom tätigen Leben (Munich: Piper, 2018), 233.
22 Roberto Esposito, *The Origin of the Political: Hannah Arendt or Simone Weil* (New York: Fordham University Press, 2017), 23.
23 Translation by the author: "The political realm according to the Greeks resembles such a continuous theatre stage, on which only appearance effectively happens, but no exit from the stage, and this realm arises directly from a togetherness, the 'participatory participation' in words and deeds." Arendt, *Vita activa oder Vom tätigen Leben*, 249. For the original see HC 198.
24 Homi K. Bhaba, "The Postcolonial and the Postmodern," in *The Cultural Studies Reader*, ed. Simon During (Oxford: Routledge, 1999), 206.
25 This reminded me also about Arendt's experiences during the Eichmann trial in Jerusalem. For Arendt the "sheer thoughtlessness" of Eichmann "predisposed him

to become one of the greatest criminals of that period" and inspired her to use the disputed term "banality of evil" (EJ 252). See Irving Howe, *A Margin of Hope: An Intellectual Autobiography* (London: Secker & Warburg, 1982), 268–74. The publication of *Eichmann in Jerusalem* ended Arendt's long-lasting friendship with Gershom Scholem and Lionel Abel and started a fierce debate with a highly polemical article in the *Partisan Review*. The critiques agreed with Jean Améry "that there is no 'banality of evil,' and Hannah Arendt, who wrote about it in her Eichmann book, knew the enemy of mankind only from hearsay, saw him through the glass cage. When an event places the most extreme demands on us, one ought not to speak of banality." See Jennifer L. Geddes, "The Banality of Evil," in *Evil: A History*, ed. Andrew P. Chignell (Oxford: Oxford University Press, 2019), 423–8.

26 Cf. Platon, *Le banquet ou De l'amour. Traduction intégrale et nouvelle suivie de commentaires de Plotin sur l'amour* (Paris: Payot, 1922), 126.
27 In *Gravity and Grace*, we can read a corresponding, much-quoted passage: "The subject of art is sensible and contingent beauty discerned through the network of chance and evil": Simone Weil, *Gravity and Grace* (London: Routledge, 2002), 148. This passage is absent in the editions of the *Notebooks*; most probably Gustave Thibon rewrote this sentence according to the following passage in the *Notebooks*: "The notion of condition of existence is for us the sole link between good and necessity. Beauty is the harmony between chance and good. The real (for man) is what is at the same time felt and thought" (NB 266).
28 Little, "Society as Mediator," 298.
29 Athanasios Moulakis, *Simone Weil and the Politics of Self-Denial* (Columbia: University of Missouri Press, 1998), 201.
30 See Brueck, *Redemption of Tragedy*, 57–8.
31 See Enikő Sepsi, *Poetic Images, Presence, and the Theater of Kenotic Rituals* (Oxford: Routledge, 2022), 79–88.
32 Moulakis, *Simone Weil and the Politics*, 201.
33 See also Charity K. Hamilton, "Troubled Bodies: Metaxu, Suffering and the Encounter with the Divine," *Feminist Theology* 22 (2013), 88–97.
34 Adriana Cavarero, *Inclinations: A Critique of Rectitude* (Stanford: Stanford University Press, 2016), 102.
35 Judith Butler, *Notes toward a Performative Theory of Assembly* (Boston: Harvard University Press, 2015), 76–7.

Bibliography

Arendt, Hannah. *Lectures on Kant's Political Philosophy*. Chicago: University of Chicago Press, 1992.

Bhaba, Homi K. "The Postcolonial and the Postmodern." In *The Cultural Studies Reader*. Edited by Simon During. London: Routledge, 1999, pp. 189–208.

Brandt, Willy. "The Political Significance of the Theatre." *Comparative Drama* 7 (1973): 222–30.

Brueck, Katherine T. *Redemption of Tragedy: The Literary Vision of Simone Weil*. New York: State University of New York Press, 1995.

Butler, Judith. *Notes toward a Performative Theory of Assembly*. Cambridge: Harvard University Press, 2015.

Cavarero, Adriana. *Inclinations: A Critique of Rectitude*. Stanford: Stanford University Press, 2016.
des Portes, Charles. "Hannah Arendt's Hidden Phenomenology of the Body." *Human Studies* 45 (2022): 139–56.
Esposito, Roberto. *The Origin of the Political: Hannah Arendt or Simone Weil*. New York: Fordham University Press, 2017.
Euben, Peter J. "Arendt's Hellenism." In *The Cambridge Companion to Hannah Arendt*. Edited by Dana Villa. Cambridge: Cambridge University Press, 2000, pp. 151–64.
Fischer-Lichte, Erika. *Theatre Sacrifice Ritual: Exploring Forms of Political Theatre*. London: Routledge, 2005.
Geddes, Jennifer L. "The Banality of Evil." In *Evil: A History*. Edited by Andrew P. Chignell. New York: Oxford University Press, 2019, pp. 423–8.
Hamilton, Charity K. "Troubled Bodies: Metaxu, Suffering and the Encounter with the Divine." *Feminist Theology* 22 (2013): 88–97.
Howe, Irving. *A Margin of Hope: An Intellectual Autobiography*. London: Secker & Warburg, 1982.
Kottman, Paul A. "Memory, Mimesis, Tragedy: The Scene before Philosophy." *Theatre Journal Baltimore* 55, no. 1 (2003): 81–97.
Kristeva, Julia. *Hannah Arendt*, vol. 1. New York: Columbia University Press, 2001.
Little, Janet Patricia. "Society as Mediator in Simone Weil's 'Venise Sauvée.'" *Modern Language Review* 65, no. 2 (1970): 98–305.
Markell, Patchen. *Bound by Recognition*. Princeton: Princeton University Press, 2009.
Moulakis, Athanasios. *Simone Weil and the Politics of Self-denial*. Columbia: University of Missouri Press, 1998.
Pirruccello, Ann. "Making the World My Body: Simone Weil and Somatic Practice." *Philosophy East and West* 52, no. 4 (2002): 479–97.
Platon. *Le banquet ou De l'amour. Traduction intégrale et nouvelle suivie de commentaires de Plotin sur l'amour*. Paris: Payot, 1922.
Sepsi, Enikő. *Poetic Images, Presence, and the Theater of Kenotic Rituals*. London: Routledge, 2022.
Sojer, Thomas. "Theatre as Creative Failure: Simone Weil's Venise sauvée Revisited." *Platform: Journal of Theatre and Performing Arts* 1 (2019): 17–30.
Trimcev, Rieke. *Politik als Spiel. Zur Geschichte einer Kontingenzmetapher im politischen Denken des 20. Jahrhunderts*. Baden-Baden: Nomos, 2018.
Van der Tuin, Iris, and Verhoeff, Nanna. *Critical Concepts for the Creative Humanities*. London: Rowman & Littlefield, 2022.
Weil, Simone. *Ecrits de Londres et dernières lettres*. Paris: Gallimard, 1957.
Weil, Simone. *Gravity and Grace*. London: Routledge, 2002.

Chapter 11

BEAUTY AS THE BEGINNING AND END OF
JUSTICE: AESTHETIC POLITICS IN HANNAH ARENDT
AND SIMONE WEIL

Catherine Craig and Sara MacDonald

Introduction

Simone Weil and Hannah Arendt were both significantly impacted by the events leading up to the Second World War. Consequently, their interest in Homer's *Iliad*, the great poem of war, is not surprising.[1] Despite significant differences in their reading of *The Iliad* and in their treatment of aesthetics more generally, Weil and Arendt come to surprisingly similar conclusions about the place of art and beauty in the creation of just communities. In brief, both women argue that the inculcation of a love of beauty, nurtured in the appreciation of works of art, encourages respect for the autonomy of others and helps to create communities of reciprocal goodwill.

Weil and Arendt each emphasize the necessity of creating and maintaining a space in which a plurality of perspectives and actions can emerge. And both argue that it is the individual's responsibility to care for the spaces we share with others, particularly those that include people who might be overlooked or oppressed. As Cecilia Sjöholm notes, works of art can aid us in taking responsibility by helping to foster an awareness of the phenomenal nature of the plurality we experience in the public sphere.[2] When engaging with a work of art, we are carried away from the immediacy of our worldly existence and the concrete realities of the artwork itself, toward that which is not currently taking place. The artist or author discloses to us a piece of their unique vision of the world. In this way, the experience of art can make us sensitive to the many diverse appearances of public life. Like works of art, other people appear before us to disclose something of their perspective. In this moment of disclosure, provided we remain attentive to the phenomenal appearance of the other and to the partial nature of that appearance, we are enabled to respond in a way that allows for revelations of the world we share. Works of beauty contribute to the plurality in which we participate insofar as they can become a part of the public sphere. The perspectives they disclose impinge upon our own, calling on us to respond to them. In this way, artwork that is of cultural significance guides public discourse by revealing diverse perspectives and ways of understanding the world.

What is more, works of beauty demand that we maintain a certain distance from them in order that they might properly be seen. This instills within us an attitude of care not just for the art but also for other people. We desire others to also encounter this beauty, sharing distinct impressions of a common experience. In caring for the plurality of beautiful images, we become attuned to the analogous care that others require from us. While art can be consumed, just as people can be used, works of beauty and culture tend to resist this wholesale consumption. Their very existence, inculcating wonder in their viewers, results in the desire not to consume but rather to care for and protect. In the same way, works of beauty might move us to realize and ultimately care for other voices that appear alongside our own.

Arendt, Politics, and The Iliad

Arendt argues that only when we are freed from focusing on the necessities of life, and in community with others, that we can truly express the "miracle" she describes as human life, namely the capacity to freely begin without any guarantee of where this "beginning" might lead. Arendt writes, "The miracle that saves the world, the realm of human affairs, from its normal, 'natural' ruin is ultimately the fact of natality, in which the faculty of action is ontologically rooted" (HC 247). No one is born of "necessity," and our appearance in the world speaks to the possibility of overcoming the necessity of nature and the natural forces that control so much of our finite existences.

Politics, Arendt suggests, is where the miracle of our birth finds fulfillment. An individual enters into the political realm where she discloses her intention to others and is put in the position of having to spontaneously respond to their reactions. In this free and reciprocal exchange of ideas, political activity is given shape. The initial principle that motivated the individual might be exchanged for another, further defined, and eventually becomes an explicit endeavor. Arendt argues that the greatest of these political endeavors, perhaps because it was the first, is depicted in Homer's *Iliad*. Leaving their homes behind, Greek kings and soldiers, united in their outrage at Paris's treatment of Menelaus, reached the shores of Troy and created a pseudo-*polis*. The outcome of the speeches and actions in their camps at Troy directed the ongoing activities of the Greek warriors. Arendt's attention to Homer's *Iliad* suggests that the beauty of the poem might incite its readers to a similar sort of political action: activity aimed at a principle of general worth enacted with the courage required when one is uncertain.

Toward the end of *The Iliad*, Menelaus confronts the Trojan Peisandros and explicitly accuses the Trojans of disrespecting the laws of hospitality made sacred by Zeus.[3] The Trojans, he notes, are insatiable, incapable of setting aside their appetites for the sake of what is just. Of course, the example par excellence is Paris's abduction of Helen. The principle of hospitality, while exemplified in different moments throughout *The Iliad*, is most notably present when Priam goes to Achilles's camp to ransom the body of his son Hector. Homer describes Priam's appearance, saying, "As when madness closes tight upon a man who, after killing someone in his own land, arrives in the country of others, at a rich man's house, and wonder grips those looking on, so Achilles looked in wonder at Priam."[4] Priam offers Achilles the opportunity to respond not with vengeance or force but rather with hospitality or what we might think of as reciprocity. Like the Greeks who set off from their homes, uncertain as to whether they would achieve their goal or even remain alive, Priam's expedition to Achilles is rooted in the spirit of freedom, something that Achilles and his men wonder at, just as we want to do because of Homer's art.

The principle of hospitality at the heart of *The Iliad* is also at the root of Arendt's account of justice. The political, Arendt argues, is dependent on a plurality of views and perspectives. In the public sphere, individuals disclose their interests and intentions to others, hoping to persuade them to work toward the same vision of the good or the just. They have no guarantee that others will see the world in the same way; instead, Arendt says:

> If someone wants to see and experience the world as it 'really' is, he can do so only by understanding it as something that is shared by many people, lies between them, separates and links them, showing itself differently to each and comprehensible only to the extent that many people can talk *about* it and exchange their opinions and perspectives with one another, over and against one another. (PP 128)[5]

Politics requires that we courageously reveal ourselves to those around us without any real expectation of their response and be entirely dependent on their hospitality. Politics asks that we all imitate Priam in front of a potential Achilles. We cannot know if others will agree with our ideas, but we must be able to reasonably count on a space within which those views can be expressed.

The beauty of art is one way to habituate people to the virtue of hospitality. Hospitality depends on our openness to the autonomy and difference of others. Rather than attempt to obliterate or overcome the distinct perspectives of others, the hospitable person understands the virtue of this difference, recognizing it as a way to ameliorate her own limited view. Insofar as art commands our attention, as it depicts the world or the ideas of the artist, it also helps us realize the many ways by which a single thing can be known or understood. Arendt describes art as memorializing the actions and speeches of people, moments of political activity that would disappear if not for the work of art that continually asks us to recollect what has occurred and why. "The whole factual world of human affairs depends for its reality ... first on the presence of others who have seen, heard and will remember, and second, on the transformation of the intangible into the tangible" (HC 95). While, as we shall see, Weil notes that the artist must renounce herself so that the beauty of what she is creating can have an autonomous existence, Arendt adds that the beauty of each piece of art is, in part, due to the particular perspective the artist brought to bear on her subject. In this, both agree, Homer is a master. To encounter a piece of art, Arendt thinks, is to enter a world of plurality, one that hospitably invites us to reflect upon not merely the particular actions of those depicted therein but also the viewpoint of the artist who produced it.

There is of course the possibility that we, like Paris, will not reciprocate the hospitality so offered. At the same time that Arendt notes the encroachment of the private sphere of necessity and desire over and against the political, she notes a congruent tendency in our approach to culture:

> Mass culture comes into being when mass society seizes upon cultural objects, and its danger is that the life process of society (which like all biological processes insatiably draws everything available into the cycle metabolism) will literally consume the cultural objects, eat them up, and destroy them. (PF 204)

While all art is in danger of succumbing to the desire to possess and consume, Arendt argues that the durability of an object, its ability to endure, is what constitutes a true work of culture. Markell notes:

> Arendt associates poetry with truth-telling—not the mere recording of information, nor the disclosure of philosophical or ... ontological truth, but a kind of disruptive faithfulness to factual reality, one that interrupts efforts to derive practical conclusions, as if automatically, from philosophically or theoretically simplified appeals to facts.[6]

In this way, poetry creates a space between action and reaction, a space wherein the other can be seen and known as they are rather than just as something to be used for our own purposes. The beauty of such things "transcends all needs and [makes] them last through the centuries" (PF 205).[7]

Works of true beauty resist our temptation to consume them. Instead, our wonder at their appearance in the world, our need to gaze at the beautiful, insists on maintaining some distance from the beautiful, if only so that it can be properly seen and admired. This distance, Arendt writes, "cannot arise unless we are in a position to forget ourselves, the cares and interests and urges in our lives, so that we will not seize what we admire, but let it be as it is, in its appearance" (PF 207). In this the viewer forgoes her own interests and is fully taken up in the being of that which she understands as beautiful. The political and the beautiful mediate the continued existence of one another. Each habituates in individuals the tendency to allow the other to appear as they are, to respect the distance that different perspectives provide, and the willingness to forget oneself in order to attend to the other (PF 215).

Arendt's treatment of Homer's *Iliad* is intriguing in this respect. As Weil notes, the majority of *The Iliad* depicts the consuming nature of force. Yet, Arendt barely references the actual battles of the war.[8] Indeed, Arendt argues that the moments spent in conversation and speech are as important, for Homer, as the moments of physical battle: "Two elements appear almost undifferentiated in Homer—the sheer strength of great deeds and the ravishing power of the great words that accompany them and sway the assembly of men who see and hear them" (PP 166). Similarly, of Achilles, Arendt says, "The stature of Homeric Achilles can be understood only if one sees him as the 'doer of great deeds and the speaker of great words'"(HC 25). Arendt argues that by showcasing the poem's physical battles alongside the speeches of the heroes, Homer shows another way for diverse communities to exist. Arendt imagines that when the men of Greece dismantled their camps and left, they, taking the lessons they learned at Troy, reimagined these same camps in their homelands, conceiving for the first time the *polis*. Now, however, rather than fighting, the emphasis is laid solely on speech, "where every victory can prove as equivocal as Achilles' and every defeat as praiseworthy as Hector's" (PP 166). By showcasing the activity and virtue of speech, Homer shows us how to live in a city.

Alongside her focus on the political activity of speech rather than the brute force of the battle, Arendt highlights the beauty of its beginning, suggesting that the Greeks who gathered and set off to Troy—uncertain of what they might accomplish, but willing to risk their lives for the same—provide us with the first illustration of the nature of politics (PP 162–3). When Arendt turns her attention to the battles that Homer depicts, she deflects the brute force that determines the winner and loser and instead focuses on the virtue, specifically the courage, of the individual characters who engage in battle with one another. Hector and Achilles serve as the example:

> What is commonly called the antagonistic spirit of the Greeks … is by no means simply a striving to prove oneself always and everywhere the best … could be understood not merely as an endeavour but also an activity that makes up the whole of life. The model for such rivalry among men was still seen as the combat between Hector and Achilles, which … gives each the opportunity to show himself as he is … by appearing in reality to become fully real. (PP 165–6)

This example, Arendt suggests, reveals the virtue of the struggle in politics to persevere and persuade others to adopt one's position and perspective (PP 171–2).

Arendt obfuscates, however. For while Achilles needs Hector to be a great warrior in order to demonstrate his own greatness, Achilles is not interested in Hector's perspective and closes the distance between them such that Hector's understanding of the world becomes a null point. Indeed, as Arendt notes, the events outlined in the poem result in annihilation, not just that of Hector but also the entire city of Troy. This war, she says, "can probably still be called the ur-example of a war of annihilation" (PP 163). As a partial explanation, Arendt points to the political nature of Homer's art. While the historical actors and particular characters, both the victors and the destroyed, have little regard for the perspective or thoughts of the other, the beauty of Homer's depiction of the events lies in his memorializing the virtue of both sides of the battle: "Homer's song does not pass over the vanquished man in silence … it bears witness as much on behalf of Hector as of Achilles … Homer celebrates this war of annihilation … in such a way that, in a certain sense … he undoes that very annihilation" (PP 163). The work of the artist and the beauty of the poem, if not the actual event, provides an example of the pluralism necessary for a just political community.

In an obvious way, Troy continues to exist in the minds and memories of those who read the poem. In this, Arendt says that Homer and artists like him grant these actions something close to immortality: "The task and potential greatness of mortals lie in their ability to produce things—works, deeds, and words—which would deserve to be and … are at home in everlastingness" (HC 19). By remembering and detailing the virtue of Hector and the beauty of Troy, Homer, Arendt suggests, invites us into a political discourse where we are witness to the virtue of both sides of the battle and asked to understand, evaluate, and judge their goodness. By making us think about the plight of the Trojans as much if not more than the Greeks, Homer accustoms his reader to look for and see the virtue of the other side. "What transforms this Homeric way of seeing into the ability to see from multiple points of view is the daily practice of public speech."[9] Homer shows us how we might appropriately approach the perspective of the other, and in our conversations with others, we should similarly seek to understand and even care for the position of the other, even those with whom we ultimately disagree.

This work of the imagination, suggests Linda Zerilli, is precisely what is required in order to understand the other from a position of empathy:

> [Arendt] invokes imagination to develop reference to a third perspective from which one observes and attempts to see from other standpoints … It is this third perspective that Arendt had in mind when she said that imaginative visiting [is] the understanding that involves coming to "see the same world from one another's standpoint, to see the same in very different and frequently opposing aspects."[10]

While Achilles eventually weeps with Priam, he does not imagine Priam's position but instead weeps in reference to Priam's similarity to his father and in his ongoing sadness with respect to Patroclus's death. As readers, however, we can imagine the perspective of each and, at the same time, recognize that our own perspective adds a third layer of meaning and thus also an element of distance. Through imagination we cross the distance between ourselves and another, yet, insofar as we know it is an act of imagination, the same distance is retained and preserved.

Notably, unlike Weil, Arendt does not speak of Priam or his expedition to Achilles that ends the poem. In many ways, Priam's actions in going to Achilles mirror the political beginnings of the Greeks who set out to Troy to wage war. Indeed, it is his virtue that makes Achilles stop and wonder, thereby creating the necessary distance for him to know and understand Priam. One possible reason that Arendt does not focus on this example is that Priam's actions are done in private for the sake of the personal. He enters Achilles's tent and asks for the release of his son's body. There are no political consequences to this event for we know that, after Hector's body has been returned to Troy and the necessary burial rites are attended to, the war continues in much the same way as before.

Yet, as Arendt presumably understands, there are nonetheless political consequences of the story of Priam's actions having been told and heard. Arendt shows us the beginning of the war, depicting the great virtue and courage of such a political undertaking. In her notebooks, she comments on the importance of our beginnings, something she, as noted, describes as miraculous. That, as finite beings, we will eventually leave this world is a given. What is more striking, miraculous even, is that we come into existence, that we begin, at all. Arendt writes,

> It is as if men since Plato have not been able to take the fact of having-been-born seriously, but rather only that of dying. [But] in having-been-born the human establishes itself as an earthly kingdom, toward which one connects, in that it searches for and finds its place, without any thought that he will one day go away again.[11]

When speaking about poetry, as the reification of actual events, Arendt initially suggests that the act of commemorating great deeds and actions transforms what was real into the "dead letter" (HC 95). Poetry in this sense is less than the actual work of politics. Yet, it is by means of poetry that the great deeds and words of individuals are memorialized and made beautiful. In this way, while poetry commemorates what is past or what has never been, it becomes part of the political by inspiring our own beginnings. Arendt does not tell us how Homer's poem ends because that end is in some way irrelevant. Instead, it is the impact the poem makes on our actions and the unknown consequences this may take that are of utmost importance in ensuring the continuation of the political.

Weil and Politics as Renunciation

For Weil, the experience of perceiving beautiful things habituates one to justice, insofar as both require limiting one's own power in order to preserve the freedom and, ultimately, being of the other. In *Forms of the Implicit Love of God*, Simone Weil describes the love of beauty as "an image of the creative renunciation of God" (WG 158). Weil argues that the creative act of beginnings is not an extension of one's power but rather a renunciation of it. The world itself begins when God thinks that which does not exist and, in so doing, creates it, emptying his being into something less than himself (WG 145, 147). This renunciation is an act of love—it treats something radically unequal as though it is equal and so gives it being. Consequently, to exist is to be sustained by a loving self-renunciation of Being itself. The continuation of the original creative act, Weil argues, is that God allows for human beings the choice to freely imitate the creative act of renunciation or to refuse it (WG 145). All creative acts in which a human being can share are imitations of the original creative act and so are renunciations of the self. The experience of beauty—of either beholding a beautiful thing or creating one—thus habituates the individual to limit themselves.

Justice is similarly understood, for justice, Weil argues, is love. It is the act of the stronger party looking at the weaker and behaving "exactly as though there were an equality" between the two (WG 143). In so doing, the stronger gives a part of herself to the weaker, thereby giving the weak "the quality of human beings, of which fate had deprived them" (WG 144). Subject to the necessities of force, the weak lose their freedom. Through justice, the strong party gives freedom back to the weak, transforming them from a piece of flesh into a human being. While the stronger person could just do as she wanted without regard for the interests of the weak, when she acts justly, she restrains her will so as to make space for the weaker party to emerge. Justice is then akin to the act of creating. The stronger party imitates God's original creative act in creating human beings, wherein he renounces himself so that we might exist. Similarly, the just individual gives the weaker party the freedom to consent to this act of love or to reject it, just as we have the freedom to accept or reject our own existence.

Nature seeks to extend power—to act justly, one must resist the motion of material necessity, whereby the strong dominate the weak. As Hamilton notes, for Weil, "the soul is subject to a kind of necessity directly analogous to the behavior of material objects in the universe."[12] To imagine that one is creating by extending their power, that is, by dominating the weak as the Athenians do at Melos, is to behave as matter behaves. In so doing, the stronger party not only ignores the supernatural good to which the soul has access but also mistakes herself as the center of the universe; she mistakes a world of unreality for what is true. For while the Athenians might be stronger than the Melians, soon after they know themselves to be weaker than the Spartans and subjected to the force of another.

Weil and Beauty as the Path to Justice

We are only able to act justly by recognizing that we are not the center of the world. By renouncing ourselves, we "awaken to what is real and eternal" (WG 159). Weil argues that one recognizes the "true center" as being outside of the material world, and in so doing, the individual consents to the "rule of mechanical necessity in matter and of free choice at the center of each soul. Such consent is love" (WG 160). For Weil, the perception of beauty is an essential beginning point that opens the individual to self-renunciation. As justice imitates the divine creative act of human beings, loving the beauty of the world imitates the creation of the material world—to love it is to give it being. The love of all beauty ultimately has universal beauty, or God, as its object. Love of beauty thus begins in "God dwelling in our souls and goes out to God present in the universe" (WG 165). The presence of the universal and eternal within the individual soul extends to, and thereby allows for the recognition of, that same presence in the material world.

At the same time, however, Weil emphasizes that loving the beauty of the natural world is incomplete because "it is felt for things incapable of responding" (WG 171). Love of matter can never be reciprocated. Consequently, love of beauty is most fully actualized in love for another person because they are capable of reciprocating it. Insofar as loving the beauty of the natural world is loving the presence of the universal in matter, loving beauty in another person, Weil argues, shows a yearning for the incarnation, or a yearning for universal beauty to look like the self and for the universal to reciprocate one's love. That is, by loving beauty in another person, one is hoping that God will make the lover his beloved.

As the love of beauty is perfected in loving another person, it redirects us to justice, for it finds its end in the reciprocity granted by others. Fundamentally, rather than seeing this reciprocity as a way of making the beautiful object one's own, loving beauty is a way of dissolving the self. The love of beauty thus realizes itself in a total negation of the self—in loving beauty, one falls away from the center of the universe and awakens to the true center. As Weil describes:

> The beauty of the world is the mouth of a labyrinth. The unwary individual who on entering takes a few steps is soon unable to find the opening. Worn out, with nothing to eat or drink, in the dark, separated from his dear ones, and from everything he loves and is accustomed to, he walks on without knowing anything or hoping anything, incapable even of discovering whether he is really going forward or merely turning round on the same spot. But this affliction is nothing compared with the danger threatening him. For if he does not lose courage, if he goes on walking, it is absolutely certain that he will finally arrive at the center of the labyrinth. And there God is waiting to eat him. Later he will go out again, but he will be changed, he will have become different, after being eaten and digested by God. Afterward he will stay near the entrance so that he can gently push all those who come near into the opening. (WG 164)

The individual is completely dissolved in the experience of beauty—they are consumed and taken up by it. This is a terrifying experience as it requires leaving the center one believes she knows and, ultimately, leaving the self.

Weil and The Iliad

Like Arendt, Weil shows the connection between beauty and justice through her extensive treatment of *The Iliad*. Weil argues that art, as a human construction, seeks to reveal the reality of the universe to the viewer (WG 168). Weil calls *The Iliad* "the purest and loveliest of mirrors" (IF 183). While the Trojan war seems to display acts of heroic greatness, as if the battlefield were a stage upon which the Greek and Trojan warriors performed, Weil argues that *The Iliad* makes force its center, illustrating the inescapable role of force in the world. Indeed, rather than showing the greatness of human personality and the preeminence of the poem's heroes, Weil argues that *The Iliad* shows the destruction of individual greatness and power and, thus, the need for humanity's decentering through love. The heroes' belief that they possess power in the battle is ultimately an illusion. Ultimately, "every human being may at any moment be compelled to submit to force" (IF 51). The warriors in *The Iliad* mistake a consequence of fortune or fate for their own power and so attempt to use it to subject others, believing that in so doing they are extending their power. Rather than illustrating individual human greatness, Weil argues, *The Iliad* shows an absolute equality between every human being in their affliction. At the same time, the beauty of the poem saves one from despair by moving the audience to love and so to be just.

On the one hand, *The Iliad* shows force by depicting heroes from one side seemingly triumphing over their foes, only to be struck down in turn. Hector's subjection to force, wielded temporarily by Achilles, is obvious—Hector dies alone in front of his city, "unaided by gods or men" (IF 198). Force's power over Hector is made all the more clear in the moment that Priam has come to recover Hector's body. By then, Hector has been made into a mere piece of flesh, dragged around by Achilles:

> He'd yoke his racing team to the chariot-harness,
> Lash the corpse of Hector behind the car for dragging
> And haul him three times round the dead Patroclus' tomb,
> And then he'd rest again in his tents and leave the body
> Sprawled facedown in the dust.[13]

Hector is reduced to matter alone.

Even Achilles, "a man like a god," is subject to force.[14] He too "must suffer what the fates spun out … the doomed fighter's life drawn that day/his mother gave him birth."[15] Unable to save Patroclus, and so subject to force, Achilles seeks to kill Hector and, in so doing, believes he can wield the power of force. At Hector's death, however, Achilles feels only "a brief joy" (IF 198). His continued despair after his apparent victory over Hector and vengeance of Patroclus reveals that his power was only an illusion; Achilles too is afflicted, for "force is as pitiless to the man who possesses it, or thinks he does, as it is to its victims; the second it crushes, the first it intoxicates. The truth is, nobody really possesses it" (IF 191). Achilles's killing of Hector shows how force seduces and tricks the individual into thinking that they are free from it, that they wield and possess it. Achilles continues to strive to free himself from force by exerting his power over Hector's body, refusing to return the body to Troy, and every night tying it to a chariot and dragging it around Patroclus's tomb three times. His very attempt to free himself by exerting his power further subjects him to force. Achilles's actions turn Hector into "a little piece of flesh, naked and inert" (WG 146). Achilles's actions similarly reduce himself. Force does violence not only to the body of the victim but also to the soul of the human being who supposedly wields it.

As force acts upon the soul, force turns human beings into matter while they are still living (IF 185). We see this in Priam, who, while still alive, is equally subject to force as is his son. Priam's city has been sacked and destroyed; his sons have been brutally killed; and Hector's body mutilated by Achilles. Each act puts Priam in the position of matter, helpless against the tragedy occurring around him. For Weil, this is the great and terrible power of force, that it makes "a human being into a thing while he is still alive. He is alive; he has a soul; and yet—he is a thing" (IF 185).

The Trojan war is the perfect canvas for depicting force, as war makes force present not only to those who die but also to all who participate in it; "our thoughts cannot travel from one day to the next without meeting death's face ... On each one of these days the soul suffers violence. Regularly, every morning, the soul castrates itself of aspiration, for thought cannot journey through time without meeting death on the way" (IF 201). War reveals force as an ever-present fact of existence, one of which the soldiers cannot help but be conscious. Part of the beauty of the poem is that Homer shows force affecting both sides equally and thus mourns both sides in the same way. Force reveals an essential and inescapable equality between human beings. When looking at the actions of the characters in *The Iliad*, one sees the effects of the faulty belief that a human being can liberate herself from force. For Weil, the idea that one can control force illustrates the misconception that one exists at the center of the universe. The strong imagines that she will never lose the capacity for force or be subject to it by anyone else, "they conclude that destiny has granted them every license and none to their inferiors" (IF 194). In so doing, they fail to see what Weil calls the "geometric" quality of force. Indeed, Weil explains, "Thus it happens that those who have force on loan from fate count on it too much and are destroyed" (IF 194).

Weil and the Politics of Empathy

Like Arendt, Weil praises Homer for portraying both sides equally: "Executioner and victim stand equally innocent, before which conquered and conqueror are brothers in the same distress" (IF 199). The reader is equally moved by the destruction of Troy and the deaths of the Achaeans far from their home, by Hector's death as by Patroclus's, by Priam and Hecuba's despair over losing Hector as by Achilles's murderous rage. By revealing this equality, *The Iliad* decenters the listener and reveals that the use of force reduces all humans, losers, and victors alike to inert matter. Weil emphasizes that no one in the poem is freed from force; there is no hero who is able to transcend it or liberate himself from it. We are not moved to despair of our condition, however, because the beauty of the poem moves us to love. Indeed, Weil argues, "Only he who has measured the dominion of force, and knows how not to respect it, is capable of love and justice" (IF 212). Rather than making us detached, Weil argues, Homer's equality of treatment draws the poet and audience closer to both sides—we more fully see ourselves and our condition reflected in them. Rather than standing in awe of the heroes, we recognize our kinship with them, not in their might but in their affliction. This recognition, Weil suggests, can move one to act justly by renouncing rather than extending the self, and in so doing creating the other.

Indeed, Weil emphasizes that the presence of force allows for the display of almost all "pure form[s] of love amongst men." These moments of love are "fleeting and sublime moments when men possess a soul" (IF 206). Rather than being consumed by force, in these fleeting moments of the soul's wakefulness, there is only courage and love. Love, Weil argues, is the discovery of the soul, in both oneself and the beloved (IF 206). As Esposito notes, for Weil, loving is understanding, for "to love reality really means to understand that reality—all reality, even the rain and the hail, even the coldest wind—is love."[16] This love is like a miracle; in the face of destruction, love allows one to participate in the creative act of justice.

Illustrating the creative possibility at its peak, Weil turns to the end of *The Iliad*. Most miraculously, we are shown, "the purest triumph of love" in Priam and Achilles. Priam comes to Achilles's tent to ransom Hector's body. When Priam approaches Achilles in supplication, asking for his son's body, rather than strike Priam down, Achilles is struck by the memory of his own father. The two weep together, sharing equally in their affliction as they mourn their lost loved ones. In turn, Weil argues that the beauty of the initial act of justice by the stronger party moves the receiver to respond with gratitude—Priam accepts Achilles's love and mourns with him. The miracle of justice is shown in the image of Priam and Achilles marveling at each other's beauty:

> And when they had put aside desire for food and drink,
> Priam the son of Dardanus gazed at Achilles, marvelling
> Now at the man's beauty, his magnificent build—
> Face-to-face he seemed a deathless god …
> And Achilles gazed and marveled at Dardan Priam,
> Beholding his noble looks, listening to his words
> But once they'd had their fill of gazing at each other.[17]

When Priam and Achilles gaze at each other, they are gazing at, and loving, beauty not only in another person but also in someone afflicted. By nature, Achilles should desire to crush Priam. But he does not. Most incredibly, Achilles cleans and returns Hector's body, telling Priam, "your son is now set free."[18] Achilles and Priam illustrate that "the purest triumph of love, the supreme grace of wars, is the friendship that stirs in the hearts of mortal enemies … it can close the gap between benefactor and suppliant" (WG 63). As Priam comes to ransom the body of his son, Achilles ransoms himself for Priam, "one gives oneself in ransom for the other" (IF 148). In this instance, we are given the perfect image of justice, as "both of them recognize that it is better not to command wherever one has the power to do so" (IF 148).

The Iliad reminds the reader that justice gives the person whom fate has given the position of matter "the quality of human beings" (IF 144). It is "giving our attention to what does not exist" and has the effect of baptizing them (IF 149, 150). In so doing, someone consents to diminish her power—she renounces her perceived control over force. This act of love is made complete when it is reciprocated by the afflicted party. By responding to charity with gratitude, Weil writes that "the afflicted man and his benefactor, between whom diversity of fortune places at an infinite distance, are united in the acceptance" of affliction (IF 148). The result of this imitation is a decentering of the self. When Priam supplicates himself to Achilles, and Achilles recognizes him in turn, they recognize an equality in each other. As Arendt illustrates, justice is only possible by fully recognizing the other and, in so doing, forgetting the self. The highest point of beauty in the poem, and an image of its greatest creative act, comes at the end. Rather than finding it in the supposed power of the actors and their beliefs in their absolute force, their creative acts are found in submission and in the mutual recognition of their affliction.

Likewise, *The Iliad* mimics the renunciation seen in love—Homer, despite being a Greek, does not seek to elevate the Achaeans over the Trojans, nor to revel in their victory. The experience of beauty mimics the creative renunciation seen in justice. The experience of submitting to or loving beauty is thus the opposite of wielding force. When one experiences something beautiful, one is moved to share it with others, to "stay near the entrance so that [she] can gently push all those who come near the opening" (WG 164). *The Iliad* serves as the mouth to the labyrinth. At the center, we find Achilles and Priam. We see ourselves naked rather than clothed in the illusion that we control force. As Weil explains:

> The only difference between the man who witnesses an act of justice and the man who receives a material advantage from it is that in such circumstances the beauty of justice is only a spectacle for the first, while for the second it is the object of a contact and even a kind nourishment. (WG 140)

The soul of the receiver is nourished; the soul of the viewer admires and is moved by the beauty of the act. In this way, art's depiction of just acts can similarly hold the viewer in awe and move her to admire the renunciation inherent in justice. In this admiration, she can be moved to imitate justice in her own life. The mirror of *The Iliad*, while perhaps terrifying, is beautiful. It is beautiful because it takes us outside of ourselves, and rather than inviting us to consume it, *The Iliad* invites us to behold. In the act of beholding something beautiful, one recognizes the center of the world as outside of oneself and so becomes capable of love.[19]

Conclusion

Weil and Arendt focus their attention on Homer's *Iliad*, using it as an example of how a work of beauty can reveal and inculcate in those perceiving it that the true nature of justice, and thus the work of politics, is a kind of empathy that requires one to relinquish their belief of themselves as the center of the world. This decentering allows for the perspective and needs of others to be brought into the foreground, so that they might be attended to with justice and with love. While *The Iliad* may not hold the same position of importance to the contemporary world, Arendt and Weil's argument still holds true. The contemporary era has witnessed an increased demand for artwork—visual, written, and performed—that features the perspectives of historically marginalized communities and individuals. Those that love the beautiful have come to understand the need for a truer representation of what beauty means and can reveal. The diversification of artistic voices that can now be witnessed both is an indication of how attention to the beautiful leads to the desire to attend to those voices that are sometimes ignored and, at the same time, expands our understanding of beauty, thereby increasing the degree to which we might lovingly respond.

Commenting on the strange concurrence of Arendt and Weil's thought, Esposito notes:

> Two of the most important thinkers of the century, both Jewish and both deeply touched by the experience of persecution and exile, never had the chance to meet, each one generating their thought in distinct and distant circles. Nevertheless—and this is the second paradox—it is precisely this conceptual distance that appears to constitute an imperceptible zone of contact, an invisible tangent, a form of mysterious convergence that is increasingly pronounced the more their explicit positions diverge.[20]

Importantly, it is precisely this "distance" that Arendt and Weil highlight as being essential to the proper disclosure of beauty as well as the possible disclosure of the position of the other. As both Arendt and Weil recognize, the majority of the activity of *The Iliad* is concerned not with gazing but with consuming—rather than admire Hector's perspective, or behold his beauty and recognize his affliction, Achilles seeks to close the gap between them and turn Hector into nothing. Rather than remain in the realm of consumption and so annihilation, Arendt and Weil argue that *The Iliad*'s equally beautiful presentation of the Trojans and Achaeans makes us aware of the need for distance and self-forgetting for justice. By recognizing a commonality with the other, we are left in awe of their beauty. We forget ourselves and, in so doing, create rather than destroy the other. So too does *The Iliad*, as a beautiful work of art, allow the reader to forget herself, thereby preparing her soul for the creative acts of justice and politics.

Notes

1. While there is no evidence that the two thinkers met or corresponded, comments on Weil's writing appear in Arendt's work, indicating that she was familiar with Weil's understanding of the world and, in some instance, actively conversing with it. Importantly, one of Arendt's most extended comments on Weil includes reference to *The Iliad*. See HC, fn 83, and Robert Esposito, *The Origin of the Political: Hannah Arendt or Simone Weil?* (New York: Fordham University Press, 2017), 6.
2. Cecilia Sjöholm, *Doing Aesthetics with Arendt* (New York: Columbia University Press, 2015), 14.
3. Homer, *The Iliad*, trans. Caroline Alexander (New York: HarperCollins, 2015), 13, 620–35.
4. Ibid., 24, 480–3.
5. See also HC 57.
6. See Patchen Markell, "Politics and the Case of Poetry: Arendt on Brecht," *Modern Intellectual History* 15, no. 2 (2018), 508. See also Ian Storey, "The Reckless Unsaid: Arendt on Political Poetics," *Critical Inquiry* (Summer 2015): 870–1.

7 Corcoran argues that for Arendt the realm of politics is an ongoing drama wherein actors disclose themselves and the world to others in the same way that a work of theater does for an audience. Paul Corcoran, "Political Recognition and Aesthetic Judgment," *Theoria: A Journal of Social and Political Theory* 55, no. 115 (2008): 78.
8 On this difference between the two philosophers, see Esposito, *The Origin of the Political*, 7.
9 Linda M. G. Zerilli, "'We Feel Our Freedom,' Imagination and Judgment in the Thought of Hannah Arendt," *Political Theory* 33, no. 2 (April 2005): 165.
10 Ibid., 176–7.
11 Arendt, *Denktagebuch* (Zürich: Piper, 2002), XIX.24.469–70. For a fuller treatment, see Jeffrey Champlin, "'Poetry or Body Politic': Natality and the Space of Birth in Hannah Arendt's Thought Diary," in *Artifacts of Thinking Book*, ed. Roger Berkowitz and Ian Storey (New York: Fordham University, 2017). See also HC 247.
12 Christopher Hamilton, "Power, Punishment and Reconciliation in the Political and Social Thought of Simone Weil," *European Journal of Social Theory* 11, no. 3 (2008): 316
13 Homer, *Iliad*, 24.17–21.
14 Ibid., 16.927.
15 Ibid., 20.149–51.
16 Esposito, *The Origin of the Political*, 72.
17 Homer, *Iliad*, 24.738–45.
18 Ibid., 24.706.
19 For more on this, Angelo Caranfo offers an excellent discussion of the significance of gazing in Weil's thought in "The Aesthetic and Spiritual Attitude in Learning: Lessons from Simone Weil," *Journal of Aesthetic Education* 44, no. 2 (2010): 63–82.
20 Espositio, *The Origin of the Political*, 1.

Bibliography

Caranfo, Angelo. "The Aesthetic and Spiritual Attitude in Learning: Lessons from Simone Weil." *Journal of Aesthetic Education* 44, no. 2 (2010): 63–82.
Champlin, Jeffrey. "'Poetry or Body Politic': Natality and the Space of Birth in Hannah Arendt's Thought Diary." In *Artifacts of Thinking*. Edited by Roger Berkowitz and Ian Storey. New York: Fordham University, 2017, pp. 143–61.
Corcoran, Paul. "Political Recognition and Aesthetic Judgment." *Theoria: A Journal of Social and Political Theory* 55, no. 115 (2008): 64–90.
Esposito, Robert. *The Origin of the Political: Hannah Arendt or Simone Weil?* New York: Fordham University Press, 2017.
Hamilton, Christopher. "Power, Punishment and Reconciliation in the Political and Social Thought of Simone Weil." *European Journal of Social Theory* 11, no. 3 (2008): 315–30.
Homer. *The Iliad*. Translated by Caroline Alexander. New York: Harper Collins, 2015.
Markell, Patchen. "Politics and the Case of Poetry: Arendt on Brecht." *Modern Intellectual History* 15, no. 2 (2018): 503–33.
Mufarech, Antonia. "Disguised Protester Smears Cake on High-Tech Glass Protecting the 'Mona Lisa.'" *Smithsonian Magazine*, May 31, 2022.
Sjöholm, Cecelia. *Doing Aesthetics with Arendt*. New York: Columbia University Press, 2015.

Storey, Ian. "The Reckless Unsaid: Arendt on Political Poetics." *Critical Inquiry* 41, no. 4 (Summer 2015): 869–92.
Zerilli, Linda M. G. "'We Feel Our Freedom,' Imagination and Judgment in the Thought of Hannah Arendt." *Political Theory* 33, no. 2 (2005): 158–88.

Chapter 12

ON THE POWER OF WORDS

Ian Rhoad

The Sophist and the Philosopher

The title of my chapter is taken from an essay that Simone Weil wrote during the year she returned from the Spanish Civil War. Originally published in 1937 with the French title "Ne recommençons pas la guerre de Troie" (roughly translated: "Let's Not Restart the Trojan War"), it appears in English as "The Power of Words" (SWA 218–38). In the essay, Weil laments the tendency of political actors to traffic in dangerous abstractions that correspond to no concrete reality. When empty of genuine content, galvanizing political slogans, she tells us, acquire their value by virtue of what we are willing to do in their name. Under the banner of various "isms," loss and sacrifice become themselves motivation for more loss and sacrifice, spurring further investment in the terms that give this a semblance of purpose. In this respect, we moderns are not so different from the ancient Greeks who allegedly persisted in a war with Troy for ten years, all in the name of a single woman whom most had not met. Helen was supposed to be a flesh-and-blood person, however. Our commitments attach to objects of fascination that are even less real: they cling, passionately, to words like "communism" or "fascism" insofar as these are *mere* words, not corresponding social realities that have been understood and soberly analyzed. In such circumstances, compared to our ancient counterparts, who made explicit space for superstition in mythology, it is we who appear dominated by superstition, which, though disavowed, has "revenged itself by invading the entire realm of thought" (SWA 222).

In the decade following the Second World War, Hannah Arendt will raise similar concerns about the pervasiveness of clichés in political discourse. For Arendt, our insertion into a shared language is a condition of possibility for self-disclosure in action. However, this positive possibility of language, which also allows us to share, preserve, and render intelligible what happens in the world of human affairs, is the other side of a danger inherent in language: that it does the work of understanding for us, allowing us to thoughtlessly appeal to clichés and outdated or poorly formulated categories when making sense of political life. Arendt's worry is not merely epistemological—that we might not know what we are doing—but political and ontological; political insofar as our reliance on clichés and outdated categories leads to a breakdown in common sense and a temptation to violence, which happens whenever the capacity for genuine speech within a community is foreclosed; ontological insofar as our capacity to "word the world" with others is a condition for a distinctly human mode of being. "The extent to which clichés have crept into our everyday language and discussions," Arendt writes in 1954, "may well indicate the degree to which we not only have deprived ourselves of the faculty of speech, but are ready to use more effective means of violence than bad books ... with which to settle our arguments" (EU 308).

Here, then, we have two philosophers warning that political vocabulary, in its dominant mode of circulation, portends catastrophic, dehumanizing consequences—a violence that will beget more violence. If we adopt Weil's famous definition of force as "that x that turns anybody who is subjected to it into a *thing*" (IF 163), we can say that "x" may stand for any signifier that has acquired such a power over us. Yet, what is perhaps more remarkable than Weil's and Arendt's disillusionment with a state of political discourse (a sentiment characteristic of intellectuals of their generation) is the conviction each has that certain words possess a positive power, namely that when properly taken up, they are points of connection to the lives of others and reminders of a forgotten mode of human relationality. It is this feature of their reflections on language that interests me here.

I shall argue that Weil and Arendt are doing something more interesting than simply repeating a traditional story that philosophers often tell themselves when they criticize popular opinions expressed in the public sphere. The traditional story I have in mind can be traced to the origins of the Western philosophical tradition. In Plato's *Crito*, Socrates's final decisive moment, when he decides whether to live or die, is presented against the backdrop of an explicit dismissal of the views of the multitude, whose opinions are seen as generally unworthy of attention.[1] In the *Gorgias*, we are invited to witness a similar dismissal of rhetoric as mere knack for gratification through flattery.[2] In each case, the suggestion—the lesson for would-be philosophers—seems to be that the linguistic practices and attitudes characteristic of the plural space of (merely) human discourse are not worth taking seriously. There are moments when Arendt and Weil seem gripped by this story; these are moments in which they understandably express dismay at a state of popular discourse. But on closer inspection, neither accepts the basic terms of this story, which opposes a wise philosopher (positioned outside the political realm) to a suspicious sophist (who dwells within it). Indeed, we shall see that they give us cause to revisit the image of Socrates in a way that challenges this binary. Nor does either thinker dismiss rhetoric as unimportant. On the contrary, Arendt and Weil give us reasons to appreciate the art of rhetoric and to take it seriously. For once we understand what our life in language is like in their terms, and how it can go wrong, then caring about an artful relationship with words, and acknowledging their power, becomes extremely important. With Arendt and Weil, I shall argue, we can reimagine rhetoric, not as an art that is useful for winning debate but rather as a kind of responsiveness through words, which is primarily a kind of listening *before* it is a kind of talking. The question of the relationship between the philosopher and the public realm can then be reframed as primarily a question of attention.

Appearance

I shall begin by considering the positive role that language plays in Arendt's account of the possibility of a distinctly human and specifically political form of life in *The Human Condition*. Arendt identifies the essence of political life with the realization of human plurality: "the fact that men, not Man, live on the earth and inhabit the world" (HC 7). This takes place through action, an activity that is only possible within a form of life possessing language. Action takes place whenever (and only when) people act and *speak* with and before one another as equals. When this happens, a "space of appearance" comes into being. A space of appearance is not a physical space—although this is required—but an intangible "in-between" that exists only so long as those gathered remain turned toward one another in the manner of word and deed. What appears in this space is the unique identities of the actors and speakers themselves, each disclosing themselves as a *who* rather than a *what* to the community (HC 175–81).

The conjunction of word and deed in this formulation is crucial. It is what marks out action, as distinct from both labor and work, as the *sine qua non* of political existence. In Arendt's account, labor is human activity determined by biological need. Cyclical and consumptive, it maintains human life at the level of animality. Work, meanwhile, transcends labor by aiming at the production of objects that endure. Insofar as objects produced through work are intended for appearance in a common world, which outlasts and houses the life secured by labor, a plural space of intersubjective meaning can be said to be at the horizon of their production. But it is important for Arendt that the people who produce these objects are not necessarily destined to appear in that space simply by virtue of their work. That is, in and of itself, work is neither necessary nor sufficient to effect the manifestation of the producer's unique identity in the common world that work constructs. For this, action—speaking and taking initiative before others—is needed. By interpreting the meaning of their deeds, which open onto an unpredictable future, the participants in a space of appearance show that they are not merely discrete instances of a biological kind but distinct *principles of beginning*: their appearance in a common space of action constitutes an irreducible beginning to a story. This demonstration of the human capacity to begin something new (natality) is thus also essentially a manifestation of human plurality. For the story of each actor is interconnected with the stories of the others.

To understand political life in Arendtian terms is to make sense of this web of interconnected stories in such a way that the plurality and natality evinced in it is not effaced. Most political philosophers, and most spaces nominally devoted to political activity, do efface these two conditions to some degree or another. Arendt's legacy as a political thinker is inseparable from the vocabulary she developed to recall these features of human life and to center them in her analysis of modernity.

The ramifications of her recovery of "the political" are many and various, but for my purposes here, there are three aspects of Arendt's account that require specific mention:

1. Self-disclosure through word and deed is presented as an inherently valuable *ontological* accomplishment. It is necessary for a distinctly human mode of existence in which *to be is to appear*. Although one cannot live their entire life in a space of appearance, a life deprived of any such disclosure, according to Arendt, is "deprived of reality, which, humanly and politically speaking, is the same as appearance" (HC 199).
2. This disclosure does not happen as a matter of course. Two people can be face to face and not appear to each other in the sense that Arendt has in mind. For this, they must be peers and relate to one another as equals. Their words cannot be intended to manipulate (in which case their utterances fail to qualify as genuine speech), and their deeds must not be violent.
3. The self that is disclosed appears primarily to others and, least of all, to the person who speaks and acts.

On the basis of the above, we can say that words facilitate *a self-manifestation that is also a self-transcendence*. By this I mean the following: if I successfully participate in a community of language in the ways that Arendt specifies, then I acquire a level of reality that I would otherwise lack. But achieving reality in this sense ("appearance") is at the same time a coming out of myself. Whereas in labor and work I may be intimately self-present, for a political mode of being I need to be a self to which I am *not* intimately present: I need to appear *over there* to others. Because I need to appear to others, I shall need to use words that will land with them. This means that I shall need to listen to them.

It is important to note that successful participation in a community of language does not exclude making political misjudgments. "Success" here simply means being able to appear at all. The must be the case because the web of human relations that makes up the world of human affairs is incredibly complicated, and the full meaning of our actions will depend on factors that we in principle cannot know. Moreover, since action expresses natality, the established language that we assume when we enter political spaces will often lag behind the reality we seek to disclose through our words. On this point, Arendt's essay "Understanding and Politics" is especially instructive.

In "Understanding and Politics," Arendt tells us that true political understanding is a never-ending process of seeking *meaning* rather than knowledge. It is not the result of obedience to a method or a training in philosophical dialectic; rather, it is an effort to make sense of what happens in the world of human affairs and is distinguished by its sustained tenacity in holding onto an original intuition of novelty that a popular and preliminary understanding first announces but then obscures. This involves working within and against the limits of intelligibility made possible by our participation in everyday discourse. If we lose all connection with everyday modes of rendering events meaningful, we will slide into "mere speculation" (EU 312). On the other hand, insofar as popular language tends to cover over the natality that it itself registers, there is a need to go beyond its limits, to challenge it while holding onto it. I would describe this as a creative work of refashioning language. It is an artful sort of work (Arendt would call it an "art of making distinctions") that must eventually issue forth into a practice of rhetoric if it is to contribute to the stories that sustain political communities. But if it is an art, it is not for that matter fanciful or pragmatic word play. It is first and foremost a practice of attention. For the principle guiding both the holding onto and the challenging of popular language is the same: to attend to and articulate the appearance of the new. Its fundamental principle is thus *to allow the new to appear and to be brought into speech and story, as such.*

Doing this successfully is not merely a cognitive achievement. Understanding, like action, is an ontological accomplishment in Arendt's account. What is at stake is the actualization of a specifically human mode of being: a way of being with others, and a way of being in time.[3] The political theorist, and the storyteller, who affirms this mode of being, affirms language in its worldliness. She is unlike the classic Platonic philosopher, who considers the world of appearances to be a mere copy of an atemporal reality and for whom language, and especially the language of "the many," represents separation from an ineffable and unchanging Truth. For an Arendtian, the region of being in which the distinctly human is accomplished and affirmed is the apparent as such, and everything worldly is understood to constitute *both* a separation *and* a connection for those who share it. That language is sometimes used for antipolitical ends, and thus functions to separate, is clear enough. Language can be used to deceive and to mystify; it can function well as a suit of armor, shielding us from the perspectives of others, if we choose to inhabit it that way. In becoming stale and rigid, we have seen that language can fail to articulate our lives in their concreteness. For the Arendtian, this simply indicates that achieving the political is hard. The work must be to patiently and provisionally, and to whatever degree possible, stitch word and deed back together, so that the meaning of what we have done and suffered can be held in common and then taken up in renewed political address.

Metaxu

The notion that a shared language is both a connection and a separation appears, albeit differently, in the work of Weil. I have in mind, in particular, an image from Weil's *Notebooks* (NB 497). As part of a discussion of the Greek concept of *metaxu* (an in-between state), Weil describes two prisoners who inhabit adjacent cells. The prisoners, though they cannot see each other, communicate by knocking on the wall that separates them. This is a metaphor for living with the absence of God, but it also suggests a way of picturing what life in language is like. Near the end of her own life, in her essay "Human Personality," we see this picture filled out, as Weil explores the idea that a life in language is a life imprisoned. The size of our cell, she tells us, is irrelevant: one can have a vast vocabulary and fantastic skills in the art of eloquent oration and yet fail to articulate anything in the proximity of truth or justice.

The carceral imagery that appears across these two texts presses us into a question: might there be a way of inhabiting the prison that is language such that the means of separation are also points of connection? To do this we would need to understand the mechanism of separation, how the walls are built, and what it can mean to turn barriers into conduits. In "Human Personality," the meaning and depth of the separation is profound and unsettling. Weil is not merely repeating the thought, as old as philosophy itself, that contemplation of the highest truths, in their unity and fundamental significance, requires solitude and silence. Weil is also—and more intensely and interestingly—calling her reader to consider our inability to become fully present to and express human affliction. "Affliction" has a technical meaning. It names the experience of nonbeing, or rather the passing over into nonbeing by undergoing annihilation. Wording this experience is implausible because holding close to an apprehension of it is implausible: "To listen to someone is to put oneself in his place while he is speaking," Weil writes. "To put oneself in the place of someone whose soul is corroded by affliction, or in near danger of it, is to annihilate oneself. It is more difficult than suicide would be for a happy child. Therefore the afflicted are not listened to" (HP 71).

A virtue ethicist might read the above as cause to counsel courage and resoluteness in the face of human suffering. Yet this would miss the radicality of Weil's reflection, which is concerned less with individual failure and more with attitudinal commitments embedded within modes of speech that must be assumed for one to participate effectively in modern politics. Weil specifically has in mind rights discourse. Discussion of rights, so central to the functioning of modern societies, foregrounds the interest of persons and can be used for good or ill. While this language may be highly useful, perhaps even necessary in certain contexts, it comes with a profound risk. If our orientation toward the possibility of justice is overdetermined by the problem of rights adjudication, a deeper, impersonal meaning of justice is ignored, and the cry of those who call out for it is deflected. Much as the meaning of politics is often covered over by institutions invested with political significance in Arendt's analysis, for Weil the meaning of justice is distorted by the very institutions that carry its banner. The experiences of the victims of profound injustice, who cry out for something impersonal and sacred, are filtered through a vocabulary that belongs to what Weil describes as *the middle region*:

> To put into the mouth of the afflicted words from the vocabulary of middle values, such as democracy, rights, personality, is to offer them something which can bring them no good and will inevitably do them much harm.
>
> These notions do not dwell in heaven; they hang in the middle air, and for this very reason they cannot root themselves in earth. (HP 66)

We have, in other words, built our prisons with very thick walls. To counter this, Weil tells us that what is needed is "a regime in which the public freedom of expression is characterized not so much by freedom as by an attentive silence in which this faint and inept cry can make itself heard" (HP 53). This raises a difficult question: how ought a community make space for silence within its discourse?

Individual abstention of speech is only so helpful. Falling silent and still might help *me* hear a muffled cry through the walls of a prison, but this is hardly sufficient to produce a regime of attentive silence. Nor will recommending this practice to others get to the heart of the matter. For the concepts that steer us away from affliction may operate on us even when we refrain from vocalizing them. Moreover, they will still be there when we begin once again to speak.

We might imagine that building places in which silence can be housed— monasteries and places of worship have often served this purpose—would constitute an advance. And to some extent this is so, as such places provide silent attention with an explicit social meaning and location. They represent an "outside" to everyday politics and commerce, which can challenge the attitudes that pervade the latter spheres. But the distance from the everyday that such places require and afford is also what makes them an inadequate solution. It is in the courtroom and on the factory floor, not just in the sanctuary, that the afflicted need articulation and audience.

Weil's answer is to create new institutions that can "put power into the hands of men who are able and anxious to hear" (HP 53) the cry of the afflicted. Yet, supposing that such people can even be found, they shall also need other words than those characteristic of current political common sense. To indulge in the prison metaphor a final time: adding more phonetic blocks of cement of the same kind to the prison infrastructure will not do; what is needed are words, and linguistic practices, that undo this infrastructure; for Weil, they must in fact undo *us* insofar as our self-conception has been constructed in the vernacular of self-concern. What is needed are words that contain an element of silence within themselves as a constitutive feature. These are words that, like the architecture of a great cathedral, suggest a higher region of significance by drawing our attention upwards. This is the suggestion of the final movement of "Human Personality," where Weil invokes the phrase with which I began: the power of words. Weil writes:

> By the power of words we always mean their power of illusion and error. But, thanks to a providential arrangement, there are certain words which possess, in themselves, when properly used, a virtue which illumines and lifts up towards the good. These are the words which refer to an absolute perfection which we cannot conceive. Since the proper use of these words involve not trying to make them fit any conception, it is in themselves, as words, that the power to enlighten and draw upwards resides. What they express is beyond our conception. (HP 76)

Examples that Weil gives are *God, truth, justice, love,* and *good*. It's important that she celebrates these words *as* words. They are signifiers, which means that they point beyond themselves, but their power lies in how they steer our attention, not in what they properly communicate. Only by refusing to have them fit any conception will they avoid the fate of those empty signifiers with which we began: "communism," "fascism," and so on. This is not easy. Such words, Weil tells us, *are like an ordeal* (HP 77). Maintaining a proper relationship with words like *truth* and *justice*, artfully weaving them into one's speech so that their silence and their promise might cast a light on the limitations of modern politics—this is the challenge that Weil leaves us with at the end of "Human Personality."

Although early in the essay Weil warns that the vocabulary of middle values will inevitably cause harm, she ends by conceding that words like *right, democracy*, and *person* are valid in their own region. The language and institutions of democratic politics simply must be sustained by an inspiration oriented toward impersonal truth and justice. Implied in Weil's distinction between the two regions, then, is the idea of a connection, and moreover the possibility of conceiving of a figure capable of moving between them. To consider the difficulties and positive possibilities of language at their boundary point is, I now want to suggest, one way to propose a bridge, a *metaxu*, between Weil and Arendt.

Unfreezing

In bringing together Weil and Arendt on the question of language, there is a risk of covering over important differences between the two thinkers. Weil's call to restructure society so that its institutions are responsive to human suffering would likely be met with suspicion and resistance by Arendt, who would hear in it a politics of compassion and a rhetoric of love that are potentially destructive of spaces of appearance. For Arendt, the attitude best suited to political life is not compassion but respect (OR 49–105). She would find the moral tenor of Weil's writings to be evidence that a sense for the autonomy of the political has been lost. For her part, Weil would see Arendt's attempt to secure the integrity of the political at the expense of addressing human needs as one more example of a discourse that has immunized itself from the presence of human affliction and, as such, contributed to disfiguring the idea of justice.

I do not wish to collapse the differences between Weil and Arendt or propose an unhappy compromise, which would detract from the force of each. Instead, I want to appreciate their works—their words—as potential sources of orientation, which might steer us down different paths of thinking about the restitution of language. And I want to end by suggesting that these paths do overlap, even if they go on to very different horizons. The point at which they come together, moreover, suggests a place from which to stage a final rejoinder to what I have called the common story about philosophy and the public realm. Their paths cross, I want to say, at the figure of Socrates.

In *The Life of the Mind*, Arendt puts forward Socrates as an ideal type that can illuminate the experience of thinking (LMT 166–93). Refusing to call Socrates a philosopher (a label she also refuses herself), Arendt finds in his image a reminder of a forgotten origin of philosophy: an experience of thinking as a *traveling through words*. To think with and like Socrates is to be carried along by the question: "What do I mean when I say 'x'?" In the Platonic dialogues, especially the early ones, the terms that Socrates interrogates typically have some bearing on the question of what it means to live well: piety, virtue, justice, and so on. Famously, Socrates's inquiries do not culminate in final definitions; his mode of traveling is one that never actually arrives at a destination. In this respect, Socratic discourse is a constant testimony to the significance of the unspoken. Yet, this constitutive absence, so beautifully captured in the concept of *aporia*, does not mean that nothing has taken place, that traveling has not occurred. For, in becoming curious about language, Socrates becomes reacquainted with experiences that lie at the origin of his vocabulary, experiences that are crystalized in words. Socratic thinking, in Arendt's account, is thus a kind of meditative process of "unfreezing" frozen thoughts and attending to their forgotten, constituent elements (LM 171). When Socrates converses in the *agora*, he then does so with an ear trained by an attentiveness to the language that he shares with his interlocutors. As much as the sophist, but in a very different way, he is fascinated with the power that words possess.

Drawn to both public conversation and solitary reflection, but neither sophist nor sage, Socrates represents an in-between: he embodies the possibility of connecting a talkative public realm and the life of thoughtful, silent reflection. And the reason he can embody this connection is because he carries within himself, whether speaking or thinking, the same language with which to travel.

Incorporating an element of Socratic curiosity about words into the rhythm of everyday life, both public and private, is deeply *morally* significant in Arendt's account. Its moral meaning is derived not only from the specific themes of the lines of inquiry that Socrates pursues but also from the general critical posture that Socratic questioning motivates (when speaking with others) and the experience of self-encounter that silent thought affords (when done alone). The former disrupts automatism of judgment (and thus, hopefully, automatism of behavior); the latter preserves the possibility of conscience. Arendt explicitly connects the moral catastrophe of Nazi Germany to a paucity of both: the unthinking adoption of a code of conduct by masses of people meant that they could proceed, as if sleepwalking, and without pang of conscience, into complicity with horrifying moral crimes.

It is therefore not accurate to simply oppose Weil and Arendt, as if the writings of one were haunted by human suffering and those of the other were not. In many ways, *The Life of the Mind* is the culmination of a long meditation on what Arendt witnessed at the trial of Adolph Eichmann, whose rule-following and inability to think from the standpoint of his victims were, in Arendt's account, internally related to his attachment to clichés and stock phrases (EJ 21–34). By calling into question pregiven rules with which to subsume particulars under universals (words, concepts, clichés, etc.), thinking frees us to judge *otherwise*. And the way we may continue to judge when no longer anchored by determining rules, Arendt tells us, is by considering how things look from the standpoint of others with whom we share a world. We saw above that Weil identifies the ability to put oneself in the place of another as the ability to listen. Arendt's liberated judgment is different in important ways from what Weil means by loving attention. But there is in each of these ideas a recognition of the moral stakes of being open to the experiences of others, and a worry that the hardness of our categories has hardened us from their presence.

There is another feature of the Socratic exemplar that needs mentioning before ending. I have so far only spoken of the moral significance of Socratic dialogue. So presented, the lesson one might take from this for rhetoric is that public discourse ought to morally edify and inspire "critical thinking" and a willingness to "speak truth to power." But there is more to it than this. A rhetorical practice that endeavors to bring a shared moral and political reality into expression ought, at the same time, to aspire to make room for an experience of beauty. In Diotima's speech in Plato's *Symposium*, where the notion of *metaxu* is introduced, Socrates is not so subtly compared to *eros*: a spirit being (*daimon*) that moves between the world of humans and the world of the gods, drawing us toward the good *and* the beautiful.[4] Beauty is what moves the soul in this picture (it "illumines and lifts up towards the good," to borrow a phrase from Weil). And the beauty that draws the characters of the *Symposium* to Socrates is certainly not physical. It is the beauty of his ideas, which shines through his words (so much so that Alcibiades, drunk and infatuated with Socrates, at one point claims that he feels compelled to cover his ears in Socrates's presence).[5]

Rhetoric should aspire to beauty because what calls out for attention is not just a sense of moral horror that is muted by contemporary political configurations (though this too, and most urgently) but *also* a positive mode of human relationality that is, indeed, rather beautiful. As beings born into language, we are ontologically primed for the possibility of expressing ourselves, interpreting the meaning of our actions, sharing and exploring the significance of common experiences, inheriting past stories, and preserving ours for future generations. To find that, when one opens one's mouth or grips a pen, one is already appealing to an intersubjective world of sense is—or should be—an endlessly gratifying and beautiful fact of our lives; it should, at least *sometimes*, feel less like a tool for getting our way and more like what (I imagine) a bird feels when it sometimes takes flight gratuitously: an activity whose performance is inherently valuable and a source of enjoyment, which expresses something basic to our nature. Beauty is an experience and reminder of this mode of enjoyment. It should lace any political discourse that seeks to construct a common space of encounter.

To avoid any misunderstanding: by concluding on this aesthetic note, I do not mean to recommend rhetoric as an art of inciting passion, cultivating prosocial emotions, or directing energies toward particular causes. That may be part of what happens in politics, but it is not what interests me here. What interests me instead is how beauty can accompany and engender the experiences of listening that I have proposed Arendt and Weil bring to our attention. Arendt's concept of liberated judgment, in which the perspectives of others enter into our mental operations, is not insignificantly modeled on Kantian aesthetic judgments, in which the mind finds that it can happily make sense of a particular object without overdetermination by a concept (LK). For Arendt, this is as close as we can come to an experience of human freedom and plurality in the life of the mind. For Weil, encountering true beauty is one way of experiencing the sacred, for it belongs to the impersonal and calls us away from our person. Holding space for beauty, then, should be part of what it means to go about unfreezing Arendt's frozen thought-objects. And it should be so (and here I will end, drawing once more on Weil's words), not simply because the beautiful is pleasant. Rather, it is because the mere presence of the beautiful in everyday life can remind us of what has been suppressed in the construction of the everyday: what is excluded by contemporary politics, what is unthinkable within the logic and economy of self-interest, and what is inexpressible in our linguistic practices. It steers our attention to what lies on the other side of the walls we have built, falling cold and hard to the point of freezing, in a state of harsh neglect:

> Beauty can be perceived, though very dimly and mixed with many false substitutes, within the cell where all human thought is at first imprisoned. And upon her rest all the hopes of truth and justice, with tongue cut out. She, too, has no language; she does not speak; she says nothing. But she has a voice to cry out. She cries out and points to truth and justice who are dumb, like a dog who barks to bring people to his master lying unconscious in the snow. (HP 73)

Notes

1. Plato, *Crito*, 46a–48a. The issue for our purposes is not whether Socrates should simply follow the guidance of popular opinion or stick to his own convictions when deciding whether to accept his execution. Rather, the issue is that Socrates's argument for the latter includes a dismissal of the views of the many as *generally* unworthy of attention because they are not based on knowledge. This is a strikingly different image of Socrates than we find in many other dialogues, where Socrates, who confesses ignorance himself, is shown to be eager to hear the beliefs of his fellow citizens and pay them close attention.
2. Plato, *Gorgias*, 462b–467a.
3. "Understanding … is the specifically human way of being alive; for every single person needs to be reconciled to a world into which he was born a stranger and in which, to the extent of his distinct uniqueness, he always remains a stranger. Understanding begins with birth and ends with death" (EU 308).
4. Plato, *Symposium*, 201e–212b.
5. Ibid., 216a.

CONTRIBUTORS

Catherine Craig is a postdoctoral scholar with the School of Civic and Economic Thought and Leadership at ASU. She received her PhD in political science from Baylor University in 2021. She is the author of "Memory and the Political Art" in *Plato's Statesman* (2023). Her work has appeared in the *Political Science Reviewer*, *Ancient Philosophy*, and *History of Political Thought*.

Pascale Devette is Professor of Political Science at l'Université de Montréal. Specialist of Albert Camus, Simone Weil, and Hannah Arendt, her current research focuses on conceptions of vulnerability and attention in political philosophy and their sociopolitical effects. She is author of "Attention, justice sociale et éducation: les apports de la philosophie de Simone Weil pour une pédagogie de l'attention" in *Politique et sociétés*; "Détachement et décentrement: l'amour 'impersonnel' d'Antigone au cœur de la cite" in *Laval théologique et philosophique*; and "Retrouver la réceptivité: écoute, attention et résonance pour débattre dans un monde polarize" in *Éthique publique*.

Marina Lademacher is a PhD candidate in Social and Political Thought in the Department of Philosophy at the University of Sussex. She is the author of "Hannah Arendt" in *Marx and Philosophy Review of Books* (2022) and a review essay of Murray Bookchin's *The Modern Crisis* (2022) and Yavor Tarinski's *Enlightenment and Ecology: The Legacy of Murray Bookchin in the 21st Century* (2021) in *Anarchist Studies*.

Kathryn Lawson is a lecturer of philosophy at Carleton University and has a PhD from Queen's University in Kingston, Ontario. Kate is the editor of *Breached Horizons: Essays on the Work of Jean Luc Marion* (2017) and author of numerous chapters and peer-reviewed journal articles, including work on Edith Stein, Simone Weil, Richard Kearney, and the *Bhagavad Gita*. Her PhD dissertation, "Decreation for the Anthropocene" (2022), focuses on Simone Weil and environmental ethics.

Joshua Livingstone is a PhD candidate at Queen's University in Kingston, Ontario. His doctoral research explores the tense relationship between philosophy and politics in the thought of Hannah Arendt, and he is the author of a chapter titled "Hannah Arendt and the Free Press" in a forthcoming volume on the work of Hannah Arendt, Edith Stein, and Simone Weil.

Lissa McCullough is a lecturer of philosophy at California State University Dominguez Hills. She is the author of *The Religious Philosophy of Simone Weil* (2014) and the editor of *Conversations with Paolo Soleri* (2012) and *The Call to Radical Theology* by Thomas J. J. Altizer (2012).

Sara McDonald is Professor and the Director of Global Great Books at Huron University. She is the author of several monographs, including *Hegelian Philosophy and the Emancipation of Women* (2008), and the coauthor of *The Coen Brothers and the Comedy of Democracy* (2018).

Marie Cabaud Meaney is an independent scholar. She is the author of *Simone Weil's Apologetic Use of Literature: Her Christological Interpretations of Classic Greek Texts* (2008), *Brücken zum Übernatürlichen: Simone Weil über das Böse, den Krieg und die Religion* (2018), and "Understanding Simone Weil's 'Science of the Supernatural' within the Context of Rationalism" in *Spaziofilosofico*.

Paolo Monti is Assistant Professor in Moral Philosophy at Università degli Studi di Milano-Bicocca, Italy. His research focuses on the ethics of citizenship, the impact of digital platforms on the public sphere, and the influence of religious pluralism in democratic societies. His latest book (with C. Ungureanu) is *Contemporary Political Philosophy and Religion: Between Public Reason and Pluralism* (2018).

Rose A. Owen is a PhD candidate at the University of Chicago's Department of Political Science. Rose holds an MA in political science from the University of Chicago and a BA in political science from Wellesley College. She is author of "A World without Men: Valerie Solanas and the Feminist Uses of Violence" in *New Political Science*, and her forthcoming dissertation is titled "Feminist Violence: Rape and Militancy in the Second Wave."

Ian Rhoad is Professorial Lecturer and Director of Graduate Studies in the Department of Philosophy and Religion at American University. He received his PhD in philosophy from the New School for Social Research in 2020 after defending his doctoral dissertation "The Ethical and the Political in Jean-Paul Sartre and Hannah Arendt." His current research explores resources in the phenomenological tradition for illuminating experiences of political resistance.

Scott B. Ritner is a professor of politics at Colorado University in Boulder. He received his PhD in politics (2018) from The New School for Social Research. Scott is the President of the American Weil Society and the author of "The Training of the Soul: Simone Weil's Dialectical Disciplinary Paradigm. A Reading alongside Michel Foucault" in *Simone Weil and Continental Philosophy* (2017).

Elvira Roncalli is a professor of philosophy at Carroll College, Helena, Montana. She is the author of *The Future of the World Is Open: Encounters with Lea Melandri, Luisa Muraro, Adriana Cavarero, and Rossana Rossanda* (2022) and the editor of *Contemporary Italian Women Philosophers: Stretching the Art of Thinking* (with Silvia Benso, 2021). Her research centers around questions pertaining to mechanisms and relationships of domination, the interplay between embodied subjectivity and living space, between power and violence, between political agency and political recognition. She is currently working on a project about the political experience of women during the Italian Resistance.

Thomas Sojer is a research assistant to the Chair of Philosophy at the Faculty of Theology, University of Erfurt. His recent publications include "Eric Voegelin's and Simone Weil's Return to Ancient Greece," *Acta Antiqua: Academiae Scientiarum Hungaricae*, and "Simone Weil's Mysticism as Corporeal Love" in *Mysticism and/as Love Theory* (2021). He is cofounder of the Simone Weil denkkollektiv.

INDEX

action 19, 22, 48, 54, 70, 157, 193–4, 200, 202
  appearance through 217–19
  dramaturgical 180–2, 185
  ethical 117–18
  and God 116
  non acting 142–3
  space of 170
  and storytelling 159–62
  uprooted 137–8
  thinking as 150
activism 137, 150
affliction 113, 120–3, 157–9, 163–6,
    170–1, 220–1
  in the Iliad 208–11
  and love 118–19
appearance 180–8, 222
  memory brings into 169–70
  of the other 199–202, 217–19
  the space of 22
  of the who 117
Aristotle 185, 194, 152
attention 4, 141–51, 157–9, 164, 169–71,
    192–3, 216–17, 219
  to the beautiful 211–12
  guiding 221–5
  vs inattention 46
Augustine of Hippo 67, 143–5
authority 22–6
  bureaucratic 48, 50–2
  of central power 45

beauty 117, 123, 188–90, 199–200, 205,
    210–12, 224–5
  of art 201–2
  event of 192–3
  and justice 206–7
  lack of 60–2
  of the world 113–14
  of writing 163
body 98, 182, 192–3, 208–10
  affliction of 121

individual 190–1
  natural/earthly 119
  social 32

capitalism 32, 35, 50–1
citizenship 134–5
  ethics of 142, 148, 150
collectivity 7, 45–6, 49, 65
  as collective mechanisms 26, 52
  as collective forms of belonging 6, 10, 29
  as political unfreedom or dogmatism
    7, 20–1
colonialism 32, 130
common sense 3, 70, 221
  breakdown in 216
communication 48, 63, 141–2, 149, 184
  as conversation 1–3, 7, 10, 14
communism 63, 67, 79
  commitment to 216
  state 33
  (*see also* politics)
contradiction 7–8, 52, 77–8, 80–2, 84–5,
    90, 116, 130–2, 163–6
conversation 1–4, 10–1, 47
  fragmented 149
  in the Iliad 202–4
  Socratic 223
  (*see also* communication)

Dante Alighieri 59
democracy 25–6, 33, 37, 49–50, 141–2,
    189–90, 220–2
  syndicalist 22
  (*see also* politics)
Descartes, Rene 19, 48
detachment 149–50, 191
dignity 5, 14, 63–4, 143, 160, 168
Doxa 64, 70, 101

Eichmann, Adolph 44, 52–4, 60–4, 69–70,
    78, 85, 90–1, 144, 147, 223

empathy 54, 204, 209, 211–12
  lack of 64
Ersatz 6, 37, 46, 71, 118, 129–30
Esposito, Roberto x, 4, 10–11, 78, 116, 146, 210, 212
evil 12, 29, 59–65, 70–73, 113, 147, 187
  banality of 52–3, 144–5
  evildoing 44, 54
  radical 68–70

force 6–8, 12, 20–1, 27, 29–31, 68–9, 72–3, 78–83, 86, 113, 123, 130, 146–8, 164–5, 187–8, 192, 202, 206, 209–11, 216
  brute 203
  instruments of 85
  in the Iliad 207–9
freedom 6, 9, 19–24, 34–7, 46, 70, 89, 149–51, 162–3, 183, 186, 201, 205–6
  of judgement 224
  of movement 54–5
  political 48–50
  public 220–1
  unfreedom 22, 27, 33, 130, 142, 147
friendship 3–4, 6, 35, 103, 114, 116, 210
  civic 149–50

God 3, 19, 61, 68, 72, 114–19, 121–3, 142–143, 191, 206–7, 219, 221
  place of 67–8
  renunciation of 205
  in service to 120
Good, The 3, 8, 36, 60–1, 71, 73, 114–15, 117, 189, 20, 221, 224
Great Beast (as society, Plato) 46
guilt 62, 66, 53

habit 62
Hegel, G. F. W. 7–9
history 7–9, 23, 31, 60–1, 69, 130, 147, 149, 166, 169
  as storytelling 161–3, 171
Hitler, Adolph 28, 62, 66–7, 71, 79, 131
Hobbes, Thomas 27–8, 32, 37, 48, 129
Homo faber 44, 48, 104

illusion (see Ersatz)
imagination 31, 33, 70, 189, 204
  figments of 63

imperialism 32, 44, 129
  forces of 35

Jefferson, Thomas 25–6, 37
judgment 70–2, 142–4, 149–50, 223–4
  ethical 52
  personal 54
justice 3–4, 6, 14, 36, 49, 66, 71–2, 78, 82, 114, 146, 201, 205–7, 209–12, 220–3, 225
  social 121, 123, 157

Kafka, Franz 43

labor 5, 19, 34, 78, 85–6, 89, 103–5, 217–18
  as in factories 51–2
law 9, 23, 43, 53–4, 60, 117, 119, 167, 183
  moral 61–6
  of nature, necessity 31, 69, 82, 100, 118
  as opposed to power 25
  replacement of 43
liberalism 22, 32, 78, 128, 186
  (*see also* politics)
liberty 26
  public liberty 37
love 35–7, 72–3, 83, 102–4, 117–19, 142–3, 163, 189–90, 206–11, 222
  beloved 167, 170
  divine 121–3
  of beauty 199, 205
  of one's neighbor 3–4, 113–14, 116
  self-giving 71–3
  of truth 63
  of World [*Amour Mundi*] 3, 71
Luxemburg, Rosa 32
lying 33, 36–7, 46, 49, 59–64, 67, 69, 143, 191

Marx, Karl 9, 24, 27, 34, 63
  as Marxism 8, 55
Metaxu [μεταξύ] 193, 219–22, 224
method 21, 31–2, 52, 218
Monsters 62, 66

narration 48, 159–60
  (*see also* storytelling)
natality 3, 14, 86, 200, 217–19

nature/natural 11, 21, 27, 60, 69, 83, 86, 100–1, 103–4, 119, 123, 130, 187, 200, 206–7
  faculties 118
  human nature 19, 30
  (*see also* supernatural)
Nazi/Nazism 5, 7, 20, 27–8, 53–4, 62–5, 77–8, 90, 128–30, 146, 158, 166, 180, 223
  neo-Nazi 157
necessity 6, 11, 19, 21, 26–9, 31, 48, 89, 104, 180, 192, 200, 202, 206
nobody (as opposed to the subject) 11, 47, 53

oppression 6, 8, 11, 27–9, 34–5, 72, 79, 129
  bureaucratic 45–6, 50–2, 55

personality 31, 117
  as human personality 207, 219–22
  legal 183
  as opposed to Impersonality
Plato 6, 7, 46, 64, 89, 115, 119, 129, 188, 194, 205, 216, 224
  the allegory of the cave 63, 119
plurality 3, 6, 12, 14, 20–2, 30, 34, 48, 88, 90–1, 99, 102, 104, 108–10, 114, 115, 117, 157, 166, 171, 182–3, 199–202, 224
  human plurality 70, 100–1, 122, 217
politics 8–10, 31, 36–7, 47–8, 77–8, 84–5, 90–1, 98–9, 102, 104, 108–10, 194, 200–1, 211, 222
  left/right politics 7
  party politics 49–50, 113
  as in the realm of the political 6
power 19–30, 33–7, 47–8, 50–2, 68, 80, 84–5, 98, 102, 108–9, 188, 215–16, 221
  systematization/centralization of 116
  violence as the opposite of 87–88
  (*see also* Force)
promise/promise keeping 34
propaganda 49, 64, 68, 70, 142–3, 180
property (ownership) 27–8, 32, 44, 51, 105

racism 47, 109, 128
revolution 23–6, 66, 87
  American 24–6, 84

French 23, 50, 85, 131
  industrial 105
  as revolutionary 30–1, 132
responsibility 47, 62, 158, 199
  moral 2, 13, 53
rhetoric 27, 85, 216, 219, 222–4
Richelieu, Cardinal (Armand Jean du Plessis) 28, 30, 129–30
Rights 6, 22, 183, 220
  human 122
  right to have rights 132–6
Robespierre, Maximilien 23
roots/rootedness 21, 36, 71, 117, 130–2, 147, 149
  of the community 7
  as rootlessness 29
  uprootedness 9

social 26–7, 31–5, 50–1, 55, 113, 130, 134, 145–7, 180–1, 189
  contract 22
  decay 165
  justice 121, 123, 157
  media 142, 148–9
  the 44, 46–8
  (*see also* Collectivity)
soul 9, 36, 115, 119, 121, 170–1, 206, 208–12, 224
  and its needs 8, 21, 130
statelessness 2, 135
  see citizenship
storytelling 157–8, 160–71
  relation to action 159
suffering 71–3, 116, 118–19, 121–2, 165, 167–8
  human 220, 222–3
supernatural 68, 71, 73, 119, 190, 192, 194, 206
  (*see also* natural)

technology 87, 104, 142
terror 59–60, 69, 88
thinking 5–7, 37, 46, 70, 97–8, 100, 143–5, 147, 150
  in opposition to thoughtlessness 53, 64
  Socratic 222–4
totalitarianism 2, 5, 9, 37, 59–60, 67–70, 116
tradition 70, 216

breakdown of 3, 97
of the Enlightenment 141
truth 49, 59, 63–4, 68, 118, 123, 165, 202, 220
speaking truth to power 224

understanding 9, 45, 109, 216, 218–19
uprootedness 129–31, 133, 147–9
(*see also* roots/rootedness)

violence 21, 77–91, 104, 132, 208–9, 216

Who [vs What] 3, 5, 13, 100–2, 107–8, 117, 159–60, 180–1, 185, 188, 193, 217

Will 144–5
to power 33
work 48, 50–2, 104–5, 131, 161, 181, 217–18
world 9, 48, 89, 97–9, 102–3, 107–10, 113–17, 161, 171, 206–7, 217
as world-creating 22
worldliness 99–101
worldlessness/world alienation 103–5
war 6, 20, 33, 45, 66, 79–81, 83, 129, 209
Spanish Civil 12, 59, 66, 77, 116, 215
Trojan 11, 78, 165, 203–5, 207, 215
World War I/Great War 26, 161
World War II 1–2, 10, 19, 22, 27, 32, 52–4, 77–8, 90, 97, 180, 194, 199

www.ingramcontent.com/pod-product-compliance
Lightning Source LLC
Chambersburg PA
CBHW071827300426
44116CB00009B/1463